CHARACTER AND COMMUNITY DEVELOPMENT

CHARACTER AND COMMUNITY DEVELOPMENT

A School Planning and Teacher Training Handbook

GORDON G. VESSELS

PRAEGER

Westport, Connecticut
London

Library of Congress Cataloging-in-Publication Data

Vessels, Gordon G., 1949–
    Character and community development : a school planning and
teacher training handbook / Gordon G. Vessels.
        p.   cm.
    Includes bibliographical references and index.
    ISBN 0–275–96133–8 (alk. paper).—ISBN 0–275–96134–6 (pbk. :
alk. paper)
    1. Moral education—United States—Handbooks, manuals, etc.
LC311.V47   1998
370.11′4—dc21   98–11132

British Library Cataloguing in Publication is available.

Library of Congress Catalog Card Number: 98–11132
ISBN: 0–275–96133–8 hc   0–275–96134–6 pb

First published in 1998

Praeger Publishers, 88 Post Road West, Westport, CT 06881
An imprint of Greenwood Publishing Group, Inc.

Printed in the United States of America

The paper used in this book complies with the
Permanent Paper Standard issued by the National
Information Standards Organization (Z39.48–1984).

10 9 8 7 6 5 4 3 2 1

Copyright Acknowledgments

The author and publisher are grateful to the following for granting permission to reprint from their materials:

Extracts from "Public and Constitutional Support for Character Education" by Gordon G. Vessels and Stephen M. Boyd, April 1996, Vol. 80, No. 579, pp. 55–62, published by NASSP. For more information concerning NASSP services and/or programs, please call (703) 860–0200.

"Core Essentials: Parent's Guide for Teaching Values (Cooperation)" by Reggie Joiner and Core Essentials Staff, November 1997. Used with permission of authors.

"Brookside's Character Corner," developed by Brookside Parent Character Education Steering Group, September 1997. Permission granted by Brookside Elementary School.

Contents

Acknowledgments

I want to acknowledge and thank contributors, reviewers, proponents and sponsors of character education in Georgia who made grant projects possible, persons who assisted with the implementation and evaluation of our grant project in Atlanta, and staff members at the model schools that were visited by teachers and administrators from Atlanta during the 1996–97 school year.

With respect to written contributions, a special thanks goes to Stephen Boyd, Eris Velma Morgan, Sherry Norfolk, and Reggie Joiner. Stephen Boyd worked with me on the April 1996 NASSP Bulletin article from which much of the content for chapter 1 was drawn. Sherry Norfolk provided the Yiddish folktale about Story and Truth plus a commentary about developing storytelling skills. Eris Velma Morgan provided a description of the inter-cultural exchange project that she arranged with students from Fain Elementary in Atlanta and the Morvant Anglican School in Trinidad. Reggie Joiner shared one of the Core Essentials' parent guides that he wrote and designed with the help of his teacher and parent associates. There were many others who shared information by telephone and/or mail including Kristie Fink, Victor Battistich, Sheldon Berman, Rudy Bernardo, Jerry Corley, Jennifer Johns, Kathy Paget, Stan Weed, James Leming, Cletus Bulach, Rose Schaffer, John Graham, Sandra Yager, Dixon Smith, Hugh Cline, Troyce Fisher, Jim Fowler, Charles Haynes, Lynn Lisy-Macon, Sheila Koshewa, Tom Lickona, Bill Parsons, and representatives from various organizations mentioned in the book.

A few busy and knowledgeable people generously took the time to review the initial and/or final drafts. Victor Battistich read and critiqued the initial and final drafts and provided valuable suggestions and a written endorsement; Kristie Fink read and critiqued the final draft and provided valuable suggestions and a written endorsement; Thomas Lickona, Rose Schaffer, and Patricia Concannon read and critiqued the initial draft; James Fowler read and critiqued the final draft and provided a written endorsement. I am sincerely grateful for their help and advice.

With respect to sponsorship, I want to thank Ron Benson, Paul Weimer, and Laura Thompson with the Georgia Humanities Council whose interest in character education, courage, and confidence in me made the Atlanta grant project and subsequent improvements in the book possible. They are largely responsible for bringing character education to the attention of educators in Georgia and making pilot programs possible.

The teachers, principals, secretaries, parents, paraprofessionals, custodians, and food service workers from the five grant-project schools in Atlanta (Blalock Elementary, Campbell Elementary, Hope Elementary, Fain Elementary, Rivers Elementary) deserve credit for implementing character education. The first year character education programs at Blalock Elementary and Campbell Elementary in Atlanta were especially successful because of the moral leadership of the principals of these two schools, Jackie Woods and Wardell Sims, and the personal commitment of key teachers like Ernestine Curry at Blalock whose desire to build character in children has been an inspiration to me.

Several people assisted me with grant-project data collection including Bill Parsons at West Point Elementary in Georgia, Brenda Logan at Hazelwood Elementary in Kentucky, Tara Terry from the University of Georgia who served as my doctoral intern and assistant during the 1996–97 school year, and Gail Williams from south Georgia who piloted the student character questionnaire for middle and high school students.

The staffs of Hazelwood, West Point, and Allen Classical-Traditional Academy in Dayton were kind enough to share their ideas with representatives from the five grant-project schools in Atlanta during our site visits to their model schools. They treated us like family, which I think we are at least in terms of our common desire to make character development the primary objective of education.

Finally, I want to thank my wife Cheryl for telling me at least once a year for the last twenty years to write a book, for putting up with me during the nearly three years it took to complete the task, and for being a supportive companion since 1962 when we were in junior high school together, and James Paul Brown who recently provided me the opportunity as a new foster parent to observe and promote the development of conscience and good character during the critical years between ages six and nine.

CHARACTER AND COMMUNITY DEVELOPMENT

Overview

Character and Community Development is for principals, teachers, parents, education students, and others who are concerned about our deteriorating social environment and convinced that schools and communities can and should be doing more to prevent and resolve social problems. It is for people who are interested in exploring the possibility that identifying "character" as our ultimate goal for children will give us the new perspective on child development and education that we need in order to truly reform schools and strengthen communities. I have been exploring this possibility for a couple of years now and have attempted to organize and communicate my knowledge and ideas in a way that will be helpful to you.

Chapter 1 defines key terms such as virtue and character, and it addresses concerns you may have with respect to public opinion about character education and relevant First Amendment issues. It makes the case that constitutional and public support for character education is quite strong.

Chapter 2 compares traditional and progressive approaches to character building and reviews relevant theories of cognitive, affective, moral, social, and friendship development. It also reviews contributions that philosophers, educators, and religious leaders have made toward defining moral character.

Chapter 3 includes a synthesis of relevant theories of development and a preschool to twelfth grade core curriculum that targets virtues and psychological processes in a developmentally appropriate manner and includes general and behavioral objectives for each of five developmental levels. These objectives reflect my conceptualization of moral character as well as an attempt to provide a framework for infusing character education into all aspects of school life.

Chapter 4 describes many instructional strategies and gives you valuable leads for obtaining materials and additional information. These strategies are organized into six learning-mode categories based on my assessment of the predominant learning mode for each strategy.

Chapter 5 presents guidelines for program planning and evaluation. It also includes detailed descriptions of many types of "direct" and "indirect" assessment techniques and presents several new assessment instruments including a school climate survey, two elementary-level classroom climate surveys, three student-character questionnaires, and a pre-coded classroom observation form.

1

Introduction to Character Education

A DEFINITION OF CHARACTER

If we are going to educate for character, we need to begin by defining the term. People from all walks of life generally agree that character implies quality and goodness, so character education is blessed with an identifying term that is unifying. When we say that people have character, we usually mean that they are predisposed to do what is right or decent and to feel and think accordingly. Because they understand right and wrong and choose what is right even if this is potentially harmful to themselves in some way, we describe them as moral. Because this inclination to know and do things that are good or right is habitual, we describe them as virtuous. Because they are capable of reasoning well and autonomously on matters of right and wrong, particularly where issues of fairness, justice, and sensitivity to others are concerned, we refer to them as ethical. When we say that people have character, therefore, we mean that they have moral character. This in turn implies that their personality is characterized by moral values and feelings (conscience), the ability to reason autonomously, fairly, and sensitively about moral issues (ethical reflection), and the habit of acting in a manner consistent with their moral reasoning and moral feelings (virtue).

A DEFINITION OF CHARACTER EDUCATION

Character education can be viewed as an emerging approach to educational reform that is driven by a shared need to resolve social problems, a shared belief that school curricula and educational priorities do not reflect a responsiveness to student and societal needs, and a shared belief that schools can make the changes needed to produce students with the virtues and moral reasoning skills needed to resolve these problems and realize their own full potential. Although there are specific programs that are exceptions to the rule, in general, character education is driven to a lesser degree by an explicit moral philosophy, well established theories of moral development, related empirical research, and quality curricula and instructional materials. Character education in its current form is a social-educational movement that could institutionalize and become a permanent feature of schools once again if it generates solution ideas that are shown to be philosophically, scientifically, and technologically sound and effective.

The fact that character education is essentially a social movement with a rather nebulous philosophy and methodology does not mean it cannot be defined with enough specificity to give interested persons a useful starting point for program planning or that there is any question about the appropriateness of its reintroduction into the schools. *Character education combines direct teaching and community-building strategies in various ways to promote personal and social integrity and the development of moral virtues, moral reasoning abilities, and other personal assets and qualities that make this possible.* When character education programs are purposeful, proactive, and comprehensive, and when they are thoroughly implemented by fully committed teaching staffs, they can transform schools morally, socially, and motivationally, and create caring communities with student and adult members who are intrinsically motivated to do what they should for themselves and others.

The term "character education" was first used early in the twentieth century by educators who employed a didactic approach. While a few antagonists continue to use the term selectively to describe only present-day programs that similarly teach specific virtues and emphasize extrinsic reinforcement and habit formation (e.g., Kohn, 1997; Wynne, 1997), most recognize its unifying potential and use it to describe all programs that promote moral-ethical, social-emotional, intellectual, and academic development with balance through all facets of school life. This broader definition includes traditional programs, progressive programs that emphasize intrinsic motivation and the creation of caring, democratic communities, and eclectic programs which combine the two.

HISTORICAL ANTECEDENTS

The belief that character building is the shared responsibility of parents and educators actually predates the first use of the term "character education" in America. Lickona (1991) stated that "wise societies since the time of Plato have made moral education a deliberate aim of schooling" and "have educated for character as well as intellect, decency as well as literacy, virtue as well as knowledge." Heslep (1995) observed that philosophers as diverse as Plato, Aristotle, St. Augustine, St. Thomas Aquinas, Spinoza, Kant, Mill, and Dewey have viewed character education as vital to society. Throughout American history persons involved in public discussions about the purpose of schools have viewed character development as an important goal and one that must be routinely achieved if democracy is to survive. Teddy Roosevelt made the point succinctly when he said: "To educate a person in mind and not in morals is to educate a menace to society."

CHARACTER EDUCATION IN THE UNITED STATES

Clearly the concept of character education is neither new nor radical, and when viewed from the perspective of American history, its neglect by educators during the last few decades can be viewed as a departure from tradition, not its introduction. The current groundswell of renewed interest among educators, parents, organizational leaders, political leaders, and other concerned citizens is encouraging and will hopefully lead to school reform characterized by a broader and more relevant curriculum. Unfortunately, the availability of knowledgeable consultants and the development of program-evaluation methods have not kept pace with the growing popularity of character education, a discrepancy that could lead to short-lived, superficial, faddish programs that fail to achieve the fundamental change reported by fully implemented programs.

During the first three decades of the twentieth century, character education was a preoccupation in the United States, and most educators saw it as an important mission of elementary and secondary education (McClellan, 1992; Leming, 1993). After the 1930s, it gradually declined in most public schools as a result of several societal changes, including increased pluralism, an emphasis on individualism, a series of U.S. Supreme Court decisions that found school systems in violation of the Establishment Clause of the First Amendment (Eastland, 1993), and a reaction to these court decisions characterized by confusion, misunderstanding, and an inclination on the part of school officials to take no chances (Haynes, 1994; Piediscalzi, 1981). Most schools and school systems abandoned formal character education during the 1950s and 1960s because they thought it could not be provided in a way that was constitutional, consistent with basic principals of progressive education, and consistent with the teachings of various cultures and religious groups.

RENEWED INTEREST

Character education regained momentum during the 1980s and 1990s because many parents, educators, and other concerned citizens from various subcultures and regions of the country saw the need for prevention programs that would counter the tide of moral decline. The results of recent opinion polls (Elam, Rose, Gallup, 1993–94) suggest that Americans can agree on what values to teach and typically agree on such values as honesty, moral courage, racial/ethnic/political tolerance, respect, democracy, fairness, persistence, compassion, and civility. The 1996 Phi Delta Kappa/Gallup pole revealed that 98 percent of Americans viewed the preparation of students for responsible citizenship as a quite important or very important role for public schools, and 86 percent viewed the promotion of cultural unity and the improvement of social conditions as important roles.

Support for character education from the federal government increased dramatically during the 1990s. It was endorsed by the U.S. Congress in 1994 (Public Law 103-301, 1994—see Appendix A) and by the President of the United States in (a) his comments (Clinton, 1994) upon signing the Improving America's Schools Act (Public Law 103-382, 1994), (b) his 1996 and 1997 State of the Union messages, and (c) his co-sponsorship of the 1995–98 White House Conferences on character education. In his speech at the White House Conference on Character Building for a Civil and Democratic Society on May 20, 1995, Clinton stated: "I personally long for the day when [character education] is once again a regular part of the curriculum of every school district in the United States" (Clinton, 1995). Since 1994 the U.S. Department of Education has awarded large character education grants to twelve states: California, Iowa, New Mexico, Utah, North Carolina, Maryland, Connecticut, Washington, Missouri, Kentucky, New Jersey, and South Carolina. In 1995 school superintendents received from Secretary Riley and the U.S. Department of Education (U.S. Department of Education, 1995) a document which was designed to dispel confusion about the implications of U.S. Supreme Court decisions concerning religious free expression and related matters including the teaching of moral values:

Teaching Values: Though schools must be neutral with respect to religion, they may play an active role with respect to teaching civic values and virtue, and the moral code that holds us together as a community. The fact that some of these values are held also by religions does not make it unlawful to teach them in school. (Riley, 1995)

In addition to promoting character education by seeking federal grant funds and using these funds to provide state coordinators and consultants, many states have promoted character education through constitutions, legislative statutes, board of education rules, and department of education policies and curricula. Greenawalt (1996) found that twenty-five state constitutions mandate moral or character education, but less than half of these states had actively promoted implementation. Nielson (1997) found that fifteen states had character education coordinators, most with other responsibilities.

Character education is also being fostered by major education associations, and some have worked in concert with groups dedicated to character building, such as the Character Education Partnership (CEP), the Communitarian Network, and the Character Counts Coalition (CCC). The Association for Supervision and Curriculum Development (ASCD) took the lead quite early by urging the teaching of values in the public schools and by devoting its 1993 issue of *Educational Leadership* to the topic. Other organizations, including the National School Boards Association (NSBA), the National Association of Secondary School Principals (NASSP), the National Association for the Education of Young Children (NAEYC), the National Education Association (NEA), and National Society for the Study of Education (NSSE), have endorsed the concept and have provided published materials. The NSSE recently published an edited book on the topic

(Molnar, 1997), and the NEA offered a workshop at its July 1997 conference in Atlanta.

Although the National Association of School Psychologists (NASP) has not endorsed character education directly, it devoted an entire issue of the School Psychology Review to the educational implications of the United Nation's Rights of the Child Convention in 1989. Article 29 (U.N. General Assembly, 1989) from this convention directed schools to promote the development of moral character by teaching children the values necessary to sustain democracies and to develop the full potential of each child. This article refers to the "development of respect for human rights and fundamental freedoms . . . respect for the child's parents, his or her own cultural identity, language, and values . . . [and respect for the] values of the country from which he or she may originate." It further refers to preparing the child for a "responsible life in a free society, in the spirit of understanding, peace, tolerance . . . and friendship among all peoples, ethnic, national, and religious groups" (U.N. General Assembly, 1989).

JUDICIAL SUPPORT AND THE FIRST AMENDMENT

Decisions of the U.S. Supreme Court and lower federal courts over the last several decades have provided substantial support for character education in the public schools. Character education was not the primary focus of these decisions, but a careful reading reveals the compatible and implicitly supportive views of many Judges and Justices with respect to teaching virtues through public school curricula. Several have referred to the obligation educators have to teach the values that support democracy and social order (Bitensky, 1995). Their decisions have consistently shown judicial restraint where matters of school curricula are concerned and an inclination to allow school systems much discretion in establishing values curricula.

U.S. Supreme Court opinions which have clarified the Free Speech rights of public school students have also established that values education is a constitutionally acceptable practice for elementary and secondary schools. Justice Brennan in *Board of Education v. Pico* (1982) wrote that while local school boards do not have "unfettered discretion" where library content is concerned, they must be permitted "to establish and apply their curriculum in such a way as to transmit community values." He referred to the "legitimate and substantial community interest in promoting respect for authority and traditional values be they social, moral, or political." In supporting curricular values education in *Bethel School District No. 403 v. Fraser* (1986), the U.S. Supreme Court said: "The public school system 'must inculcate the habits and manners of civility as values in themselves conducive to happiness and as indispensable to self-government in the community and the nation.'" The U.S. Supreme Court also upheld curricular values education against student claims of free speech violations in Hazelwood School District v. Kuhlmeier (1988). The majority U.S. Supreme Court opinion in *Ambach v. Norwick* (1979) stated:

Public school teachers perform a task "that go[es] to the heart of representative government." . . . The importance of public schools in the preparation of individuals for participation as citizens, and in the preservation of the values on which our society rests, long has been recognized by our decisions. . . . Other authorities have perceived public schools as an 'assimilative force' by which diverse and conflicting elements in our society are brought together on a broad but common ground. . . . Within the public school system, teachers play a critical part in developing students' attitude toward government and understanding of the role of citizens in our society. . . . Further, a teacher serves as a role model for his students, exerting a subtle but important influence over their perceptions and values. . . . This influence is crucial to the continued good health of democracy. . . . [A] State properly may regard all teachers as having an obligation to promote civic virtues and understanding in their classes, regardless of the subject taught.

Even though these and other decisions indicate that the U.S. Supreme Court is disinclined to interfere in matters related to public school curricula and will support character education as evidenced by its commentary about values education, it is useful to consider the ways in which character education could be challenged in the federal courts.

One possible basis for litigation would be the claim that a character education program violates the Establishment Clause of the First Amendment. The Court has already decided that a number of school practices violate this clause including Bible reading, religious instruction, school sponsored prayer, teaching creation or "creationism" as science, and moments of silence that were clearly intended to encourage prayer. Since first introduced in *Lemon v. Kurtzman* (1971), the Court has found that laws and actions are constitutional under the Establishment Clause if they (a) have a secular or civic purpose, (b) have the primary effect of neither advancing nor inhibiting religion, and (c) avoid excessive entanglement with religion.

The "endorsement" test proposed by Justice O'Connor as a replacement for the "Lemon" test would find government actions invalid if they create the perception in the mind of a reasonable observer that the government was either endorsing or disapproving of religion. It is unlikely that Georgia's recent inclusion of "respect for the Creator" in a list of virtues to be taught in the public schools (Georgia H.B. 393, 1997) would pass even this less stringent test of the Establishment Clause if challenged in court.

The many Establishment Clause cases decided by the U.S. Supreme Court give school systems and states every reason to expect a strict interpretation of this Clause and a strict application of the separation principle. Nevertheless, school systems and state governments that have restricted their focus to moral, civic, and prosocial values can expect support from the Court. Those that have not are advised to restrict themselves to the area of common ground described by Horace Mann (1880s): "There is a secular morality which is not opposed to religious morality . . . but is the result of human experiences, is recognized by all civilized people, is taught by the philosophers of all nations, and is sanctioned by all established creeds."

The First Amendment's Free Exercise Clause has been used to challenge school curricula and related activities (not formal character education programs) that were constitutional under the Establishment Clause but allegedly in violation of the religious Free Exercise Clause. In deciding these cases the U.S. Supreme Court has used a four-part test known as the "Sherbert" or "compelling state interest" test (*Sherbert v. Verner*, 1963). To claim protection under this Clause, a person must show (a) that his or her actions were motivated by a sincere religious belief and (b) that his or her beliefs have been substantially burdened. If the answer is "yes" to both, the school system will still prevail if (a) it is acting in the furtherance of a "compelling state interest" such as a public safety need and (b) it has pursued this interest in a manner least restrictive or burdensome to the religious beliefs in question (*Wisconsin v. Yoder*, 1972; Barnette v. West Virginia State Board of Education, 1943). If objecting parents can meet the four parts of this test, they will have a legally protected basis for insisting that their child be excused from a particular class, activity, or assignment.

Very few "free exercise" claims have succeeded in meeting all four parts of this "compelling state interest" test. The Ninth Circuit Court of Appeals in Grove v. Mead School District (1985) and the Sixth Circuit Court of Appeals in Spence v. Bailey (1972) applied the "compelling state interest" test by excusing students from using school materials and courses they felt were in conflict with their religious beliefs. Such findings are extremely rare and are unlikely to occur in situations where excusal is precluded by the infusion of character education into all aspects of school life, including both curricular and extracurricular activities. The disinclination of the federal courts to rule against school officials when dissenters claim values-related curricula violate religious "free exercise" rights has been established, but no cases in this area have yet been reviewed by the U.S. Supreme Court. Chief Judge Lively from the Sixth Circuit Court of Appeals wrote in *Mozert v. Hawkins County Board of Education* (1987):

The [Supreme] Court has almost never interfered with the prerogative of school boards to set curricula, based on free exercise claims. . . . It is a substantial imposition on the schools to require them to justify each instance of not dealing with students' individual, religiously compelled, objections. . . . Therefore . . . under the Supreme Court's decisions . . . school boards may set curricula bounded only by the Establishment Clause.

Justice Jackson wrote in *McCollum v. Board of Education* (1948):

If we are to eliminate everything that is objectionable to any [religious group] or inconsistent with any of their doctrines, we will leave public schools in shreds; nothing but educational confusion and a discrediting of the public school system can result from subjecting it to constant law suits.

In *Smith v. Mobile County* (1987), the Eleventh Circuit Court of Appeals found that textbooks did not establish "secular humanism" at the expense of the "free exercise" rights of students, and that they had the effect of instilling democratic values without precluding the possibility that religion was the original source of these values. Many felt that this decision weakened the four-part "compelling state interest" test and diminished the rights of students to freely exercise their religious beliefs. Their dissatisfaction with this decision resulted in the Religious Freedom Restoration Act (Public Law 103-141, 1993). It was designed to strengthen the "compelling state interest" test but was soon ruled unconstitutional by the Supreme Court in *City of Boerne v. Flores and the United States* (1997).

ACHIEVING CONSENSUS THROUGH INCLUSION

A common factor among successful character education programs is the process of building community consensus and commitment through inclusion. Nielson (1997) found that thirty-one states were able to initiate programs without controversy and that this was typically attributed by state coordinators to early community involvement in the identification of values to be taught. He also found that several state legislatures had developed lists of virtues without major controversy.

Several publications provide guidelines for formulating character education programs in a manner that minimizes alienation and helps people from different religions and cultures realize their common values (Lickona, 1993; Boston, 1993; Ditwiler, 1993; Huffman, 1995; National School Boards Association, 1987). Haynes (1994) and his associates teach citizens how to use the triad of social virtues that flow from the First Amendment to find common ground: freedom of conscience (Rights), the obligation to guard this freedom for oneself by guarding it for all others (Responsibility), the need to maintain dialogue by taking stock of how we debate as well as what we debate (Respect). Heslep (1995) points out that character education is not the business of just one institution and that it must begin with mutual respect among those who are to share responsibility for it. Nielson's findings and anecdotal reports from schools and school systems indicate that many communities have followed ethical guidelines such as these without controversy.

Efforts to initiate character education programs have failed in a few situations where respectful and inclusive approaches were not used (Ditwiler, 1993; McQuaide & Pliska, 1993). These failures were caused by state personnel choosing core values to be taught and failing to anticipate the concerns of constituencies predisposed to erroneously view character education programs as an attempt to substitute "secular humanistic" values for Biblical values. For the most part, reasoned proponents of character education have succeeded in persuading all religious constituencies that character education teaches core ethical, moral, civic, and prosocial values that enable pluralistic democracies to survive, and that it can be carried out in a manner not hostile to those for whom such values are based on deeply held religious convictions.

In 1991 the Georgia State Board of Education and its staff in the Department of Education developed a list of core values with input from the community at seven regional meetings. This was too early to ride the popular wave of "character education" although it was encouraging core elements of character education. This model initiative was followed in 1997 by a legislated list (Georgia H. B. 393, 1997) that was not preceded by community input, that gave the department of education little time to develop or select a curriculum, and that included "Respect for the Creator" as a virtue after its legal council advised that this could provoke First Amendment litigation. The author of the initial version of this legislation had good intentions, but the final version may do more to harm than help the character education movement. By contrast, the governor, state legislature, state board of education, state department of education, and local school systems in Utah have actively promoted character education without serious controversy or provocative legislation and without mandating the teaching of specific values or virtues.

CONCLUSIONS

Schools, school systems, and states that wish to plan and implement character education programs without controversy or litigation must (1) demonstrate an awareness of relevant constitutional principles and Court opinions that support character education; (2) focus on widely shared civic, moral, and prosocial values that transcend cultural and religious differences, as articulated by Horace Mann; (3) respectfully include persons from all points of view in discussions of what values to teach and how to teach them; and (4) communicate effectively with parents, students, and school personnel on the purposes and goals of character education. The prospects for success have increased greatly during the last decade thanks to the rapid growth of public, governmental, and organizational support for character education programs that satisfy this criteria.

LEGAL CITATIONS

Ambach v. Norwick, 441 U.S. 68 (1979).
Bethel School District No. 403 v. Fraser, 478 U.S. 675 (1986).
Board of Education v. Pico, 457 U.S. 853 (1982).
City of Boerne v. P. F. Flores, Archbishop of San Antonio, and the United States, 117 S.Ct. 2157 (1997).
Georgia H.B. 393, *Education, State Board to Develop Character Curriculum*, Code Sections –20-2-145 (1997).
Georgia State Board of Education Rule 160-4-2-.33 adopted June 13, 1991: *Values Education*.
Grove v. Mead School District, 753 F.2d 1528 (9th Cir.), *cert. denied*, 474 U.S. 826 (1985).
Hazelwood School District v. Kuhlmeier, 484 U.S. 260 (1988).
Lemon v. Kurtzman, 403 U.S. 602 (1971).
McCollum v. Board of Education, 333 U.S. 203 (1948).
Mozert v. Hawkins County Board of Education, 827 F.2d 1058 (6th Cir. 1987), *cert. denied*, 484 U.S. 1066 (1988).
Public Law 103-141. *Religious Freedom Restoration Act of 1993*. 107 Stat. 1488–1490.
Public Law 103-301 [S.J.Res.178]. *National Character Counts Week—Proclamation of 1994*. 108 Stat. 1558–1559.
Public Law 103-382. *Improving America's Schools Act of 1994*. 108 Stat. 3518.

Sherbert v. Verner, 374 U.S. 398 (1963).
Smith v. Board of Commissioners of Mobile County, 827 F.2d. 684 (11th Cir. 1987).
Spence v. Bailey, 465 F.2d 797 (6th Cir. 1972).
West Virginia State Board of Education v. Barnette, 319 U.S. 624   (1943).
Wisconsin v. Yoder, 406 U.S. 205 (1972).

REFERENCES

Bitensky, S. (1995). A Contemporary Proposal for Reconciling the Free Speech Clause with Curricular Values Inculcation in the Public Schools. *Notre Dame Law Review*, 70, 769–843.
Boston, J. (1993). In search of common ground. *Educational Leadership*, 51 (3), 38–40.
Clinton, B. (1994). Comments upon signing the Improving America's Schools Act of 1994. In *Weekly Compilation of Presidential Documents*, October 28, 1994, p. 2088; also in *CEP Character Educator*, Winter 1995, p. 3.
Clinton, B. (1995). Speech at the White House Conference on Character Building for a Civil and Democratic Society, May 20, 1995. In *Weekly Compilation of Presidential Documents*, May 29, 1995, p. 877.
Ditwiler, F. (1993). The tale of two districts. *Educational Leadership*, 51 (3), 24–28.
Eastland, T. (1993). *Religious Liberty in the Supreme Court: The Cases That Define The Debate Over Church and State*. Washington, D.C.: The Ethics and Public Policy Center.
Elam, S., Rose, L., and Gallop, A. (1993–94). The 25th annual Phi Delta Kappa/Gallop Poll of the public's attitudes toward the public schools. *Phi Delta Kappan*, October 1993, 137–52; The 26th annual Phi Delta Kappa/Gallop poll of the public's attitudes toward the public schools. *Phi Delta Kappa*, September 1994, 41–56.
Greenawalt, C. (1996). *Character Education in America*. Harrisburg, PA: The Common- wealth Foundation.
Haynes, C. (Ed.). (1994). *Finding Common Ground: A First Amendment Guide to Religion and Public Education*. Nashville, TN: The Freedom Forum First Amendment Center at Vanderbilt University.
Heslep, R. D. (1995). *Moral Education for Americans*. Westport, CT: Praeger Publishers.
Huffman, H. (1995). *Developing A Character Education Program: One School District's Experience*. Washington, D.C.: CEP Clearinghouse.
Kohn, A. (1997). The Trouble with Character Education. In A. Molnar (Ed.), The Construction of Children's Character. Chicago, IL: The National Society for the Study of Education; distributed by The University of Chicago Press.
Leming, J. (1993). In search of effective character education. *Educational Leadership*, 51 (3), 63–71.
Lickona, T. (1991). *Educating for Character: How Our Schools Can Teach Respect and Responsibility*. New York: Bantam.
Lickona, T. (1993). The return of character education. *Educational Leadership*, 51 (3), 6–11.
Mann, H. (1880s). *Wisconsin Journal of Education*.
McClellan, B. (1992). *Schools and the Shaping of Character: Moral Education in America, 1607–Present*. Bloomington, IN: RIC Clearinghouse for Social Studies/Social Science Education and the Social Studies Development Center, Indiana University.
McQuaide, J. and Pliska, A. (1993). The challenge to Pennsylvania's educational reform. *Educational Leadership*, 51 (3), 16–21.
Molnar, A. (Ed) (1997). *The Construction of Children's Character*. Chicago: The National Society for the Study of Education; distributed by The University of Chicago Press.

National School Boards Association (1987). *Building Character in the Public Schools: Strategies for Success*. Alexandria, VA: NSBA.

Nielson, L. (1997). Research summary: The status of character education from the perspective of state departments of education. Paper presented to U.S. Department of Education staff and federal grant recipients in Washington D.C. on June 11, 1997. A summary is to be published by CEP and the CA Council for Social Studies.

Piediscalzi, N. (1981). A survey of professional efforts to establish public education religion studies. In *Public Education Religion Studies: An Overview*, by P. Will, et al. Chico, CA: Scholars Press.

U.S. Department of Education, R. Riley Secretary (1995). *Religious Expression in the Public Schools*. Included with a letter to school superintendents from Secretary Riley dated August 10, 3-6. Copies available by calling 800-USA-LEARN.

Wynne, E. A. (1997). For-Character Education. In A. Molnar (Ed.), The Construction of Children's Character. Chicago: The National Society for the Study of Education; distributed by The University of Chicago Press.

2

Relevant Philosophy and Theory

TRADITIONAL VERSUS PROGRESSIVE CHARACTER EDUCATION

The terms character education, moral development, sociomoral development, moral education, values education, virtue ethics, deontological ethics, values clarification, civic education, and socialization have been used to describe various approaches to promoting morality, ethical decision making, and responsible citizenship that have been offered by philosophers, social scientists, educators, and theologians. These terms may appear synonymous and interchangeable, but to proponents of each approach, they reflect subtle philosophical and theoretical differences. The most basic traditional-versus-progressive difference has been in evidence for more than a century.

Process-oriented "progressivists" have emphasized developing the student's autonomous capacity to reason or deliberate in a morally principled way. Content-oriented "traditionalists" have emphasized transmitting specific moral facts, perennial truths, and codes of conduct. The indirect progressive approach can be traced to Dewey, Kant, Plato, Socrates, and cognitive-developmental psychologists including Piaget and Kohlberg; the direct traditional approach can be traced to Eliot, Durkheim, Fourier, Aristotle, and many other philosophers and religious leaders whose ideas have spawned social systems and world religions. Traditionalism as defined here includes, or is essentially synonymous with, virtue ethics, which seeks to develop moral people by studying and conveying what virtuous people would do in "moral" situations; progressivism as defined here includes, or is essentially synonymous with, deontological ethics, which focuses upon moral principles and seeks to develop in students the capacity to independently reflect in novel situations where these principles are in conflict and the right action is not immediately apparent.

Some traditionalists have criticized child-centered progressivists for "moral relativism," or a reluctance to teach specific moral facts or precepts. They allege that progressivists overemphasize individualism (in the tradition of open, democratic, and pluralistic societies) and neglect the emotional and motivational aspects of morality. Some inheritors of progressivism, in turn, have criticized culture-centered traditionalists for "moral dogmatism" or indoctrination. They allege that traditionalists overemphasize collectivism (in the tradition of nondemocratic and nonpluralistic societies) and neglect developmental constraints upon morality and learning.

Traditional Moral Education

Traditionalist philosophy predominated in American education during the final decade of the nineteenth century and the first two decades of the twentieth century. By the end of the third decade, most educators favored the indirect teaching of morals through all school subjects and activities rather than the direct teaching of morals through courses designed for that purpose, and other inculcative strategies including lists of virtues and the application of rewards and punishments in accordance with codes of conduct (Golightly, 1926:88; Charters, 1928:161). The decline in popularity of the direct, traditional approach was due in part to Hartshorne and May (1928, 1929, 1930) who found in their study of deceit and public service that honesty was situation-specific, and who encouraged character educators to focus less on lecture and exhortation and more on school climate and service learning (Leming, 1997). Their criticisms were similar to those made much earlier by John Dewey who was calling at the time for fundamental school reform (1893, 1916, 1975):

Moral education in school is practically hopeless when we set up the development of character as a supreme end, and at the same time treat the acquiring of knowledge and the development of understanding . . . as having nothing to do with character. On such a basis, moral education is . . . reduced to . . . catechetical instruction, or lessons about morals. (Dewey, 1916:354)

Certain traits of character have such an obvious connection with our social relationships that we call them moral in an emphatic sense. . . . To call them virtues in their isolation is like taking the skeleton for the living body. . . . Morals concern nothing less than the whole character. . . . To possess virtue does not signify to have cultivated a few nameable and exclusive traits. (Dewey, 1916:357)

Traditionalists can be subdivided into "emotionalists" and "collectivists." Both approaches view moral education as socialization, that is, a top-down process of transmitting or inculcating a collective moral code from the community to the individual through direct instruction, consistent modeling, and external incentives. During the first three decades of the century, "emotionalist" moral educators emphasized "training the will" in accordance with strict morality codes. The views of present-day "emotionalists" are similar. Green (1984) called for a renewed understanding of the "moral" in moral development and a recovery of the concept of "conscience" as an organizing center for character education. Sommers (1993) stressed that "basic ethics" or "plain moral facts" can be taught and that effective moral education appeals to the emotions as well as the mind.

The "emotionalist" perspective can be contrasted with the "collectivist" perspective reflected in the moral socialization of Durkheim (1961, 1973, 1979), the social engineering of Fourier, the social constructionism of Hogan and others (Turiel, 1989; Chazan, 1985), and the somewhat more eclectic modern-day communitarianism of Etzioni (1993). "Collectivism" is less concerned with emotion and conscience as internal regulators of prosocial and moral behavior and more concerned with instilling a sense of obligation or duty to sociocultural and/or religious standards, norms, rules of conduct, beliefs, and, in some cases, duty to individuals whose moral authority is not to be questioned within a nation or culture. The sociologist Durkheim identified three elements of being moral: to respect discipline, to be committed to the group or society, to have knowledge of the reasons for expected conduct (Durkheim, 1961:120). "Collectivists" claim that their socialization initiatives are not indoctrination because they include explanations of standards and because the method of choice is "suasion" and not coercion (Etzioni, 1993:38).

Progressive Moral Education

The progressivist approach to moral education emerged as part of the "progressive education" movement early in the twentieth century. In contrast to the traditional approach, it encouraged open-mindedness, holistic moral development, interactive learning, allowing children to develop naturally, and the cultivation of children's ability to make moral judgments through social experience within classroom and school communities. These ideas re-emerged during the 1960s, following a twenty-to-thirty year period during which neither traditional nor progressive moral instruction was formally occurring in most schools (McClelland, 1992; Pietig, 1976).

During the 1960s and 1970s, cognitive developmentalists and values clarificationists reformulated and reintroduced progressive moral education in the public schools. These approaches shared an emphasis upon reflection based on moral principles, teaching the whole child, and fostering intrinsic motivation and commitment. They commonly viewed autonomy as a distinguishing feature of true morality. The cognitive-developmental reformulation of progressive moral education focused exclusively upon reason rather than both reason and emotion for the origins of morality, and it was not until the 1970s and 1980s that affective-developmentalists offered some balance by proposing that morality emerges from emotional reactions or feeling states present at birth (Hoffman, 1977, 1982, 1983; Kagan, 1984; Damon, 1988). Kohlberg (1970, 1983, 1985) thought that cognitive-developmental constraints precluded the didactic teaching of virtue and that morality should be fostered through dialogue and discussion, and through participation within just democratic communities, that is, guided experience in moral reasoning. He viewed justice as the highest moral principal. Values clarificationists felt that specific moral precepts should (*rather than could*) not be taught directly and sought to facilitate prosocial behavior by teaching a values-clarifying process that was largely subjective and placed more emphasis upon emotion. In contrast to developmentalists, they were essentially individualists who believed that no person has the authority to impose a set of moral norms on another, that morality is located in the individual, not the community, and that it is not centered upon any single principle such as justice.

Reminiscent of Dewey's disparaging reference to "a few nameable and exclusive traits," Kohlberg (1970) scornfully referred to traditionalists' morality codes and related lists of desirable character traits as a "bag of virtues." He also criticized the "emotivism" of values clarification, a criticism that can be logically extended to Green's "moral emotions" and "voices of conscience," Sommers' claim that effective moral education appeals to the emotions as well as the mind, Gilligan's (1987) ethic of care, and the conclusion of Hoffman (1977, 1982, 1983), Kagan (1984), Damon (1988), and Hay (1994) that morality emerges, via social experience, from "universal emotional reactions" present in a rudimentary form at birth. Traditionalists including Sommers (1993), Bennett (1993), and Green (1984), in turn, have criticized Kohlberg and other progressivists for over-intellectualizing morality and for wrongly assuming that children will learn right and wrong indirectly through natural development and through facilitation, guidance, and social experience.

Eclectic Moral Education

The influence of progressivism and traditionalism on moral education has vacillated throughout most of the twentieth century (Ravitch, 1985). It was not until the 1980s that the idea of a combined approach began to grow in popularity. Many who had advocated an exclusively indirect approach during the 1960s and 1970s began to write about the compatibility of traditional and progressive ideas and the failure of values clarification. (Many who had advocated a direct approach were much less flexible and accommodating.) Even Kohlberg acknowledged late in his career that the teacher must socialize or teach content and not merely facilitate moral development through Socratic and Rogerian methods and the establishment of a just community within the classroom. He displayed no flexibility with respect to the importance of emotion and saw no need to balance his ethic of justice with an ethic of care.

Dewey

Like so many contemporary ideas in education, the notion of a combined approach may have originated with Dewey (Chazan, 1985; Pietig, 1976). His criticisms of extant character education programs obscured his belief that the process-content dichotomy in moral education was meaningless. He proposed that moral people reflect and reason about moral issues, confront moral issues with feeling and passion, learn moral principles through participation in communities, display prosocial habits and dispositions, and are an organic self in the sense that their actions reflect a consistent pattern. For Dewey, the teacher was both a transmitter of society's values and an organizer of democratic group experiences that promote the development of moral deliberation and passion.

Lisman

Lisman (1996) proposed that the direct traditional approach to moral instruction or moral development is more justifiable at the elementary school level, and that the indirect progressive approach, or deontological ethics, is more appropriate with older students whose autonomous moral reflection can be significantly improved through critical discussions of moral issues. He suggests the need for an age-appropriate balance of the two approaches by clarifying the basic problems presented by programs that rely too heavily on one or the other. He concludes that the problem with an approach that promotes moral growth mainly through ethical reflection is that it fails to acknowledge the difference between being able to figure out the right thing to do and feeling the need to do it, or having the will to do it. He concludes that the basic problem with an approach that relies on instilling virtue is that it assumes the virtuous person will either know or figure out what to do in situations where ethical principles are in conflict:

In our zeal to mold moral beings through direct moral instruction, we can jeopardize independence of character . . . at times we need direct moral instruction. There is a time to make clear to young people . . . that we are on the side of honesty, compassion, and justice. However, many ethical issues of the day involve conflicts, not over whether or not one should be moral, but over how to apply these moral norms or principles in concrete situations. . . . Assuming young people have developed some of the virtues of the moral person, they need assistance in developing the ability to think critically about ethical issues. Being able to critically analyze ethical issues and make effective ethical decisions is as important as the will to be moral. (Lisman, 1996:5)

Consistent with his view that both traditional and progressive or virtue ethics and deontological ethics have their place in moral instruction, he endorses liberal communitarianism, which may be closely related to Heslep's (see subsequent section) theory of moral agency. Liberal communitarianism, as he describes it, proposes that we acquire an understanding of ourselves as social beings who feel a fundamental obligation to promote the good of all and a fundamental need to promote a sense of community. It further proposes that we fulfill this obligation and satisfy this need not by merely exercising the freedom to pursue our own good and our own lifestyle—within the constraints of fairness and respect for the autonomy of others— but by being willing to "uphold those customs and practices that provide for . . . bonds of trust" among members of the community (Lisman, 1996:67).

Fowler and Lickona

Fowler (1992) suggested that specific core virtues can be formulated and nurtured (within an environment of caring and accountability) through the stimulation of natural development as articulated by Kohlberg and others, the development of "voices of conscience" or moral attitudes as articulated by Green, the provision of knowledge and information, and the use of literature as a primary tool for conveying moral orientations, motivations, and identifications. His model went beyond simply combining basic traditional and progressive ideas and integrated them to some degree. Similarly, Lickona (1991) viewed experience within moral communities as the primary means of teaching respect and responsibility. He integrated the knowing/thinking of Plato and the practicing/doing of Aristotle with "moral affect," which he described as "a motivational bridge between knowing what is right and actually doing it." By looking at moral knowing, moral feeling, and moral doing, he also initiated a true synthesis of traditional and progressive ideas and contributed toward a more useful definition of morality.

Iheoma and Peters

In building his case that religious education promotes moral education by fostering commitment, Iheoma (1986) provided a rationale for a combined progressive-traditional approach to all moral education. He explained that only a combined approach satisfies Peters' (1966) criteria for effective teaching and learning:

Moral education is concerned with . . . the transmission of moral values, habits and fundamental principles of conduct. Moral education must have a worthwhile moral content. . . . Moral education is not therefore just a matter of "values clarification" or "cognitive development," both of which . . . reject any kind of directive moral education. . . . Furthermore, moral education does not consist merely in passing on . . . isolated pieces of information about moral values and rules. The moral educator must aim at securing commitment to the values he is trying to inculcate . . . and to develop a sense of moral responsibility. . . .

[T]he moral educator must be engaged in the transmission of knowledge and understanding of moral issues and principles. He must not be content with merely passing on the inherited moral code of his society in an uncritical manner. The moral educator must show respect for the truth and encourage critical thinking and genuine discussion of the moral and social issues of the day. . . .

Moral education, therefore, does not consist in imposing one's point of view on others. All forms of indoctrination and authoritarianism are incompatible. . . . One of the aims of the moral educator, then, must be to develop in his students the ability to think for themselves about moral issues and to make autonomous moral judgments. (Iheoma, 1986:143)

The Child Development Project

The developers of the best researched eclectic approach to character or "socio-moral" development, the Child Development Project, contrasted their relatively progressive model with extreme traditional and extreme progressive approaches to socialization which they referred to as the "societal transmission of values" and "self-construction of sociomoral values" or constructivism, respectively (Battistich et al., 1991). As described by Battistich and colleagues, the former transmits norms and values through direct instruction and reinforcement and seeks to transform external regulation into internal regulation via affective conditioning; the latter allows the child to construct sociomoral values naturally through participation in social groups and interpersonal interaction. They stated:

We see the societal transmission and self-construction models as contrasting, but essentially complementary perspectives, that, together, provide a more comprehensive framework for understanding sociomoral development than either does by itself. Central to our "integrative" view of socialization and sociomoral development is the concept of self-other balance. (Battistich et al., 1991:97)

Damon

Damon (1988, 1995) combined his cognitive-interactionist theory of moral development with the "affective-developmental" ideas of Kagan (1984) and proposed that "children's morality is a product of affective ["natural emotional reactions"], cognitive, and social forces that converge to create a growing moral awareness" (Damon, 1988:119). In addition to this synthesis of affective and cognitive-interactionist propositions, he provided a scientific rationale for avoiding (1) approaches to moral education that emphasize moral habit at the expense of moral reflection, and vice versa, and (2) approaches that are either too child-centered (constructivist) or too adult-centered. With respect to the latter polarity, he suggested that only a combined approach enables the teacher to engage children in an essential process of interaction, and he describes socialization as a process of "bridge building" and "respectful engagement" that effectively links the child's subjective experience with the ideas and values that adults must transmit. He wrote:

Like all socialization practices, moral instruction must touch children's goals as well as their beliefs, skills, and feelings. . . . Influencing the child's goals means sharing the child's agenda while at the same time moving it in a new direction. This can only take place when an adult assumes a role of leadership. . . . The leadership . . . cannot be in the form of an arbitrary, tyrannical force that the child perceives as external. . . . In order to have a lasting, positive influence . . . the adult must exert leadership within a participatory, collaborative relationship. . . . Effective socialization encourages children both to respect moral authority and to learn to think on their own . . . to respond habitually to moral concerns and to reason well about moral problems. (Damon, 1995:150–51)

Children acquire moral values by actively participating in adult-child and child-child relationships that support, enhance, and guide their natural moral inclinations. Children's morality is little affected by lessons or lectures for which they are . . . passive recipients. (Damon, 1988:118)

If . . . we want democratic citizens, we should provide for them relationships in which they can think, argue, and freely make choices. . . . This does not mean that schools should pretend to be value-neutral; or that teachers and administrators should refrain from clear moral instruction and explanation. Children need adult guidance. They also need to develop morally responsible habits. But reasoning can only strengthen and enlighten such habits. (Damon, 1988:146)

Heslep

Heslep (1995) contrasted his theory of "moral agency" with individualism, communitarianism, moral developmentalism, and social liberalism. He gave social liberals credit for overcoming some of the deficiencies of individualism and communitarianism by acknowledging that individuals become autonomous only through experience in social groups that encourage autonomy, but he challenged social liberals for restricting their instructional focus to prudential reasoning and civic virtues (public values) such as freedom, justice, and equality. He proposed a beginning theory of "moral agency" that locates morality in the interaction between members of a moral group rather than in the individual or the community. And in contrast to social-liberal philosophy, he included among other forms of moral reasoning virtues other than civic. He defined a moral agent as one who willfully does something that influences another and explained that the norms of "moral agency" contain criteria for moral rights, duties, values, and virtues that enable moral agents to reconcile conflicts between self-interest and the social good. For Heslep, the aim or moral education is to produce people with the characteristics of knowledge, autonomous reasoning, empathy, charity, justice, and friendship. He separated character education into two parts: nonmoral, which includes prudential (learning to take care of one's self), cultural (understanding persons from other backgrounds), social (social roles and manners), and civic (laws and political ideals); and moral, which provides an instructional context of moral principles for the four nonmoral components of character education.

Nucci, Benninga, Kirschenbaum

Since the 1980s many have followed the lead of Dewey, Kohlberg, Damon, and the Child Development Project by proposing combined approaches. Nucci (1991) offered a research-based rationale for an approach to moral education that is nonindoctrinative and nonrelativistic. Benninga stated that "effective programs . . . must focus on concern for justice and human welfare as well as the sound rules and organizational structures underlying social conventions and regulations" (1991a:266). Benninga (1991a; 1991b) and Nucci (1991, 1989) encouraged a synthesis by inviting proponents of direct and indirect approaches to contribute to their books. Kirschenbaum (1995) proposed a combined progressive/traditional approach in his "comprehensive moral education" model and used the instructional categories of inculcation, modeling, facilitation, and skill development as a framework for presenting and describing numerous instructional strategies.

Berkowitz

Berkowitz (1995) pointed out that leaders in the field of moral education are beginning to reconstruct the complete moral person. He argued that the correct question is not which theory is right but how best to promote moral growth given the information provided by all theories. His seven-part taxonomy provided a way of judging the completeness of the various theories, philosophies, and methodologies: moral behavior, moral values, moral character, moral reason, moral emotion, moral identity, and meta-moral characteristics. He elaborated that moral behavior is intentional, that moral values reflect beliefs and attitudes that have an affective component, and that moral character is reflected in personality or a stable disposition to act in moral ways. He viewed moral reasoning as necessary in novel and unanticipated situations; he viewed moral identity as having at its core a sense of being or trying to be a moral person. He defined meta-moral characteristics as those which serve the moral person but are not inherently moral such as self-discipline and motivation.

DEFINITIONS OF MORALITY

Ethicists, philosophers, theologians, psychologists, sociologists, educators, and many others have endeavored to define morality. The definitions offered by social scientists lack the specificity and perhaps the substance of those offered by ethicists, philosophers, educators, and theologians, and this is understandable given their view of child development as a natural process that imposes constraints upon learning at different age levels, and their focus upon the important role of social interaction and community experience, that is, the "when" and "how" of moral education rather than the "what." The social science literature includes "conceptualizations" that aptly describe morality as internally driven, but the literature largely fail to specify what is "right" and "good" and what is not.

Damon (1988:5) summarized six ways in which social scientists have conceptualized morality: an evaluative orientation that distinguishes good and bad and prescribes good conduct, a sense of obligation toward standards of a social collective, a sense of responsibility for acting out of concern for others, a concern for the rights of others, a commitment to honesty in interpersonal relationships, and a state of mind that causes negative emotional reactions to immoral acts. Piaget (1948, 1965) stated that the essence of morality is respect for rules and that acting on internalized principles represents a higher level of morality than blind conformity. Havighurst (1953) stated that the essence of morality is doing what is right and good and that one achieves this by internalizing the demands of society. He implied that the more altruistic person is the more moral person. Kohlberg (1970) stated that true morality is demonstrated by persons who feel compelled by self-chosen principles of conscience to act unselfishly to bring about moral justice. In contrast to most social scientists, Hartshorne and May (1928) defined morality in terms of specific virtues, including honesty and cooperation.

In comparison to the definitions of morality offered by social scientists, those offered by ethicists, philosophers, educators, and theologians appear to be more substantive, at least in the sense that they list specific moral principles and virtues and thus distinguish between right and wrong. Many of the authors of these definitions, however, seem to assume that children of all ages can understand and display most if not all moral principles and virtues. Some appear to discount evidence pointing to natural stages of moral development and developmental constraints upon what can and cannot be learned and understood at a given point in a child's development. The task of adapting these definitions and lists to the various age levels, to the extent that this can be done, is left to teachers. Interestingly, Aristotle (with whom many modern-day ethicists, philosophers, and traditionalist educators like to identify) and Plato apparently had a more complete understanding of developmental constraints upon moral development than many moral philosophers and traditionalist moral educators today. They, in fact, laid a philosophical foundation for theories of moral developmental that emerged in the twentieth century.

The Ancient Cardinal Virtues

The so-called classical or cardinal virtues of prudence, justice, fortitude, and temperance have been studied by Socrates, Aristotle, Plato, and many others throughout history (Eastman, 1967; Simon, 1986). Prudence and justice are the intellectual virtues and can be linked with the thinking or reasoning part of Plato's conscious life or "soul"; fortitude and temperance correspond, respectively, to the spirit or mettlesome part of the "soul" and the appetite or sensuous part of the "soul." The primacy of reason in Greek philosophy is reflected by Plato's statement that the spirit enforces dictates of reason and that the passions obey. Socrates referred to temperance as "a course steered between abstinence and indulgence by a pilot called the mind," that is, moderation and self-restraint in matters pertaining to pleasure (Eastman, 1967). Fortitude, for Aristotle at least, pertained to the type of courage displayed on the battlefield. Prudence can be defined as the practical wisdom or good judgment that brings order to acquired knowledge and provides direction no matter how unprecedented the circumstances might be. Justice concerns relations with other people and the community. Aristotle distinguished between general justice, which embraces all virtues, and particular justice, which is subdivided into distributive justice and corrective justice. General justice or legal justice covers what is owed to the community by individuals; distributive justice covers what the community owes individuals based upon rules of merit and need. Corrective justice is activated when the rules that govern just exchange (called commutative justice) are violated. Finally, in response to those who have justly criticized these classic philosophers for totally neglecting the importance of compassion, Socrates valued friendship above all other things except clear and honest thinking.

Green's Five Voices of Conscience

Green (1984) proposed that conscience (defined as reflexive judgments of conduct accompanied by emotions such as shame, guilt, and pride) speaks to us in five different voices: craft, membership, responsibility, memory, and imagination. The conscience of craft involves making habitual a desire to do things well. The conscience of membership involves forming bonds or attachments to the community. The conscience of membership also requires individuals to refrain from criticisms unless improvements can be proposed, to continually examine whose interests are being served, and to guard against self-serving behavior. The conscience of responsibility essentially involves a sense of duty and obligation and the need to keep one's promises. The conscience of memory involves being rooted in one's cultural past through stories, myths, and so forth, and keeping faith with the people and traditions that formed us. Finally, the conscience of imagination involves claiming solidarity with and feeling responsible for generations yet unborn.

Starratt's Ethical School

Starratt (1994) may not describe himself as a moral philosopher, but in conjunction with his guidelines for building an ethical school, he included a section on the special qualities of ethical people. These moral qualities are autonomy, connectedness, and transcendence. He stated that truly ethical people act as autonomous agents within the constraints of relationships, and act in ways that transcend immediate self-interest. For Starratt, autonomy implies choice, responsibility, and ownership of one's actions. He links his concept of connectedness to Green's "conscience of membership" and the importance of empathy in becoming interpersonally connected. His concept of transcendence concerns reaching for excellence, valuing heroism, possibly being heroic in some way, and going beyond self-absorption to share with and help others as an individual or as part of a collective action. He wanted these qualities to be viewed not as virtues to acquire but as aspects of personal integrity which are developed through action and choice, or "doing-constantly-repeated." Starratt juxtaposed his three qualities with an analysis of "ethical systems of thought" or types of ethics: critique, justice, and care.

Religions of the World

In spite of the fact that most religions over the centuries have linked morality and religious beliefs, few proponents of moral education in the public schools have acknowledged the important role that religions have played in the formulation and transmission of prosocial and pro-environmental values, and the powerful incentives for moral action that religious beliefs provide for many people. Their timidity is primarily attributable to a fear that any reference to religion might elicit arguments against moral education based on the First Amendment separation of church and state. Their timidity is perhaps less frequently attributable to the belief that religion and morality can and should be logically separated in order to ensure the development of rational and autonomous moral thinking in children rather than passive adherence to authoritarian moral principles (Iheoma, 1986).

Obviously, religious doctrines or beliefs vary greatly and are sometimes contradictory. Even religions that are relatively similar in terms of virtues taught tend to differ in terms of emphasis. Nevertheless, there is a nucleus of values or virtues commonly taught by most religions (Eastman, 1967; Carmody, 1974, 1988).

The Golden Rule or "reciprocity" has been articulated as a virtue by Jesus (Christianity), Hillel (Judaism), Muhammad (Islam), and Confucius (Confucianism) and is included among the seven cardinal virtues of Maat (an Egyptian moral principle), to mention a few. The "fundamentalisms," including Christianity, Judaism, and Hinduism, and various sagacious religions including Buddhism and Confucianism, teach that the good person is controlled by sympathy and compassion rather than reason as taught by the Greek philosophers. The Western concept of justice flows from a union of this emphasis on compassion and the Greek's more intellectual analysis of justice. Justice is listed as an important virtue by all major religions and is the primary virtue of Judaism.

Jesus emphasized the worth of each individual, laid the groundwork for various groups to escape discrimination, and modeled the virtues of compassion, courage, humility, nonviolence, unselfishness, sincerity, forgiveness, and reciprocity. Gandhi and Martin Luther King modeled these virtues as they endeavored to eliminate discrimination, and these virtues have been taught by Christianity and other religions for centuries. In addition to its primary emphasis on social justice, Judaism teaches peacemaking, serious study, involved charity, and the Ten Commandments. Compassion is the paramount virtue of Buddhism, followed by a belief in the sanctity of life and other virtues, including helpfulness, peacefulness, happiness, truth, kindness, generosity, and the capacity to control one's anger, desire, and the urge to return hate. The five ethical precepts of Buddhism (not to kill, lie, steal, commit unchaste acts, or take intoxicants) have counterparts among the Ten Commandments shared by Judaism and Christianity and the forty-two Admonitions or Declaration of Innocence of Maat in the religious tradition of Egypt.

Confucianism teaches principles of interpersonal relations including the truthfulness, equality, and liberty that justice demands (yi). It also teaches virtues of character such as goodness (jen), wisdom (zhi), courage (yong), proper behavior or propriety (li), faith or trust (xin), the summation of all virtues in the moral life that has been variously translated as human relatedness, benevolence, and compassion (ren), moral commitment and steadfastness (zhong), treating others as one would like to be treated (shu), which Confucius described as the whole of moral practice, and various other virtues. These include dignity, mercy, tolerance, the duty of reverence, the sacredness of work, and the need for leaders to be well educated (Tan Tai Wei, 1990; Eastman, 1967; Carmody, 1974, 1988).

Many religions share with Hinduism an emphasis on the importance of duty and the belief that people cannot escape the consequences of their evil and righteous actions (karma, which is often mistakenly interpreted as fatalism). A similar principle is articulated in Christianity by St. Paul, who stated that people reap what they sow. The ideal human being according to Hinduism is humble, upright, truthful, slow to wrath, charitable, tender toward the suffering, kind toward all living things, patient, courageous, modest, and unrevengeful. Taoism teaches simplicity, humility, persistence, objectivity, satisfying work, selflessness, and objectivity. Some have alleged that Islam places less value on world peace and the sanctity of life than other major religions and more value on submission to Allah (God), but like most major religions, it teaches patience, kindness, justice, hard work, respect for others' rights, temperance, and responsibility for the needy.

The ancient Egyptian principle of Maat (personified by the goddess Maat) is communicated in seven cardinal virtues or rules that are shared by most other religions and that remain the moral foundation of the Egyptian people: truth, order, justice, balance, righteousness, harmony, and propriety/reciprocity. Shamanism and Animism (the latter a more inclusive term) identify another ancient belief system that continues to be practiced in a variety of forms within traditional or relatively nonindustrialized tribal societies on all five continents, including Native Americans in the United States and isolated tribal cultures in Africa and South America. It shares with Shintoism, an indigenous religion or mythology in Japan, a reverence for nature and a feeling of interdependence with nature that uniquely sustains a strong conservation ethic and an aesthetic sensitivity that has special relevance in a modern world characterized by diminishing resources, pollution, animal extinction, and over-population.

Miscellaneous Lists of Virtues and Moral Principles

Hutchins (1917) authored the Children's Morality Code, which outlined ten laws of right living. These ten laws were used by many school systems across the country in the 1920s and 1930s: self-control, good health, kindness, sportsmanship, self-reliance, duty, reliability, truth, good workmanship, and teamwork. Presented in the form of categories for his book of stories, Bennett (1993) listed self-discipline, compassion, responsibility, friendship, a work ethic, courage, perseverance, honesty, loyalty, and faith. The Josephson Institute of Ethics (1992) identified six Pillars of Character: respect (courtesy, nonviolence, nonprejudice, acceptance), responsibility (accountability, pursuit of excellence, self-restraint), trustworthiness (honesty, integrity, promise keeping, loyalty), caring (kindness, compassion, empathy, unselfishness), justice and fairness (equity, openness, reasonableness, consistency), and civic virtue and citizenship (lawfulness, service learning, voting, protection of the environment).

Some commercially available character education curriculums target specific virtues. The Heartwood Institute in Pittsburgh, Pennsylvania, focuses upon seven core virtues: courage, loyalty, justice, respect, hope, honesty, and love. The Center for Learning in Rocky River, Ohio, lists twenty-five values deemed vital to responsible and ethical behavior: adaptability, citizenship, compassion, consideration, courage, diligence, endurance, equality, faith, family commitment, freedom, gratitude, initiative, integrity, justice, loyalty, peace, responsibility, privacy, respect, self-actualization, self-discipline, service, teamwork, and truth.

Although few schools in Georgia used the list developed by the Georgia Department of Education in 1991, it is among the best available and is broken down into primary categories of citizenship, respect for others, and respect for self, and secondary categories of patriotism (courage, loyalty), democracy (equality, justice, freedom/liberty, tolerance, respect), respect for the environment, altruism (civility, compassion, courtesy), integrity (honesty/truth, trustworthiness), accountability (commitment, perseverance, self-control, frugality), self-esteem (accomplishment, cooperation, dependability, diligence, pride, productivity, creativity), and work ethic (knowledge, moderation, respect for health). A similar scheme was adopted in 1992 in the state of Utah. They built upon a solid legislative base (Section 53-14-4.3, Utah Code Annotated, 1953) by targeting the principles of self-worth and the courage of one's convictions, self-motivation, respect for others, moral judgment, and critical thinking. Each of these desired outcomes was operationalized in the form of several abilities. One would show respect for others, for example, by listening to another point of view, disagreeing without becoming angry, and so forth (Utah State Department of Education, 1992).

Some of the most successful character education programs are structured around values words or lists of virtues. The Allen Classical/Tradition Academy in Dayton, Ohio, began using a virtue-of-the-week strategy several years ago, and their reported success caused many other schools across the country to adopt the strategy, including West Point Elementary in Troup County, Georgia, the first school in Georgia to use this strategy successfully. Allen and some of its clones chose a values word for each week of the first semester and then repeated with synonyms for the second (e.g., respect and consideration, responsibility and dependability, honesty and truthfulness, self-control and self-discipline, kindness and generosity, courage and bravery, helpfulness and cooperation, courteousness and politeness, patience and perseverance, loyalty and patriotism).

The Core Essentials scheme (CorrEss@aol.com), which was developed by parents for parents and teachers, also uses pairs of values words with each pair chosen to convey one of eighteen character concepts or qualities that they hope parents and teachers will work together to develop in their children: determination and responsibility, endurance and patience, discipline and orderliness, resourcefulness and initiative, conviction and virtue, respect and obedience, joy and contentment, loyalty and commitment, courtesy and kindness, individuality and uniqueness, love and friendship, gratitude and humility, generosity and compassion, peace and cooperation, forgiveness and acceptance, truth and honesty, courage and confidence. Their brief description of the eighteen qualities corresponding to these word pairs is interesting and reflects an organizational clustering of virtues which is structurally similar to the clustering I used in my core curriculum, which is presented in chapter 3.

The Fort Washington School District in California used seven categories of character qualities (Sparks, 1991): honest (trustworthy, truthful, ethical); responsible (dependable, accountable, conservation minded); respectful (courteous, obedient to legitimate authority, patriotic); dedicated (courageous, involved, faithful); perseverant (industrious, self-disciplined, diligent, resourceful); self-respecting (self-accepting, confident, resilient, health-minded); concerned for others (friendly, helpful, considerate, fair, cooperative, civic-minded). The SMILE program in Utah uses seven core values or principles: worth and dignity, rights and responsibility, fairness and justice, care and consideration, social responsibility, effort and excellence, and personal integrity.

Among the many schools that use lists of virtues and/or principles, Boyer's (1995) "basic schools" and Joseph Gauld's (1993) "character first" schools are among the best conceived. As articulated by Boyer, "basic schools" must be committed to character, must bring people together to build a community, must develop a coherent curriculum, and must create a climate for learning that promotes effective learning and teaching. Character building in the "basic school" relates to the entire school experience and is taught through curriculum, climate, and service. The seven virtues of the "basic school" are respect, compassion, honesty, responsibility, self-discipline, giving, and perseverance.

Character growth is the centerpiece or foundation for the Hyde Schools rather than academic achievement, and academic achievement is viewed as a part of character and a means of achieving one's dreams and unique potential. The five virtues that comprise the Hyde motto effectively convey the objectives of the curriculum: the courage to accept challenges, the integrity to be truly oneself, concern for others, the curiosity to explore life and learning, and leadership in making the school and community work. In addition, the school has five guiding principles: "each of us is gifted with a unique potential that defines a destiny" (destiny); "we trust in a power and purpose beyond ourselves" (humility); "we achieve our best through character and conscience" (conscience); "truth is our primary guide" (truth). While these lists of virtues and guiding principles may suggest a didactic approach, nothing could be further from the truth as conveyed in Headmaster Malcolm Gauld's recent comments:

Character is inspired rather than imparted; we don't pour character into our students; we summon it forth with values-forming challenges and experiences. . . . I believe that many contemporary educators who seek to "teach character" are engaged in a futile game of deficit reduction. . . . If we truly seek to teach character we must begin to build community with a new triad: student-teacher-parent(s). (Hyde School Website, May 1997)

RELEVANT DEVELOPMENTAL THEORIES

As mentioned in the previous section, Aristotle and Plato laid a foundation for theories of moral development that emerged in the twentieth century. These philosophers did much more than identify and define the cardinal virtues. They offered a beginning explanation for how children develop into moral beings and what adults must do to facilitate this development. Aristotle viewed habituation as necessary in early life to prepare the "soul" for rational teaching (Aristotle, 1985). His levels of ethical development (ethics of fear, ethics of shame, ethics of wisdom) correspond to Plato's (Eastman, 1967; Colby, 1987) three parts of the conscious life or "soul" (appetites, spirit, reason), and they resemble Kohlberg's preconventional, conventional, and post-conventional levels of moral development (Burnyeat, 1980). Aristotle implied, and Plato later stated, that these parts of the "soul" or "psyche" must be educated sequentially (Simon, 1986).

Piaget's Moral and Cognitive Stages

Piaget's (1948 and 1965) ideas about moral development have been inaccurately described as being limited to two stages: a morality of constraint or heteronomy, which is based on respect for rules that are external to the child and imposed by authority, and a morality of cooperation or autonomy, which is based on an understanding of moral principles developed through social experiences with peers. While this description captures the concept most central to his thoughts on moral development, it falls short of reflecting his elaborate analysis, which reads more like Plato or Aristotle than the work of a cognitive-developmentalist. He approached the topic from several perspectives, each articulated in the form of stages that must be integrated for a full understanding.

First Piaget viewed the rules of children's games as an important origin for morality, and he delineated four stages that reflect the "practice of rules" and three that reflect the "consciousness of rules." Stage two of his four stages of rule practice, called egocentrism, was described as an intermediate stage between the purely individual play of toddlers and the socialized behaviors of children age seven and older. This egocentric stage, which lasts until about age six, includes playing with others without an interest in winning. At the third stage, which emerges at about age seven and called the stage of cooperation, players want to win but have only a vague notion of the rules. The fourth stage, which begins at about age ten, is characterized by the codification of rules. The difference between stages three and four is one of degree, with stage-three children not yet knowing the rules in detail and stage-four children mastering the rules and exhibiting an intense interest in them.

With respect to rule consciousness, rules are regarded as sacred and unchangeable during stage two, which begins at about age six (during the practical egocentric stage described above) and ends at about nine or ten (midway through the practical cooperation stage). Rules at this stage are regarded as obligatory, and this is a product of unilateral respect for constraining, external authority. This is preceded at age four and five by a rather casual attitude toward game rules. During the third and final rule-consciousness stage, rules are viewed as a free product of mutual consent and are no longer viewed as sacred and unalterable. Piaget felt that constraints necessarily imposed by authority during early stages of child development effectively maintain egocentrism and that only cooperation and reciprocity, born of mutual respect, can deliver children from unconscious egocentrism and heteronomy into the realm of moral autonomy, where they feel the desire to treat others the way they wish to be treated. He suggested that during this transition, rules and commands are "interiorized" and generalized.

In an analysis separate from his analysis of rules, Piaget concluded that the child's acquisition of a sense of justice requires nothing more for its development than the mutual respect and solidarity that holds among children. He contrasted this with rules initially imposed by adults and describes justice as an imminent product of social relationships. With respect to retributive justice, he defined expiatory punishment inherent in the relations of constraint and punishment by reciprocity. He defined three stages of justice beginning with equating "just" with what is commanded by authority (evident up to the age of seven or eight), followed by equalitarianism, which comes from solidarity and mutual respect among children (between ages eight and eleven), followed by a more subtle form of justice he calls equity, which involves taking into account the circumstances of individuals involved (at age eleven or twelve).

Piaget stated that parent-child relationships have other features besides constraint. He referred to mutual affection, which promotes acts of generosity and kindness, and he viewed this as the starting point for the "morality of good." He stated that this morality develops alongside the "morality of right or duty," but he did not attempt to analyze in detail this morality of good.

According to Piaget's general theory of cognitive development (1952), two- to six-year-old children cannot "decenter" or take the perspective of others, are impervious to adult reasoning, cannot comprehend classes and subclasses, assume that you know what they know, are highly imitative, must rely on others for correction, cannot think about their own thinking, are perceptual rather than conceptual in their thinking, and cannot solve a problem in their mind (preoperational). Seven- to eleven-year-old children willfully engage in social cooperation, can take the perspective of others, begin to move from perceptual to conceptual thought, cannot reason abstractly or imagine events that are not also real events, and are beginning to solve problems in their mind by manipulating objects symbolically (concrete operations). Children twelve and older can think both logically and abstractly, manipulate symbols in their mind, consider many viewpoints, can imagine hypothetical as well as real events, can introspect and think about their own thinking, and tend to be more self-conscious than younger children.

Kohlberg's Cognitive-Moral Stages

Influenced by Dewey's emphasis on the social nature of learning, Kant's formalistic emphasis on the duties and obligations of moral people, and Piaget's emphasis on stages of cognitive development, Kohlberg proposed that ethical judgments for young children have more to do with external consequences than an understanding of intrinsic goodness. He suggested that children come to understand "justice" by initially viewing "good" as behavior that gains the approval of others (ages four to ten), and then viewing "good" as behavior that adheres to rules that extend beyond the immediate situation. His six stages of moral development reflect qualitatively different styles of thinking which serially focus on punishment, pleasure, acceptance, status, law, and justice. Stages one and two involve thinking that is "preconventional" and thus self-serving; stages three and four involve reasoning that is "conventional" and thus other-serving or group-serving; stages five and six involve reasoning that is "post-conventional" and thus serves moral principles rather than the self or others.

Kohlberg proposed that children progress from being good to avoid punishment (an egocentric perspective), to viewing right as that which satisfies their needs with or without an exchange of favors (a concrete, pleasure-seeking, reward-seeking, individualistic perspective), to gaining approval from significant others by being caring and accommodating (an interpersonal, Golden-Rule, approval-seeking, disapproval-avoiding perspective), to dutifully following rules and respecting authority (a societal or organizational need, censorship-avoiding perspective), to an understanding of mutual obligation, standards, and rights within society as a whole (a combined moral/legal point of view which centers upon community welfare concerns), to acting according to principles of conscience that are thought to have universal application (a truly moral perspective which centers upon a need to avoid self-condemnation). The key concepts in his theory are justice and social perspective-taking, which are gradually acquired.

Damon's Fairness and Social-Affective Stages

Damon's (1977) original theory applies to children in the four-to-ten range and focuses on the development of four aspects of social knowledge: positive justice (sharing and fairness), friendship, authority, and social regulations. He saw the "roots of justice growing in the soil of early friendships" (Damon, 1977:138), and he saw children's knowledge in both areas growing and changing throughout their development. His research and related theoretical propositions suggested that other developmental theorists, including Kohlberg, have been too heavily influenced by the subservience of young children to authority and too quick to conclude that the most primitive forms of morality are characterized by fear-induced adherence to externally imposed rules. He acknowledged the importance of the child's authority-obeying perspective and need to relate to authority figures, as evidenced by his six levels of authority, but he did not find in this the origins of morality. According to his model, even five- and six-year-old children operate on the basis of internal principles of justice that change and improve with age in a predictable sequence of six stages.

According to Damon's six-stage theory of positive justice, four-year-old children at level 0-A feel they should get more because they want more, and they make no attempt to justify their choices. Five-year-old children at level 0-B feel a need to justify their choices but do so in an after-the-fact, self-serving way (e.g., I deserve more because I am the biggest or I am a girl). Levels 1-A and 1B are egalitarian. Many early elementary children are at level 1-A, where fairness and related choices are based on a principle of strict equality that serves to prevent troublesome consequences caused by competition. Other early elementary children are at 1-B, where fairness emerges as a value in its own right and where choices are based on notions of reciprocal obligation and merit (e.g., he shares his things with me so I have to share my things with him). At level 2-A fairness is considered a general right of all persons, especially the needy who are in an unequal position to begin with. Typical seven- and eight-year-old children at this level recognize disparate claims to justice as legitimate and try to mediate through compromise (e.g., "He should get the most because . . . but she should get some too"). Levels 2-A and 2-B have benevolence in common. By age ten children are typically at level 2-B and realize that justice is context dependent. Children at this level take into account the claims of various persons and the demands of the situation, and exclude all but the best claims, but they are unable to view the situation from a perspective wider than the parties involved and have not reached full maturity in terms of notions of fairness (e.g., an adult selling a piece of candy for five dollars would be acceptable if it was acceptable to the adult and the child).

For relationships with authority Damon proposed six levels beginning with an inclination at level 0-A for the child to distort the authority's commands to fit his wishes. At level 0-B the child senses authority as an obstacle to satisfying desire and still has no sense of a necessary function of authority. At level 1-A authority is confused with power to enforce, and the authority is viewed as having the right to be obeyed, that is, might makes right. At level 1-B there is some recognition that authority figures have talents other than strength and power and that obedience can be legitimately exchanged for the benefits derived from these talents. The authority is seen as deserving obedience because of past, present, and future favors or help, and obedience for the first time is voluntary. At level 2-A those with leadership knowledge are considered to have more legitimate authority, and authority is viewed as a relationship between people with equal rights but different experience. At level 2-B, which is typically achieved by age ten, authority is viewed as a situational role adopted by consensus in response to a problem.

In formulating his more recent "affective-cognitive-social" theory of moral development, Damon (1988, 1995) drew heavily from Kagan (1984) and Hoffman (1977, 1982, 1983) who were the first to suggest that morality emerges from feeling states which are present at birth in a rudimentary form. He proposed that early emotional reactions provide a natural base or energizing structure for moral learning which is inextricably tied to the cognitive and social aspects of children's development. He proposed that through active participation in (1) peer relationships that promote the development of perspective-taking skills and introduce norms of reciprocity and standards of sharing, cooperation, and fairness, and (2) adult relationships that introduce social standards (substance), foster respect for social order, and offer moral-developmental guidance through "respectful engagement," children's natural emotional reactions are transformed into enduring moral values (Damon, 1988).

Hoffman and Kagan on Moral Emotion

Kagan (1984) and Hoffman (1977, 1982, 1983) proposed that emotion rather than cognition provides the foundation for morality. They proposed that the potential for moral-emotional reactions is present at birth and that natural feeling states provide a "platform upon which a set of universal, or principled, moral standards can be built" (Kagan, 1984:123). They proposed that empathy begins in infancy as discomfort at others' distress (referred to by Hoffman as "global empathy") and develops by age one or two into feelings of genuine concern that constrains aggression. They proposed that moral emotions such as this emerge during the first two years as cognitive development brings the ability to take the perspective of others (the cognitive component of empathy). Kagan identified as core moral emotions (1) fear of punishment, disapproval, or failure; (2) empathy towards those in distress; (3) guilt over callous and irresponsible behavior; (4) disgust from the over-satiation of desire; and (5) anxiety over the awareness of inconsistency between beliefs and actions.

Youniss and Selman's Friendship Stages

Youniss (1978) and Selman (1980, 1990) focused specifically on friendship. Youniss' findings suggested to him that children's friendship knowledge moves from conceptions based on the sharing of material goods and pleasurable activities at about age six to conceptions based upon the mutual sharing of private thoughts and feelings. He found that the friendship stories of six-year-old children are about sharing toys and playing, those of ten-year-old children are about playing only, and those of thirteen-year-old children are about children assisting each other. Selman studied friendship from the perspective of social perspective-taking. According to his model, children at level 0 (three to six) define friends as those who live nearby, those with whom they happen to be playing, or those whose toys they want. They cannot distinguish between their own perspective and that of others. At Level 1 (six to eight), friendship is characterized by subjectivity and "uneven-handed" reciprocity. At this stage children are aware that others may have a different perspective and they can respect others' views, but they can only focus on one view and will gravitate toward and rationalize their own. At level 2 (eight to ten), friendship is defined by a cooperative and more even-handed reciprocity. At this level children have a better understanding that people have different viewpoints and that they can have more than one viewpoint or mixed feelings about a situation themselves. At level 3 (ten to thirteen), mutual understanding replaces reciprocal interest in friendships. Here children are able to step outside a situation and view its complexities. Level 3 friendships can withstand conflicts between friends that "fair weather" friendships at level 2 cannot. At Level 4 (middle to late adolescence), autonomous interdependence replaces the exclusivity of level 3. Friends at this level are close and intimate yet grant one another the autonomy and independence to have other close friends.

Havighurst and Erikson on Developmental Crises

In the psychoanalytic tradition, Havighurst (1953) and Erikson (1950, 1968, 1980) viewed development in terms of a series of "bio-socio-psychological tasks" (Havighurst) or developmental "crises" (Erikson) that must be achieved or resolved at the proper time by children in order to avoid (1) difficulty with later tasks or crises, (2) social disapproval, (3) unhappiness, (4) a lack of success in life, and (5) troublesome personality characteristics. Havighurst may have been the first to use the terms "teachable moment" in his description of the child's need to achieve these tasks when they are imposed through physical maturation, societal pressure, and personal desires and values. Both proposed that babies, during their first year, must gain a sense of trust and optimism that results from dependable and affectionate parental care, and that this trust or lack thereof becomes part of the total personality. Both proposed that the toddler will meet the challenge of achieving autonomy or self-direction and avoid becoming self-conscious, self-doubting, over-dependent, and hostile if treated firmly but tolerantly by parents. Both proposed that children in early childhood (preschool level) must successfully take initiative and will display excessive guilt as children, and either fail to realize their potential as adults or over-compensate (by deriving too much of their self-worth from accomplishment) if they fail to meet this challenge. Both proposed that the basic challenge of middle childhood (elementary grades after kindergarten) is to gain a sense of industry and competency (a sense of being able to make and do things well) and that the danger of failing to do so is the emergence of an enduring sense of inadequacy and inferiority and an inability to work well with others.

Havighurst addressed morality or the development of conscience in more detail than Erikson. However, Erikson's elaboration of the emergence of conscience in middle-childhood (elementary grades) is very similar to Havighurst's, and he alluded to the moral-developmental relevance of resolving conflicts at each developmental level by proposing that the healthy personality "weathers" these conflicts and emerges and re-emerges "with an increased sense of inner unity, with an increase of good judgment, and an increase in the capacity to do well, according to the standards of those who are significant to him" (Erikson, 1980:52). Havighurst referred to the early-childhood/preschool stage as the "beginning of moral responsibility and the dawn of conscience" (Havighurst, 1953:20). Nevertheless, he and Erikson described the third stage (middle childhood) as the stage during which conscience becomes an "inner moral guide" or "governor" of initiative (Havighurst, 1953:21). They contended that if properly installed through love (which promotes identification with adult care givers) and a form of discipline that is neither too excessive nor too permissive, the young child takes into himself the controlling voice of his parents and begins to feel appropriately guilty even for thoughts and for deeds that his parents have not witnessed. Havighurst referred to this inner moral voice of the parents as an "authoritarian conscience" and proposed that it is gradually replaced during elementary school by a "rational conscience" (Havighurst, 1953:53). He compared this rational conscience with Piaget's morality of cooperation and shared with Piaget the view that this rational conscience is acquired through peer group identification and peer group activities made possible through rules and a growing understanding of their function. Finally, he proposed that adolescents internalize a complete set of moral principles used to judge oneself and others.

Erikson had little to say about moral development during and after the middle-childhood or early elementary years, but he alone among psychoanalytic theorists articulated in detail the crises or conflicts that must be addressed by adolescents (identity versus role diffusion/confusion), young adults (intimacy versus isolation), middle age persons (generativity versus self-absorption), and old persons (integrity versus despair). His descriptions of adolescents have some implications for moral instruction. He proposed that adolescents are driven by a concern for how they are perceived by their peers and are seeking to integrate or consolidate their social roles and identifications into an ego identity characterized by sameness and continuity. He suggested that as they grapple with this challenge, they tend to over-identify with individuals and groups and tend to be clannish, intolerant, and cruel in their exclusion of individuals from groups to which they belong. Erikson stated that the intolerance and stereotyping typical of adolescents should be treated with understanding since it is "difficult to be tolerant if deep down you are . . . not sure if you will . . . ever be attractive, that you will be able to master your drives, that you really know who you are, that you know what you want to be, that you know what you look like to others, and that you will know how to make the right decisions without . . . committing yourself to the wrong friend, sexual partner, leader, or career" (Erikson, 1980:98).

Hay's Synthesis of Prosocial Development Research

Hay's (1994) beginning theory of prosocial development (defined as actions which benefit others or promote harmonious relations) was based on more than seven hundred empirical studies. He presented five developmental hypotheses. He proposed that a basic impulse toward prosocial interaction emerges during the first two years of life and then declines during the preschool years because children learn that prosocial behaviors are not always socially appropriate. He proposed that prosocial behavior during childhood becomes more differentiated on the basis of gender and that individual differences in prosocial feelings and actions are shaped by both biological and social forces. Finally, he proposed that both a lack of prosocial behavior and an excess of empathy places children at risk for behavioral and emotional disorders. He referred to research showing that by their third birthday children are able to distinguish moral rules from social conventions and have developed a conscience in the sense that they regulate their behavior in accordance with the expectations of absent adults. He also noted that the moral emotions of shame (the reaction felt when violating others' standards) and guilt (the reaction felt when violating standards set by oneself) are normally acquired before children enter school and that preschoolers become aware of reciprocity in their dealings with people and use prosocial behaviors to establish friendships.

REFERENCES

Aristotle. (1985). *Nichomachean Ethics*, translated. Terence Irwin. Indianapolis, IN: Hackett, 1985.

Battistich, V., Schaps, E., Solomon, D. and Watson, M. (1991). The role of school in prosocial development. In H. E. Fitzgerald et al. (Eds.), *Theory and Research in Behavioral Pediatrics, Volume 5.* New York: Plenum Press.

Bennett, W. (Ed.) (1993). *The Book of Virtues: A Treasury of Great Moral Stories.* New York: Simon and Schuster.

Benninga, J. S. (1991a). Synthesis and evaluation in moral and character education. In J. S. Benninga (Ed.), *Moral, Character, and Civic Education in the Elementary School.* New York: Teachers College Press.

Benninga, J. S. (Ed.) (1991b). *Moral, Character, and Civic Education in the Elementary School.* New York: Teachers College Press.

Berkowitz, M. (1995). *The Education of the Complete Moral Person.* Hilton Place, Aberdeen, Scotland: Gordon Cook Foundation.

Boyer, E. (1995). *The Basic School: A Community for Learning.* Princeton, NJ: The Carnegie Foundation for the Advancement of Teaching.

Burnyeat, M. F. (1980). Aristotle on learning to be good." In A. O. Rorty (Ed.), *Essays on Aristotle.* Berkley: University of California Press.

Carmody, D. and Carmody, J. (1974). *Shamans, Prophets, and Sages: A Concise Introduction to World Religions.* Belmont, CA: Wadsworth Publishing Company.

Carmody, D. and Carmody, J. (1988). *Peace and Justice in the Scriptures of the World Religions: Reflections on Non-Christian Scriptures.* New York: Paulist Press.

Charters, W. W. (1928). *The Teaching of Ideals.* New York: Macmillan.

Chazan, B. (1985). *Contemporary Approaches to Moral Education: Analyzing Alternative Theories.* New York: Teachers College Press.

Colby, A. and Kohlberg, L. (1987). *The Measurement of Moral Judgment, Volume 1.* Cambridge, MA: Cambridge University Press.

Damon, W. (1977). *The Social World of the Child.* San Francisco: Jossey-Bass, Inc., Publishers.

Damon, W. (1983). *Social and Personality Development: Infancy Through Adolescence.* New York: W. W. Norton & Company, Inc.

Damon, W. (1988). *The Moral Child.* New York: The Free Press.

Damon, W. (1995). *Greater Expectations: Overcoming the Culture of Indulgence in America's Homes and Schools.* New York: The Free Press.

Dewey, J. (1893). Teaching ethics in the high school. In *Early Works, Volume 4.* Carbondale: Southern Illinois University Press.

Dewey, J. (1916). *Democracy and Education.* New York: Free Press, Macmillan.

Dewey, J. (1960). *Theory of Moral Life.* New York: Holt, Rinehart and Winston.

Dewey, J. (1975). *Moral Principles in Education.* Carbondale, IL: Arcturus Books, Southern Illinois University Press. Originally published in 1909, Boston: Houghton Mifflin.

Durkheim, E. (1961). *Moral Education.* New York: Free Press.

Durkheim, E. (1973). *Moral Education: A Study in the Theory and Practice of the Sociology of Education.* New York: Free Press.

Durkheim, E. (1979). *Essays on Morals and Education,* W. S. F. Pickering, (Ed.), London: Routledge and Kegan Paul.

Eastman, M. (1967). *Seven Kinds of Goodness.* New York: Horizon Press.

Erikson, E. H. (1950). *Childhood and Society.* New York: W. W. Norton & Company;

Toronto: George J. McLeod Limited.

Erikson, E. H. (1968). *Identity: Youth and Crisis*. New York: W. W. Norton & Company; Toronto: George J. McLeod Limited.

Erikson, E. H. (1980). *Identity and the Life Cycle*. New York: W. W. Norton & Company; Toronto: George J. McLeod Limited.

Etzioni, A. (1993). *The Spirit of Community: The Reinvention of American Society*. New York: Simon & Schuster, a Touchstone Book.

Fowler, J. (1992). Character, conscience, and the education of the public. In F. Clark Power and D. K. Lapsley (Eds.), *The Challenge of Pluralism: Education, Politics, and Values*. South Bend, IN: University of Notre Dame Press.

Gauld, J. W. (1993). *Character First: The Hyde School Difference*. San Francisco: Institute for Contemporary Studies Press.

Georgia State Board of Education (1991). Rule 160-4-2-.33 adopted June 13: *Values Education.*

Gilligan, C. (1987). Moral orientation and moral development. In E. F. Kittay and D. T. Meyers (Eds), *Women and Moral Theory,* Totowa, NJ: Rowman and Littlefield.

Golightly, T. (1926). *The Present Status of the Teaching of Morals in the Public High Schools*. Nashville: George Peabody College for Teachers.

Green, T. (1984). The formation of conscience in an age of technology. *American Journal of Education*, Nov., 1–38; a similar lecture was delivered at the 1984 joint meeting of the John Dewey Society and American Association of Colleges of Teacher Education and is available through the Syracuse University School of Education, Syracuse, New York, 13210.

Hartshorne, H. and May, M. A. (1928, 1929, 1930). *Studies in the Nature of Character: Studies in Deceit (Vol.1), Studies in Service and Self Control (Vol 2), Studies in Organization of Character (Vol 3)*. New York: Macmillan.

Havighurst, R. J. (1953). *Human Development and Education*. New York: Longmans, Green and Company.

Hay, D.F. (1994). Prosocial development. *Journal of Child Psychology and Psychiatry and Allied Disciplines*, 35 (1), 29–71.

Heslep, R. D. (1995). *Moral Education for Americans*. Westport, CT: Praeger Publishers.

Hoffman, M. (1977). Moral internalization: current theory and research. In L. Berkowitz (Ed.), *Advances in Experimental Social Psychology, Vol. 10*. New York: Academic Press.

Hoffman, M. (1982). Development of prosocial motivation: empathy and guilt. In N. Eisenberg (Ed.), *The Development of Prosocial Behavior*. New York: Academic Press.

Hoffman, M. (1983). Empathy, guilt, and social cognition. In W. F. Overton (Ed.), *The Relationship Between Social and Cognitive Development*. Hillsdale, NJ: L. Erlbaum Associates.

Huffman, H. (1995). *Developing a Character Education Program: One School District's Experience*. Washington, D.C.: CEP Clearinghouse.

Hutchins, W. J. (1917). *Children's Code of Morals for Elementary Schools*. Washington: Character Education Institute. (This four page pamphlet can be found in the Library of Congress.)

Iheoma, E. O. (1986). The role of religion in moral education. *Journal of Moral Education*, 15 (2), 139–49.

Josephson, M. (Ed.) (1992). Youth leaders choose core language for character education. (A follow-up to the Aspen Conference during which discussions moderated by Diane Berreth produced the Aspen Declaration and Six Pillars of Character). *Ethics*, Issues 19 & 20 (double issue), 64–81.

Kagan, J. (1984). *The Nature of the Child.* New York, NY: Basic Books.

Kirschenbaum, H. (1976). Clarifying values clarification: Some theoretical issues. In D. Purpel and K. Ryan (Eds.), *Moral Education: It Comes with the Territory.* Berkley, CA: McCutchan Press.

Kirschenbaum, H. (1977). *Advanced Values Clarification.* La Jolla, CA: University Associates.

Kirschenbaum, H. (1995). *100 Ways to Enhance Values and Morality in Schools and youth settings.* Needham Heights, MA: Allyn & Bacon.

Kohlberg, L. (1970). Education for justice: A modern statement of the Platonic view. In N. F. Sizer and T. R. Sizer (Eds.), *Moral Education: Five Lectures.* Cambridge, MA: Harvard University Press.

Kohlberg, L. (Ed.) (1983). *The Psychology of Moral Development.* San Francisco: Harper & Row.

Kohlberg, L. (1985). A just community approach to moral education in theory and practice. In M. W. Berkowitz (Ed.), *Moral Education: Theory and Application.*

Leming, J. (1993). In search of effective character education. *Educational Leadership*, 51 (3), 63–71.

Leming, J. (1997). Research and practice in character education: A historical Perspective. In A. Molnar (Ed.), *The Construction of Children's Character.* Chicago, IL: The National Society for the Study of Education; distributed by The University of Chicago Press.

Lickona, T. (1991). An integrated approach to character development in the elementary school classroom. In J. S. Benninga, *Moral, Character, and Civic Education in the Elementary School.* New York: Teachers College Press.

Lisman, C. D. (1996). *The Curricular Integration of Ethics.* Westport, CT: Praeger Publishers.

McClelland, B. E. (1992). *Schools and the Shaping of Character: Moral Education in America–Present.* Bloomington, IN: ERIC Clearinghouse for Social Studies/Social Science Education and the Social Studies Development Center.

National School Boards Association (1987). *Building Character in the Public Schools: Strategies for Success.* Alexandria, VA: NSBA.

Nucci, L. P. (Ed.) (1989). *Moral Development and Character Education: A Dialogue.* Berkeley, CA: McCutchan Publishing Corporation.

Nucci, L. P. (1991). Doing justice to morality in contemporary values education. In Benninga, J. S. (Ed.), *Moral, Character, and Civic Education in the Elementary School.* New York: Teachers College Press.

Peters, R. S. (1966). *Ethics and Education.* London: Allen and Unwin.

Piaget, J. (1948/1965). *The Moral Judgment of the Child.* Glencoe, IL: The Free Press; New York: Free Press.

Piaget, J. (1952). *The Origins of Intelligence in Children.* New York: International Universities Press.

Piaget, J. (1978). *The Development of Thought.* Oxford: Blackwell Publishers.

Pietig, J. (1976). John Dewey and character education. *Journal of Moral Education*, 6 (3), 170–80.

Power, C., Higgins, A. and Kohlberg, L. (1988). *Lawrence Kohlberg's Approach to Moral Education.* New York, NY: Columbia University Press.

Ravitch, D. (1985). American education: Has the pendulum swung once too often? In D. Ravitch (Ed.), *The Schools We Deserve: Reflections on the Educational Crises of Our Time.* New York: Basic Books.

Selman, L. (1980). *The Growth of Interpersonal Understanding: Developmental and*

Clinical Analyses. New York: Academic Press.

Selman, L. and Schultz, L. H. (1990). *Making a Friend in Youth*. Chicago: The University of Chicago Press.

Simon, Y. R. (1986). *The Definition of Moral Virtue*. New York: Fordham University Press.

Sommers, C. (1993). Teaching the virtues. *Public Interest*, No. 111, 3–13.

Sparks, R. K. Jr. (1991). Character development at Fort Washington Elementary School. In J. S. Benninga, *Moral, Character, and Civic Education in the Elementary School*. New York: Teachers College Press.

Starratt, R. J. (1994). *Building an Ethical School: A Practical Response to the Moral Crisis in Schools*. Bristol, PA: The Falmer Press.

Turiel, E. (1989). Multifaceted social reasoning and educating for character, culture, and development. In L. P. Nucci, *Moral Development and Character Education: A Dialogue*. Berkeley, CA: McCutchan Publishing Company.

Weed, S., Buck, J., Skanchy, G. and Weed, M. A. (under development 1995). *SMILE: A Character Education Curriculum*. Ogden, UT: The Institute for Research and Evaluation.

Wei, T. T. (1990). Some Confucian insights and moral education. *Journal of Moral Education*, 19 (1), 33–37.

Youniss, J. and Volpe, J. (1978). A relational analysis of children's friendship. In W. Damon (Ed.), *New Directions for Child Development, Vol. 1: Social Cognition*. San Francisco: Jossey-Bass.

3

A Developmentally Based Core Curriculum

DESIGN CONSIDERATIONS

Good instructional models for character development take into consideration the need to (1) define for students what is good and right and to keep the definitions simple and "learnable"; (2) develop in students a sense of moral responsibility and commitment to the virtues taught; (3) develop in students the ability to think independently about moral issues or to make autonomous moral judgments; (4) know what children at various stages of development can learn, how they think and feel, and under what conditions they will learn best; (5) infuse and suffuse moral instruction into all aspects of school life rather than adding isolated lessons; (6) keep all stakeholders informed and motivated about the program (students, teachers, parents, administrators, school board members, interested citizens); (7) operate within First Amendment constraints upon what can be taught in schools and to be respectful of the religious beliefs of all students and parents; (8) bring together interested citizens and school personnel starting at the program planning stage and to design programs that match the unique combination of people, problems, and resources within each community; and (9) approach design and implementation in an organized and strategic manner with plans of action, review, evaluation, and improvement.

AN OPERATIONAL DEFINITION OF MORAL CHARACTER

Moral character is appropriately viewed as personal and social integrity. With respect to personal, people with moral character are predisposed to (1) show kindness and compassion with empathetic understanding; (2) show the courage to be honest and principled irrespective of circumstances; (3) acquire a wide range of abilities that enable them to independently resolve problems, analyze situations where moral values and principles may be in conflict, and adapt to change in a personally and socially constructive manner; and (4) display a high level of effort in their daily work, and a high level of commitment to individual and group goals and standards. With respect to social, people with moral character are predisposed to (1) show an interest in and concern for others in the spirit of friendship and brotherhood and to act on these concerns routinely, (2) perform as responsible and other-directed team members within families and other groups, and (3) view the preservation of social institutions and the improvement of both self and community as civic duties.

From this description of the moral person, we can extract, categorize, define, and elaborate specific qualities that can be described as (a) virtues, for persons who have been habitually predisposed to act accordingly, and (b) a collection of moral values and metamoral characteristics, for those who are aspiring to be virtuous (referred to hereafter as virtues). A content extraction such as this provides a values vocabulary and a simple conceptual structure for curriculum development and lesson planning. This extraction is offered with some reservations, however, since the various psychological processes involved in moral functioning can only be inferred from such lists of isolated words and definitions (psychological processes such as judging, feeling, perceiving, valuing, perspective taking, reflecting, needing, thinking critically, being intrinsically motivated, reasoning autonomously, empathizing, and understanding), and since providing such a list may increase the chances that educators will conclude that moral character can be instilled through instruction that includes little active student participation (e.g., guided and independent practice and natural discovery). To guard against such an outcome, this extraction of content will be balanced by an extraction and clarification of emotive and cognitive processes that are essential ingredients of moral functioning.

Extracted Psychological Processes

Persons with moral character have the will and ability to think for themselves about any issue, including issues where their moral values and ethical principles are in conflict. They can also critically and objectively evaluate themselves and others using their critical thinking skills, objectivity, situational perceptiveness, and knowledge gained from past experience. Their connection with other individuals and communities is characterized by a sense of obligation and responsibility that may supercede self-interest in some situations and demand self-interest and personal excellence in others. This sense derives from learning and internalizing social-role expectations and moral principles (beginning with rules imposed on children by adults), and from the capacity to feel and understand the needs and circumstances of others (beginning with a purely affective form of empathy in early childhood and later including perspective taking that adds the cognitive component of empathy). They are motivated by a sense of social obligation and a related empathetic concern for others, and by self-regulating and self-reinforcing inner feelings (e.g., pride, shame, guilt, fear). These feelings are accompanied by automatic or reflexive judgments about one's thoughts, feelings, and actions. Without autonomy and the will and ability to think critically, and without the acquisition of a social-empathetic, emotionally self-regulating conscience that is reflexive and compelling, their moral character cannot develop fully.

Extracted Virtues

The extraction of content yields a categorized list of virtues, or values terms that might be appropriately referred to as a combination of moral values and metamoral characteristics, that is, characteristics which are not in and of themselves moral but which help make moral action possible. The two foundation categories for this list are *personal integrity* and *social integrity*. Personal integrity includes the virtues of *kindness, courage, ability,* and *effort;* social integrity includes the virtues of *friendship, teamwork,* and *citizenship.* These seven virtues will be referred to hereafter as primary virtues; the twelve terms listed with each of the seven primary virtues will be referred to hereafter as "elaborative" virtues. These elaborative virtues appear beneath each of the seven primary virtue terms (see below) and effectively elaborate each primary-virtue concept. They are listed in order of increasing abstractness or complexity with the most abstract or complex elaborative virtues appearing at or near the bottom of each list of twelve, and the most concrete or elementary elaborative virtues appearing at or near the top of each list of twelve. This categorized list of virtues will be followed by definitions for each of the seven primary virtues and each of the eighty-four elaborative virtues.

Virtues That Reflect Personal Integrity

Kindness	Courage	Ability	Effort
nice	honest	attentive	hard-working
loving	exploring	creative	energetic
gentle	brave/heroic	prepared	determined
cheerful	sorry/remorseful	skillful	competitive
thankful	independent	organized	studious
friendly	risk-taking	knowledgeable	self-disciplined
comforting	decisive	realistic	ambitious
courteous	assertive	flexible	dedicated
sensitive	self-disclosing	objective	optimistic
interested	self-evaluating	deliberate	idealistic
compassionate	persevering	prudent	persistent
empathetic	principled	resourceful	conscientious

Virtues That Reflect Social Integrity

Friendship	Teamwork	Citizenship
helpful	on-task	peace-loving
sharing/giving	respectful	rule-following
fair/just	cooperative	drug-free
forgiving	productive	law-abiding
patient	responsible	health-conscious
considerate	positive	rights-respecting
supportive	mediating	volunteering
understanding	punctual/prompt	educated/employed
trustworthy	humble/modest	socially conscious
devoted/loyal	genuine/sincere	culturally literate
charitable	compromising	historically literate
altruistic	temperate	family-valuing

Definitions of Primary and Elaborative Virtues

Since the primary virtues should be taught at all developmental levels, they are defined in simple terms so that even five- and six-year-old children can understand them. The elaborative virtues are divided, for definitional purposes, into those targeted for elementary school and those targeted for middle and high school. The definitions of the elaborative virtues taught at the elementary level use simple terms like the primary-virtue definitions and should be suitable for all ages beyond four. Definitions for the virtues taught at the middle or high school level are written for students in grades six through twelve and are not suitable for most elementary school children.

Primary Virtue Definitions:

Kindness: making others feel better by knowing how they feel and either sharing or causing good feelings.
Courage: being strong enough to do what is right when you are afraid to do so.
Ability: having the skills to figure out what is right and good and to make yourself and your world better.
Effort: doing your best and not giving up even when things are very hard.
Friendship: treating others the way you want to be treated.
Teamwork: helping to achieve group goals by doing your part and working well with others.
Citizenship: following rules and laws and trying to make yourself and your community better.

Elaborative Virtues Defined—Elementary:

ambitious: a strong need to be or do something special; knowing what you want to do or what you want to be and not letting anything stop you.

attentive: keeping your eyes, ears, and thoughts on the person who is speaking or leading your group.

brave/heroic: doing or saying the right thing when you are scared.

cheerful: being so happy and in such a good mood that you make others happy.

cooperative: working together to do more than you can do by yourself, and doing what you can to get everyone to help and get along while working together.

comforting: making someone's sadness, pain, or problem seem easier by acting interested, concerned, nice, and loving.

considerate: thinking about the feelings of others and what they need, and sometimes doing what is best for them rather than what is best for you.

courteous: being polite or helpful in a respectful way that makes someone feel important such as holding a door and not interrupting.

creative: using your imagination to make something that has never been made or seen before; solving new and different problem when you are not sure how to do this at first.

determined: to know in your heart that you really want to do your best and that nothing can stop you.

drug-free: showing concern for yourself and your health by never using drugs.

exploring: looking for and learning about new places and things even when this is a little scary to do.

fair/just: making sure that people get what they deserve after thinking about their needs, rights, and behavior.

forgiving: telling someone it is OK when they say they are sorry, and not being mad or sad any longer.

friendly: showing that you want to talk with people and do things for them and that you enjoy spending time with them and want to bring joy to their lives.

gentle: showing a soft and sweet touch and voice, and being kind when being rough and loud might cause others to be scared or feel bad.

hard-working: doing your best and not stopping until you are finished even when your work is not very fun.

health-conscious: doing what you must do to keep from getting sick or hurt and to make yourself strong.

helpful: aiding or helping others when you have something they need or when you know something that will help them do something right or solve a problem.

honest: telling the truth and not stealing or cheating others; telling how you really think and feel about things; admitting what you have done wrong.

independent: doing things by yourself or on your own even when it might be easier to let someone else do it for you; telling your own ideas and feelings about things and not letting others talk you into doing things you should not do.

law-abiding: knowing that laws are like class rules, except that all people in the state and country must follow them, and making sure that you follow both.

loving: feeling and showing love, warmth, and caring in a very special way toward a person or animal who is special to you.

mediating: helping to solve arguments and fights between others in your class and school by asking them to listen to each other and to find a way to get along.

nice: being one of many different kinds of people that other people like to be around because they do good things and never treat others badly.

on-task: keeping your mind on your work even when others try to bother you, and even when your teacher is out of the room.

organized: keeping your things neat and where you can find them, and planning when you will do things so it all is completed on time.

patient: being willing to wait for something you really want and not cheating, griping, pushing, or crying to get it right away.

peace-loving: showing a desire to get along with others by staying out of arguments and fights, and by working out problems with others without violence.

prepared: being ready to do what you need to do by having supplies, getting lots of sleep, having a good attitude, doing your homework and chores, and planning ahead.

productive: helping yourself or others by getting lots of important jobs finished.

punctual/prompt: being where you need to be and doing what you need to do on time so that others will not have to wait on you or help you.

responsible: doing what you are supposed to do as a student and citizen and showing you can be trusted to do so on your own without others reminding you.

respectful: treating others right because you feel they deserve it, and behaving the way you should toward parents, teachers, older people, other adults, disabled people, smaller children, children your age, and people who are different from you in some way such as their color or religion.

rights-respecting: knowing that all people have rights such as the right to be free and to say what they think and feel, and not doing anything that might keep them from doing what they have a right to do.

rule-following: showing that you want to be a good citizen by knowing the rules of your class, school, and community and following these rules all the time.

sharing: giving others some of what you have when they have less than you or when they have given you some of what they have; telling people how you really feel about important things.

self-disciplined: doing things without being told; getting a job done all by yourself; doing what you should do when you should do it even when you do not want to do it.

skillful: being very good at things like art, reading, and sports after learning from others, practicing and working very hard.

sorry: feeling badly that you have hurt or disappointed someone, and telling them how you feel.

studious: having a very serious attitude about school and about learning even when others are making fun or acting like they do not care about learning.

thankful: feeling glad that you were helped by someone who did not have to help you, and telling them how happy you are that they took the time to help.

Elaborative Virtues Defined—Secondary

altruistic: having an unselfish regard for the welfare of others.

assertive: expressing one's self boldly, confidently, and without aggression even when efforts are being made to intimidate or dominate you.

charitable: being full of love and generous goodwill toward others you may not know personally.

compassionate: being aware of the distress of others and having the desire to alleviate it.

competitive: striving to improve upon an earlier performance, or striving as an individual or team member to outperform others in the spirit of fairness and respect.

compromising: resolving an interpersonal disagreement by making concessions in response to those made by others, or by offering to make concessions if others will reciprocate.

conscientious: acting in a manner consistent with the dictates of one's conscience, that is, in accordance with the feelings and reflexive thoughts about right and wrong that enable one to self-regulate and consider others.

culturally literate: having knowledge of one's cultural heritage and enough knowledge about the cultural norms, traditions, and belief systems of others to communicate and work with them effectively.

decisive: making decisions confidently and without hesitancy, self-doubt, or troublesome delay after considering enough relevant information to make a good decision.

dedicated: to be so committed to another person, cause, or goal that slothfulness and quitting are virtually impossible.

deliberate: thinking slowly, carefully, and thoroughly about all aspects of a problem or issue and gaining a full understanding as a result.

devoted/loyal: being faithful to a group, person, or country, and placing the needs of this group, person, or country above one's own.

educated/employed: having the knowledge and skills needed to be a productive and resourceful member of the local, national, and world communities.

empathetic: being able to understand another person's situation and to feel what they feel to some degree without forfeiting objectivity or being blinded by sympathy and over-identification.

energetic: being routinely active, vigorous, and tireless in one's endeavors and interpersonal interactions.

family-valuing: understanding that it is difficult for people to remain happy, healthy, and productive without the support of a few people whose commitment to one another supercedes all other interpersonal commitments and personal interests, and to act in a way that fosters close interpersonal relationships and mutual helping and among members of these special support groups.

flexible: being open to new information and capable of generating new and different ideas, and being able to change one's position or course of action.

genuine/sincere: meaning what you say and/or do without considering potential gain or loss to yourself.

historically literate: knowing enough about the past to place current events into their appropriate historical context, and enough to teach others.

humble/modest: viewing yourself in a manner characterized by an absence of alienating pride, vanity, conceit, boastfulness, arrogance, and vindictiveness and acting accordingly so others do not feel devalued or inferior.

idealistic: being guided by your vision of a more perfect self, organization, community, or world, and adhering to this vision in the face of practical matters that tend to cause you to lose sight of your vision.

interested: connecting with others in a way that communicates through questions, gestures, and feedback a desire to be fully informed about their situation and thus capable of serving them as a trusted advisor, critic, or supporter.

knowledgeable: knowing enough about a particular subject to be able to communicate intelligently with experts in the field, and achieving this level through purposeful study and practical experience.

objective: being able to look at a person, problem, or situation factually or without distortion due to personal feelings and prejudices.

optimistic: anticipating the best possible outcome both personally and collectively, and avoiding any negative thinking, feeling, and action that might prevent this best possible outcome.

persevering: persisting or not giving up in an endeavor or situation in spite of counter influences, opposition from others, unanticipated obstacles or hardship, and personal feelings of discouragement that naturally accompany barriers to success.

persistent: continuing resolutely and stubbornly for as long as it takes to achieve your original objective and not concerning yourself with those who might object to your constant presence and unyielding spirit.

positive: maintaining a frame of mind free of self-disparagement and self-devaluation and free of thoughts and actions which might disparage others or diminish the quality of the relationships on which group harmony and optimum group achievement depend.

principled: having an internalized code of conduct or internalized standards of right and wrong and adhering to these standards in the face of threats to your status and personal well being.

prudent: being wise, discerning, cautious, self-governing, and circumspect in making decisions and judgments that will effect yourself and others.

realistic: setting goals that are clearly achievable given your skills and potential, and being aware of and guided by facts rather than fantasies.

resourceful: being able to find or devise ways and means to handle unanticipated problems, and possessing a repertoire of skills and personality qualities that make it possible to cope with such challenges.

risk-taking: being willing to venture into new situations and endure feelings of insecurity, frustration, and failure because this is necessary for personal growth.

self-disclosing: sharing, exposing, or revealing things about yourself that will allow others to know you well and to see you as you really are.

self-evaluating: having the humility and objectivity to assess your thoughts, feelings, and actions and to self-correct or change accordingly.

sensitive: being delicately aware of the needs, attitudes, and feelings of others in real and imagined situations.

socially conscious: being aware of real world problems and intrinsically motivated to do your part to create a better world.

supportive: being there for others when they need you the most and doing what you should to put them in control or keep them in control.

temperate: showing moderation in action, thought, and feeling particularly in situations where over-indulgence and extreme passion could be harmful to yourself or others.

trustworthy: displaying a pattern of conduct that causes others to feel that they can believe you, depend on you, and have confidence in you.

understanding: acting in a way that causes others to conclude that you are fully aware of their feelings and circumstances and are willing to make adjustments to lesson or limit their difficulties.

volunteering: noticing needs and problems within a community and freely offering to help in some way without compensation.

SEVEN LEARNING MODES

Students acquire personal and social virtues through (1) a supportive environment that includes relationships with parents, teachers, and other "respectfully engaging" and authoritative adults (as opposed to permissive or authoritarian); (2) unstructured peer group interaction and play that minimizes adult intrusion; (3) developmentally appropriate discipline and reinforcement that treats students with dignity and respect; (4) exposure to virtuous models with whom children and adolescents can identify; (5) didactics or developmentally appropriate direct teaching about moral standards and desirable virtues; (6) active participation within just, democratic, and caring communities where virtuous behaviors and autonomous moral reasoning can be practiced in real and dramatized situations; and (7) meaningful real-world experiences within various communities outside the school.

There are noteworthy similarities between this seven-mode scheme (see chapter 4 for specific strategies) and those implied or specified by others including Kevin Ryan's scheme of Example, Explanation, Ethos (climate), Experience, and Expectations, and Stan Weed's SMILE curriculum, which includes stimulating interest in the moral principle (S), modeling it (M), integrating it with existing knowledge (I), linking with parents through homework (L), and extending the principle into real life situations (E). From the Child Development Project list of strategies, one can extract or identify the predominant modes, which are active student participation, didactics through literature, and interpersonal support. Their strategies include highlighting and exposing children to prosocial values, providing opportunities to help others, using cooperative learning, helping students to understand and respect others through literature and class experiences, and using developmental discipline, which combines creating a caring community with social skills instruction and an instructional approach to discipline. An analysis of the "12-point comprehensive approach to character education" offered by Lickona and the Center for the 4th and 5th Rs shows that six modalities are utilized including active student participation (cooperative learning, democratic decision making in classrooms, ethical reflection, using conflict resolution skills), didactics (teaching values through the curriculum, direct instruction in conflict resolution, direct instruction related to moral discipline and good craftsmanship), discipline and reinforcement (moral discipline), exposure to virtuous models (the teacher as model and mentor, conscience of craft), supportive environment (caring classroom community, teacher as care giver, parent-school-community partnerships, caring beyond the school, moral school culture), and experience within the community (partnerships among parents, educators, and the broader community).

CORE CURRICULUM OVERVIEW

The author's effort to satisfy the need for a conceptual/methodological framework for developmentally appropriate character education begins with descriptions of children at five developmental levels. These descriptions provide a guide for formulating instructional goals, objectives, and content, and for selecting appropriate strategies and materials. The first developmental level includes kindergarten (K) and pre-kindergarten (pre-K), and the second includes the first and second grades. The third and fourth levels include three grades each: third through fifth and sixth through eighth. The final developmental level includes all four high-school grades. These descriptions are a product of the author's (1) experience with children of all ages and dialogue with the teachers of these children, (2) synthesis of relevant developmental theories, and (3) use of Elkind's (1994) and Wood's (1994) practical descriptions.

To facilitate the integration or synthesis of developmental theories, key propositions from each theory were charted together (see Appendix B). The information presented in this chart suggests that these theories are more consistent with respect to the specific stages they identify and define than the ages at which these stages emerge. This is illustrated by a comparison of Damon's conclusion that children view fairness in terms of strict equality at the early elementary level and Piaget's conclusion that this occurs at the late elementary level. Progressive early childhood educators argue that theorists of the past have underestimated young children because of their characteristic egocentrism and perceptual thought. It is also conceivable that children are developing more quickly than they did fifty years ago when theorists such as Piaget, Erikson, and Havighurst were active. The author suspects that both of these explanations apply and that current progressivist, humanistic early-childhood educators are reactively over-estimating what young children can do and causing traditionalists to discount decades of developmental research.

PRE-KINDERGARTEN AND KINDERGARTEN/EARLY CHILDHOOD

Play is the heart and soul of development during the preschool years and the primary means through which the child's need to take initiative is satisfied. One might reasonably argue that play itself is a need that must be satisfied at this level. Through play children can safely take chances and express feelings, and they can satisfy wishes that are not otherwise realizable. The imagination that is evident in their play and that accounts for their interest in stories is the seed-bed for early abstract concepts such as binary opposites (e.g., survival and destruction).

Preschool children show in their make-believe play with peers a consciousness of rules underlying real-world relationships and interactions, and they mold their play to conform to these rules without allowing these symbolic connections with reality to restrict their imaginations. Through make-believe interactions involving boys and girls and/or same-sex playmates, they step outside themselves to symbolically imitate and practice what they have learned about human roles and relationships in the real world. The symbolic nature of their play is coupled with a sense of self that is also symbolic in that it is organized around their names and related pronouns such as I, me, and mine.

Social play or cooperative make-believe play is the predominant form of play for four- and five-year-old children and is one of the first forms of truly cooperative and reciprocal social interaction, but parallel play is still fairly common. They exhibit a beginning "tit-for-tat" form of reciprocity that is more of a way to get their way than anything approaching a sense of moral obligation. They define friendship in terms of playmates and sharing and will behave prosocially to attract playmates even though their prosocial behavior is becoming more selective. Although they do not always choose to share and are inclined to be more generous to themselves than others, they know that they should share and are motivated by an empathetic understanding of how doing so or failing to do so will make their playmates feel. They are well aware of the inner feelings of others and will normally feel guilty if they hurt the feelings of others.

There is a flipside to the wonderfully playful, imaginative, and affectionate nature of kindergarten and pre-kindergarten children, and their willingness to ask permission and accept rules without compulsively testing limits like older children. They are primarily driven by passion and curiosity and not by a need to be in harmony with others in their environment. They will act impulsively to satisfy their desires and will either make no attempt to justify their actions or justify them in an after-the-fact, self-serving manner unless external consequences, both positive and negative, condition them to inhibit their impulses and/or to engage in prosocial behavior. Although they can follow adult expectations in the absence of adults due to conditioning, imitation, and modeling, they have not internalized adult expectations in a manner that would enable them to self-regulate or self-correct in a deliberative manner. They can feel badly when they fail to meet adult expectations, but this also reflects conditioning and anticipated consequences rather than shame or guilt in a thoroughly internalized sense. Four- and five-year-old children depend heavily upon authoritative parenting to learn to control their impulses and tendency to react physically in conflict situations, but the averseness of conflict with peers plays a role as well and often leads to purposeful conflict-avoidance behaviors without adult involvement. The intense conflict that often occurs over toys and the sharing of toys is rooted in the fact that they do not differentiate between themselves and preferred objects and tend to view these objects as an extension of themselves.

Adults tend to talk over the heads of pre-K and kindergarten children because their "why" questions (typical at four years of age), interest in knowing what things are for and what they do (typical at five years of age), interest in "big person" jobs, and extensive imitative use of big words and phrases suggest levels of comprehension far beyond their capabilities. Adults also tend to expect too much from four- and five-year-old children in terms of paying attention, staying still and seated, controlling anger, remaining on-task, not talking, not spilling, dropping, and falling out of their chairs (sideways), holding pencils and other objects properly, not exaggerating, and thinking logically.

The thinking of children at this age level is limited to immediate perceptual experiences, the memory representations that these experiences elicit, a transductive or event-to-event type of cause-effect reasoning, and concept formation that precludes the nesting of classes within broader classes. This preoperational thinking precludes such things as a unit concept of number, and it accounts for their unfounded inferences about one action causing another, their hypersensitivity to perceptual cues, and their exaggerated fears.

No matter how much moralizing adults may impose when K and pre-K children misbehave, their level of intellectual development precludes analyzing their thoughts, feelings, and motivations, and they cannot independently escape their self-centered perspective to distinguish and compare their own viewpoint with the view-point of adults or children with whom they come into conflict. They can, however, identify or empathize with the feelings of others if they have been taught a feeling vocabulary, have learned that all people experience the same feelings, and are guided toward identification with another's feelings by an adult's interjection of perceptual cues (e.g., You hurt . . .). Their role-taking or perspective-taking ability is quite limited as evidenced by not being able to tell a story from the perspective of different characters, but it exists in a beginning form as reflected in the roles they assume in cooperative social play and their spontaneous reciprocal communications with each other, and it tends to be task specific and teachable to some degree.

Instructional Implications and Recommendations

Interpersonal and Environmental Support

Pre-K and K children need to feel loved and protected by the adults they depend on, and they must be provided with teachers who feel comfortable touching them affectionately and talking to them in an affectionate, reassuring voice. They also need teachers who appreciate their need for uninhibited exploration of their social and physical world. Finally, they need teachers who are aware of their unrealistic fears and who will avoid exacerbating these fears by carefully selecting stories to be read, avoiding threats and hostile reprimands, and being willing to talk with individual children in a personal and caring way about their specific fears.

Unstructured Peer-Group Play

Informal, child-initiated play at this level is critical to many types of development and must be scheduled for significant amounts of time during the school day—at least a couple of hours. If the adults in their lives have sufficiently exposed them to things from their real world and have made them feel that any type of make-believe play is permissible provided aggression does not occur, they should not have to worry about play being developmentally relevant and educational. Their role should be restricted to feeding children knowledge and stimulating them prior to free play with all types of materials and information, and making the play environment one which promotes imaginative imitation of the world they share with adults and older children.

Discipline and Reinforcement

Since social interactions with peers at this age are more incidental than instrumental (as they will be in the next stage), and since the students are inclined to justify their inappropriate actions, will do as they please if allowed, and need to take initiative, authority figures need to balance clear limits, firm consequences, much structure, and much patience with affection and many opportunities for children to freely explore their social and physical world. Children at this age will learn classroom rules best through consequences, both positive and negative, rather than didactic instruction. When their rule violations are relatively minor, they need an assertive, matter-of-fact "no!" without nagging moralism or lecturing, and without preliminary threats that inappropriately give them a choice between defiance and compliance. When the rule violations of children are serious and upsetting to others, adults should point out how their actions made others feel, and should respond in a firm, nonaggressive way by temporarily removing them from the opportunity to satisfy any of their desires (timeout). Students should not be forced to carry out restitutional or amendatory prosocial behavior since the association with negative feelings might reduce the already decreasing frequency of such behaviors in nonconflict situations. In addition to the preventive function of modeling and other methods, teachers can prevent conflict and misconduct to some degree by arranging cooperative or team-learning activities that are noncompetitive limited to a few children. Finally, teachers should reward virtuous behavior through simple compliments at the time the behavior is observed, and should reward it in more formal and elaborate ways such as issuing Good Friend of the Month or Peacemaker of the Month awards.

Observation and Modeling

Teachers should make a point of modeling targeted virtuous behaviors in a way that children can easily imitate, and they should call attention to and clearly label these prosocial behaviors when they are displayed by their students and others. Teachers should also model social problem solving in interpersonal conflict situations, and this should be one of the predictable consequences of interpersonal conflict. Teachers can model empathy (without using this term) by sharing aloud the thoughts and sensitivities that are a part of sharing another's feelings and thoughts, and they can promote empathy by labeling feelings as they are observed and by encouraging identification with story characters and peers in distress.

Didactic Teaching

Children at this age love to have stories read and told to them, so storytelling and reading stories to children should be primary instructional strategies (see chapter 4 for ideas on identifying stories that will help build character). Teachers should also take advantage of the fact that all elementary children find stories affectively engaging and are ostensibly able to learn abstract concepts best through stories by presenting all possible lessons in a story-like rhythm that sets up expectations or a dramatic tension at the beginning and resolves this tension at the end (see chapter 4 for details on Egan's teaching-as-story-telling methods).

Teachers should not have children memorize classroom rules, and they should not teach targeted virtue words and feeling words and definitions in this manner either. Rather, they should call attention to rule-following and rule-violating, virtuous and unvirtuous behavior, and all types of feelings as they occur by labeling and describing them. Virtue words and feeling words need not, or perhaps should not, be made visible in print, but they can be illustrated through the display of real life pictures and by classroom puppets or cartoon characters with names that reflect specific virtues and feelings.

Many of the targeted virtues can be viewed as skills or as having a skill component (e.g., being nice, being thankful, being helpful, sharing, and, with respect to peace-loving, dealing with teasing, dealing with being mad, dealing with losing, learning how to relax, accepting "no" or consequences). Some class time should be devoted to direct social skills instruction along these lines using a Skill-streaming type approach that involves modeling, role playing, and practice. With respect to social problem solving or interpersonal conflict mediation, the steps of the process should be learned through the observation of actual conflict resolutions within the classroom. However, those who have attempted to teach early social problem solving have found that the social problem-solving process is enhanced by teaching pre-problem-solving words including feeling words and concepts such as same-different, some-all, might-maybe, before-after, and now-later, and by teaching pre-problem-solving skills such as listening and identifying feelings in oneself and others.

Active Participation Within Classroom and School Communities

Preschool children learn by doing things that occupy their bodies as well as their minds and by interacting with adults, each other, and materials. Therefore, teachers must focus their efforts on planning and preparing the instructional environment so that (1) many types of action and interaction can occur, (2) children have plenty of room to move about freely, (3) their primary role as teacher during class time is that of facilitator, (4) children have to make the choices they are developmentally ready to make (e.g., choosing from alternative activities), (5) children have some responsibility for maintaining a pleasant, student-centered classroom (e.g., chores and helping with displays), (6) early forms of peer cooperation and sharing are promoted rather than competition and conflict, and (7) role-playing occurs both spontaneously and by design and thus capitalizes on their natural imitativeness. Role-playing should be the central feature of planned social skills instruction and should also be used in conjunction with storytelling and story reading. Children should be taught songs about character such as those written and recorded by Garry Smith (a former kindergarten teacher), and be given many opportunities to sing them together. They should also spend considerable time on cooperative group games. Teachers are not advised to involve preschool and kindergarten children in classroom rule-making, but they can involve the entire class in teacher-guided mediations of interpersonal conflicts (interpersonal or social problem solving) and should have disputants in these conflicts do as much of the work as possible in resolving these conflicts whether or not teacher intervention is required.

Experiences Within the Larger Community

Teachers should encourage parents to expose their children to all types of activities, events, and places within their community and encourage them to involve their preschoolers in extensive free play and organized recreational activities with peers. Some field trips should be chosen with character development goals and objectives in mind. At least one whole-class service learning activity should be planned that gives students the opportunity to demonstrate kindness to the needy, keeping in mind that they do not yet see fair in terms of equity.

Instructional Focus

Targeted Virtues

The primary focus for pre-kindergarten and kindergarten children is *Kindness* and the elaborative virtues of *nice, loving, gentle, cheerful, thankful, and friendly*. Other targeted virtues include *Courage* and the elaborative virtues of *honest and exploring, Ability* with the elaborative virtues of *attentive and creative, Effort* with the elaborative virtue of *hard-working, Friendship* with the elaborative virtues of *helpful and sharing, Teamwork* with the elaborative virtue of *on-task*, and *Citizenship* with the elaborative virtue of *peace-loving*.

Targeted Psychological Processes

The process focus for pre-kindergarten and kindergarten children is threefold: nurturing, strengthening, and eliciting—through prompts—an *affective form of empathy* that emerges developmentally before perspective-taking (the cognitive component of empathy); encouraging both *initiative* and *conditioned conformity* to adult-imposed rules; and preventing children from becoming overly selective with their prosocial feelings and actions (i.e., *prosocial with all* peers).

Primary Instructional Modes

The emphasis at this level is upon active student participation in the classroom and providing opportunities for unstructured peer group play. K and pre-K children need to feel free to explore, make choices, and learn in a natural way within the context of firmly and quickly enforced boundaries and the constant modeling and verbal labeling of their virtuous behavior. Discipline, social reinforcement, and modeling are very important for basic habit formation, but the use of these modes needs to take place within this active environment for the most part. With respect to interpersonal and environmental support, adults must be careful not to stifle initiative as they seek to provide the feedback and structure necessary for habit formation. They also need to encourage fours and fives to be concerned about the feelings of others and to constrain their selfishness and aggression by using feeling words to help them understand how their behavior has affected others. When student conflicts occur, teacher-mediated social problem should be used with input from the entire class when possible, that is, a combination of didactics and active student participation. Didactic teaching should include planned and spontaneously infused social skills instruction, much storytelling and story reading, and the presentation of lessons in a story-like rhythm whenever possible (see chapter 4). The targeted virtue words and related feeling words should be used extensively to describe what occurs in the classroom.

General Instructional Objective

The general character development objective for K and pre-K students is to cultivate the seven primary virtues within a learning environment that encourages exploration, with an emphasis on (a) kindness and the development of an affective form of empathy through consciousness-raising dialogue, (b) habitual good conduct and prosocial feelings through direct instruction and reinforcement, and (c) initiative through adult encouragement and facilitation.

Behavioral Objectives

1. Students will show concern for others and stop behaving in any way that is harmful to others when they see—or an adult helps them to see—how their behavior has made others feel.

2. Students will learn the meaning of kindness and display their understanding by accurately labeling their actions and those of others as kind, nice, loving, gentle, cheerful, thankful, and friendly, and by being kind to others without adult prompting.

3. Students will learn what it means to be honest and exploring and that this is not always easy (i.e., it takes courage), and they will display their understanding by labeling these behaviors in themselves and others, by being honest about themselves and others, and by exploring all aspects of their learning environment with adult encouragement.

4. Students will learn what it means to pay attention and to be creative and imaginative, and they will display their understanding by accurately labeling these behaviors in themselves and others and by being attentive and creative when given the opportunity.

5. Students will learn what it means to make a good effort and to be hard-working, and they will display their understanding by labeling these behaviors in themselves and others and by trying as hard or harder than most children their own age.

6. Students will gain a beginning understanding of friendship, defined in terms of sharing and helping, and will display their understanding by accurately identifying friendships, sharing, and helping, and by sharing with and/or helping at least one person each day.

7. Students will begin to learn the meaning of teamwork by staying on task to complete their work and by helping to keep order in the class by following rules and directions with minimal adult prompting.

8. Students will learn what it means to be peace-loving and peaceful and display this understanding by (a) labeling this behavior in themselves and others, (b) not being the first to hit or be mean, (c) telling the teacher when someone is mean to them rather than hitting or crying, and (d) participating in teacher-led whole-class conflict resolution.

EARLY ELEMENTARY/MIDDLE CHILDHOOD

Early elementary school children are more interested in real things and how they work than the fantasy and fairy tales that were attractive during early childhood. They are also more creative, artistic, spontaneous, optimistic, and physically active than they will be at the late elementary level, although all gradually diminish during this period. As they enter first grade, they tend to be impatient, demanding with parents, aggressive in play, prone to tattling and jealousy, and overly interested in winning and being first. At the second grade level they are more serious, more sensitive to embarrassing criticism and exposure, less active, more interested in friends, more polite and considerate with parents, more demanding with teachers, and more inclined to feel unfairly treated. Between six and seven, children typically move from being overly assertive and rather insensitive to being relatively unassertive and overly sensitive due to an emerging awareness that they are being evaluated by others. Coupled with this emerging awareness is an emerging understanding of self in terms of comparisons with others and a gradual departure from an understanding of self in terms of a collection of separate and unrelated characteristics such as how they look, what they can do, and how they feel from moment to moment.

All early elementary children like to learn to play games with rules, but sixes do not learn game rules well and are overly competitive. The ability to follow game rules well by age seven is made possible by the emergence of concrete operational thinking that includes deductive and syllogistic reasoning and reversible mental operations. All early elementary children have a need to make and do things well as evidenced by a strong desire to show their school work to their parents. Sixes enjoy the process of creation more than the product and are highly industrious, loud, and hurried. Sevens are preoccupied with producing perfect products, tend to overuse their erasers, and tend to be much more self-conscious, quiet, moody, slow-working, and inward than sixes.

Early elementary children intentionally use people and things in their environment to satisfy their wants and desires. They are now truly social where they were only moving in this direction earlier, but their cooperation with others has a predominant instrumental or self-serving quality that is reflected in descriptive words and phrases such as "uneven-handed reciprocity," "reciprocal obligation," and "exchanging favors to satisfy needs." At school they exchange their compliance with teacher expectations for help in satisfying their need to be productive and competent. At home they exchange obedience and conformity for support and assistance. Friendships are often based upon whether another child will go along with what they want to do rather than an awareness of shared values or goals, and these friendships tend to last only as long as both parties feel that they are benefitting. They can be very loving and kind, as they have demonstrated in the past, but unless they see a personal advantage or have received extensive reinforcement for kindness, they are likely to act in pursuit of their goals and objectives with little or no regard for the feelings and needs of others.

One might reasonably conclude that children at the beginning of this level sense their capacity to satisfy their desires at the expense of others or through manipulation and deception if necessary, and their need for mechanisms, both external and internal, to keep this corrupting power under control. This inner sense may be reflected in their eventual tendency to view rules, including game rules, as sacred and unalterable, their inflexibility in applying these rules to others, the fact that they begin to internalize the controlling voice of firm but loving adults with whom they identify (authoritarian conscience), their inclination to accept as just the actions of authority, their willingness to exchange obedience for adult assistance, and an emerging awareness that problems caused by competing desires among peers can be prevented through equal treatment (egalitarianism). They tend to use the terms equal and fair synonymously, and tend to be more interested in equal treatment when they receive less than when they receive more.

Instructional Implications and Recommendations

Interpersonal and Environmental Support

First and second grade students are still very dependent, but they do not need as much affection and reassurance as preschool and kindergarten children. Because children at this level gradually become more aware of being evaluated by others and more sensitive to criticism, teachers should be alert to negative moods and willing to provide immediate support. They also need to be alert to the emotional difficulties of children who have been over-protected by parents and therefore lack the independence and self-confidence to deal with the social and academic demands of school. Finally, they will need to encourage initiative and to be patient with children who have progressed from simply wanting to do things (typical of age six) to wanting to do them well (typical of ages seven and eight).

Unstructured Peer-Group Play

Although the nature of free play becomes less symbolic and more social and rule-bound as children move out of kindergarten and into the first and second grades, it continues to be critical for social and moral development. Early elementary children need at least an hour of free play. During this time games and activities should not be led by adults. Teachers and other adults should do nothing more than remain in the area to intervene when children are unable to resolve their conflicts peacefully.

Discipline and Reinforcement

An elaborate classroom discipline system with visible charts and hands-on components is appropriate for these high-energy children who have a natural interest in rules, a natural tendency to be competitive, a natural tendency to run over each other in pursuit of their desires and interests, an awareness of their partial dependence on authority to achieve self-control, and a natural tendency to internalize rules if authority figures who impose them can combine firmness with enough love to promote personal identification with authority.

When reprimanded, first and second grade children should not be subjected to moralizing but should be asked to repeat the rule they violated, told that they must follow the rules even when they want something badly, and, if the rule violation is sufficiently serious, placed in timeout as a clear way of communicating that the cost of getting what they want at the expense of the rules and others is to *not* get what they want for a specified time period. Timeout will be needed to handle serious misbehavior, and a sequence of levels of timeout, each more seclusive and restrictive than the preceding, should be planned in advance and consistently applied in order to encourage children to choose self-control, thereby avoiding increased restrictions (e.g., pushed away from the group, timeout corner, timeout outside the classroom, detention, suspension).

Peer mediation is not recommended at this age (unless much older students are the mediators), but an adult-guided search for nonviolent solutions to minor conflict can be effective and will be the most effective when children have already learned about prospective alternatives through previous mediations and/or stories. Some type of restitutional or reparative penalty rather than, or in addition to, timeout may be appropriate, depending on the amount of remorse shown.

Since first and second grade children can take the perspective of others and engage in prosocial behavior unconditionally but are too preoccupied with satisfying their own needs to do so voluntarily much of the time, they should be told the behaviors that are good, encouraged to be the first to show these behaviors, given ample opportunities in free play and cooperative learning activities to exhibit these behaviors, socially rewarded whenever they display these behaviors, and given special attention through consequences such as monthly awards for prosocial behavior or adding their name and deed to a Good Deed Tree. Prevention of conflict can also be achieved by taking their natural competitiveness and selfishness seriously, taking time to clarify game rules, and strategically legitimizing competition in some activities and structuring it away in others by using cooperative conditions. Totally eliminating competitive activities as some have suggested is unnatural and unrealistic for this age level.

Observation and Modeling

Adults responsible for teaching first and second grade children must take special care to be consistent in modeling the virtues they teach or they may suffer the criticism of their students. They should also use in their interactions with students the virtue words targeted for this level and those targeted at the preschool level. Their emphasis should be on calling attention to and labeling virtuous models within and outside the classroom. Pairing students with older student buddies within the school, or adult buddies from outside the school, is highly effective with this age group.

Didactic Teaching

Teachers should display the seven primary virtues and definitions in their classrooms along with the "elaborative" virtues that are targeted for these grades. The latter should be presented in an interesting format such as identifying them as virtues that the cartoon character Arthur possesses. Students should be asked to learn the definitions for the seven primary virtues since they are very simple. This learning should occur through hands-on activities such as posters, art work, journals, and bulletin board displays rather than rote memorization. Students should also have these words infused into their reading and writing and have the concepts underlying all fifteen of the virtue words for this level infused into language arts and social studies through stories, drama, art, and music.

Some of the targeted virtues and elaborative virtues (comforting, courteous, brave, sorry, forgiving, patient) can be viewed as social skills and should therefore be systematically modeled, role played, and practiced apart from other parts of the curriculum (see subsequent descriptions of the Skillstreaming approach). Other targeted virtues need to be associated with feeling words through direct instruction and labeling (e.g., shame and embarrassment related to being sorry). With respect to social problem solving, children at this level should be taught the basic steps, but these steps should be carried out through teacher-guided and classroom-assisted mediations and not conventional peer mediation unless older students are the mediators.

Students should not be asked to memorize classroom rules, but they should have some involvement in their formulation. These rules should be clearly posted and referred to when they are being followed or violated. More than likely, many of the students will learn the rules well and take pleasure in catching others who violate them. Once the rules are created, every effort should be made not to bend them since children at this level view rules as sacred and unchangeable.

Active Participation Within Classroom and School Communities

Students at this level should be given choices, as they were earlier, but they do not need to move about as freely as preschool children and do not need as much time for discovery learning or free exploration. Since they do not view rules as an alterable product of mutual consent as they will in late childhood and early adolescence, their contribution to the formation of class rules should be limited. The extent to which cooperative learning techniques can be used at this level is limited, so the teacher should focus primarily on prerequisite skills like learning to be patient and considerate of others during teacher-led small group instruction and being able to follow rules in simple game play. The assignment of learning partners and cluster group seating can be introduced during the second grade or during the first grade if prerequisites are in place. Active participation of students at these ages should be in age-appropriate forms such as role-playing as a part of social skills training, classroom dramatizations of stories read and events studied in class, speaking and reading in front of peers, routine center time activities with puppets, construction toys, housekeeping toys, and so forth, class meetings, cross-grade buddies activities, giving input during teacher-mediated interpersonal problem solving, making comments, asking questions, and answering questions during teacher-led didactic instruction, and working as peer tutors for those who are academically and socially ready for this responsibility.

Experiences in the Larger Community

Teachers should plan field trips to places where the needy are being served, plan and carry out school and community service projects and an intercultural exchange project, and give homework assignments that are related to the targeted virtues and psychological processes.

Instructional Focus

Targeted Virtues

The primary focus for first and second grade students is *Friendship* and the elaborative virtues of *fair, forgiving, patient,* and *considerate.* Other targeted virtues include *Kindness* and the elaborative virtues of *comforting* and *courteous; Courage* and the elaborative virtues of *brave* and *sorry; Ability* and the elaborative virtues of *prepared* and *skillful; Effort* and the elaborative virtues of *energetic, determined,* and *competitive; Teamwork* and the elaborative virtue of *respectful;* and *Citizenship* and the elaborative virtue of *rule-following.*

Targeted Psychological Processes

The process focus for first and second grade children includes expanding their natural affective form of empathy to include a *beginning* cognitive or *perspective-taking* component, promoting the process of internalizing adult rules to form an *authoritarian conscience*, promoting the development of a beginning notion of *fairness that appreciates equality* but not necessarily equity, promoting the transition from simply wanting to do things (initiative) to wanting to do them well (*competence*), and encouraging *early forms of cooperation and friendship* that will be unavoidably limited by one-way social perspective that is inherently self-serving, unevenly reciprocal, and instrumental.

Primary Instructional Modes

Once again, teachers must balance an emphasis on active student participation and unstructured peer interaction and play with enough didactic instruction, modeling, reinforcement, and interpersonal support to ensure that children learn the virtues and related feeling vocabulary, and learn adult rules and expectations in a manner that will promote the normal formation of an authoritarian conscience. Adults need to continue to be loving and firm with clear consequences for disregarding rules, and they need to be sensitive to those students who begin to display perfectionistic tendencies or a desire to do things well. Didactic instruction should continue to focus on the infusion of character themes into all possible lessons and the use of storytelling and reading stories to students that support character development objectives. Interpersonal conflicts should be addressed through teacher-led mediation with class input where possible, and teachers need to take the time to ask the questions and give the prompts that students will need to begin taking the perspective of others. Social skills training should occur daily using a Skillstreaming type model that combines didactics and active participation. The use of discipline/reinforcement as a learning mode should include a classroom management system that provides an ongoing, interesting, visible account of each child's current status in terms of acceptable versus unacceptable behavior and includes some type of hands-on component. Teachers need to control excessive competitiveness by using more cooperative than competitive activities. Finally, active student participation in the classroom should include daily class meetings, cross-grade buddies activities, beginning cooperative learning in pairs or groups of three, school service, service learning, and an intercultural exchange project with another class in another school.

General Instructional Objective

The general character development objective for first and second grade students is to cultivate the seven primary virtues in an active-student environment with an emphasis on friendship and the development of (a) a beginning perspective-taking ability (elicited through prompts and questions), (b) an authoritarian conscience (i.e., internalized adult expectations) through quality student-teacher relationships and clear rules, and (c) a sense of competence as children begin to move from merely wanting to do things to wanting to do them well.

Behavioral Objectives

1. Students will begin to take the perspective of others, will internalize adult rules, and will begin to show a desire to do things well. They will demonstrate this growth through their responses to teacher questions and their expressed feelings and attitudes, and by behaving in accordance with adult rules and expectations when adults are not present.

2. Students will expand their understanding of kindness to include being comforting,

courteous, and polite, and they will demonstrate this understanding by using gentle talk and touch and offering to play with peers who are upset, and by adding to their repertoire of social skills the habitual courtesies of saying "good morning" and "excuse me" and not interrupting the teacher when she is talking to someone else.

3. Students will learn that being brave and being sorry are forms of courage, and they will demonstrate their understanding by accurately labeling the bravery of others and by showing that they are sorry for wrongdoing through nonverbal and/or verbal behaviors that reflect associated feelings and attitudes as judged by their teachers and parents.

4. Students will learn what it means to be prepared and skilled and the importance of both, and they will demonstrate their understanding by accurately labeling these behaviors in themselves and others, by remembering their materials and homework, by practicing before performing for others, and by acquiring reading and math skills at expectancy.

5. Students will expand their concept of effort by learning the meaning of energetic, determined, and competitive, and they will demonstrate their understanding by accurately describing others as energetic, determined, and competitive, and by being energetic, determined, and competitive in a socially appropriate way.

6. Students will broaden their understanding of friendship to include treating others fairly, forgiving others, being patient with others, and considering the effects of their behavior on others. They will demonstrate this understanding by taking turns and treating peers fairly, by not staying angry with peers for more than a few minutes following minor conflicts, by waiting their turn without complaint or cheating, and by listening when the teacher uses perceptual cues to describe how their behavior is affecting others.

7. Students will learn that being a good team member involves treating others with respect, and they will demonstrate this understanding by accurately labeling respect and disrespect among peers and story characters, by not making fun of others, and by not teasing, hitting, and name calling.

8. Students will learn what it means to be law-abiding as a citizen and the relationship of this social responsibility to following rules in class, and they will demonstrate this understanding by following class rules and by not complaining and denying wrongdoing when caught breaking the rules.

LATE ELEMENTARY/LATE CHILDHOOD

For third, fourth, and fifth grade children, the family continues to be a very important influence, but the peer group is the primary growth center in their lives and a critical foundation from which a rational conscience and true cooperation develops. At this stage children view "right" as that which gains approval from peers and adults, and they manage to gain approval by being caring and accommodating toward significant others and living by a golden-rule standard that reflects an understanding of even-handed reciprocity in friendships. They begin this stage by viewing justice and fairness in terms of equality and begin to view it more benevolently with a new appreciation for unequal needs among people (equity). For the first time they can make reasoned decisions by considering disparate claims to justice or fairness and the circumstances within which these claims are made, but their perspective continues to be limited for the most part to a particular situation and the persons involved. As they acquire the capacity to distinguish between the intentions of others and the effects of their actions at about age nine, they tend to give more weight to the intentions of others when they make judgments about fairness.

Late elementary children no longer view authority figures as different from themselves in terms of rights, and by age ten or eleven, they no longer feel compelled to test limits imposed by authority. They recognize that relevant superior knowledge and skill justify the superior status of leaders and authority figures. Their willingness to conform to adult expectations derives from this understanding rather than from a fear of authority, unless persons in authority are intimidating. They know the function of rules, become infatuated with the details of game rules, and willfully adhere to them. By the end of this stage, children no longer assign greater importance to their own desires than those of the group, even though they may not act accordingly, and they are capable of true cooperation. They can take the perspective of others both intellectually and emotionally and compare the perspectives of others with their own. They develop an appreciation for relationships or affectional bonds and see the value of life accordingly. Their self-understanding is based on comparisons with others to a large degree, and begins to include the real and potential effects of their characteristics on others.

Upon entering the third grade, children tend to be concerned about what their parents and teachers think about them, but they begin to form close friends and are more interested in peers than the teacher. They tend to be very judgmental of themselves and others and very sensitive about incompetencies, such as being a poor reader. They are very industrious and competitive but tend to be self-critical, overly competitive, and very serious, as well as worrisome and generally negative by age ten. Their tendency to be judgmental increases somewhat as they enter the fourth grade, and it includes the dispassionate appraisal of parents, teachers, and themselves, and an ability to accept blame and responsibility for their actions. The close same-sex friendships that began in the third grade continue with greater intensity at the fourth grade level and are accompanied by a beginning polarization between the sexes that peaks at eleven.

In contrast to third graders, fourth graders are more inner directed and more attracted by materials and information. They are also much more positive and seem to have an instinct for cooperation that makes group activities work extremely well. By the end of the fourth grade, they are typically less judgmental and critical, enjoy better relationships with parents and teachers, and are generally as adapted to their world as they will be for years. This adaptation begins to crumble somewhat as children begin the growth spurt that leads them into the new hopes and anxieties of early adolescence. By the end of the fifth grade, many children have become noticeably more active, ill-mannered, unpredictable, defensive, argumentative, easily embarrassed, and independent, but they continue to work well in groups. By age eleven children can think deductively, reason abstractly, and view the world from many perspectives.

Instructional Implications/Recommendations

Interpersonal and Environmental Support

Children in this age range do not need their teacher to serve as a second mother or father, but they need to feel that they are liked by the teacher in spite of their typical negativeness at grades three and five. They also need a classroom and school environment that is child-centered, and one in which adults do not demean, insult, threaten, and ridicule them in public.

Unstructured Peer-Group Interaction

Children at this level also need time with peers outside of their structured classroom activities, and this includes recess and after-school clubs, sports, and recreational activities that allow them time before, during, and after adult-organized activities to interact freely and spontaneously.

Discipline and Reinforcement

Since this stage marks the beginning of rule codification or intense interest in game rules, and since students now fully comprehend the role of rules and authority, teachers can spend more time on rule creation with significant student input and activities designed to achieve over-learning of rules. They may not have to adhere to the general rule of having just a few class rules. They are advised to build some type of game-like, team-based, competitive approach to classroom management where students are not always on the same team, and where chronic offenders, if there are a few, are put on a team of their own. Their system should include both group and individual contingencies (see Discipline and Reinforcement strategies in chapter 4 for more details). Consequences for rule infractions that clearly violate the rights of others should have some type of restitutional, amendatory, or positive-practice over-corrective consequence, and consequences should be determined in advance with student input when possible. Behavioral contracting is a very effective tool at this stage. This is the first age at which it is critical to provide a grading system that rewards individual progress (e.g., letter grades for individual progress as reflected through pre-post testing and taking ability into account, and number grades to show mastery of grade-level material).

Observation and Modeling

Children in this age range are ideally suited to serve as role models for younger children through a buddy system. At-risk younger children should be paired with the most virtuous and accomplished older students. Children enjoy spending time with adult buddies or mentors from adopting businesses and concerned organizations. Prospective buddies from businesses who are rookies should be oriented by a team including the teacher, principal, and counselor or school psychologist. Students in this age range are also ideal for a "He Is My Hero" program in which students are encouraged to study, write about, write to, and, if possible, communicate with their hero inside or outside the school.

Didactic Teaching

Teachers should introduce, define, and infuse in every subject possible the nineteen words that identify the target virtues for this age range, but this direct instruction should not be used as the primary instructional method. Teachers should also become preoccupied with identifying exemplars of these virtues, and they should encourage their students to do the same and to bring in stories from outside of school. Students could read and report on books that teach about one of the targeted virtues, and this could be facilitated in advance by cataloging library books by the virtues and moral principles they teach (see chapter 4). Social skills instruction in the Skillstreaming mode should continue from the previous level and should focus on social skills related to the nineteen virtues targeted at this level (e.g., listening as a skill related to showing genuine interest in others, showing sportsmanship even when one loses, taking the initiative to mediate conflicts among teammates other than oneself, being assertive in resisting pressure to become involved in drugs and law-breaking, etc.). Finally, children need to learn the basic steps in social problem solving well enough to eventually serve as peer mediators without adult involvement (see chapter 4).

Active Participation Within Classroom and School Communities

This cluster of grades is the best time to begin emphasizing cooperative learning strategies, class meetings that address serious interpersonal and ethical problems and that employ group counseling techniques, the full inclusion of students in the writing of rules, the introduction of peer mediation, intercultural exchanges with students of the same grade from another school and culture, and service learning projects that serve the needy outside the school. Decisions with respect to intercultural exchanges and service learning should include student input. Cooperative learning should be the most commonly used instructional strategy beginning at the fourth grade.

Experiences Within the Larger Community

This is the ideal age for children to become involved in organized recreational activities, clubs, scouts, and other youth groups. This is so important that school personnel should make sure that every child is involved in something after school or outside of school. The primary virtue emphasis at this level is teamwork, and actually being on teams inside and outside of school is the best way for students to learn. Parents could also be encouraged to build upon school-organized service learning initiatives by becoming involved in such efforts as a family.

Instructional Focus

Targeted Virtues

The primary focus for third, fourth, and fifth grade students is *Teamwork* and the elaborative virtues of *cooperative, productive, responsible, positive, mediating,* and *punctual/prompt.* Other targeted virtues include *Kindness* and the elaborative virtues of *sensitive* and *interested; Courage* and the elaborative virtue of *remorseful; Ability* and the elaborative virtues of *organized, knowledgeable,* and *realistic; Effort* and the elaborative virtues of *studious* and *self-disciplined; Friendship* and the elaborative virtue of *supportive*; and *Citizenship* and the elaborative virtues of *drug-free, law-abiding,* and *health-conscious.*

Targeted Psychological Processes

The process focus for late elementary children is threefold includes promoting the transition from an early authoritarian conscience (internalized heteronomy) to a *beginning rational conscience*, promoting a *beginning understanding of equity*, and encouraging a *need for approval from responsible peers* via reciprocal cooperation and friendship—all made possible by the transition from perceptual to conceptual or concrete operational thinking and a more mature but still limited ability to take the perspective of others.

Primary Instructional Modes

The primary mode at this level is once again active participation in classroom and school communities with an emphasis on cooperative learning techniques, intercultural exchange, cross-grade buddy systems, class meetings, service learning, and extracurricular activities. Discipline and reinforcement and didactic teaching are also important since students are interested in the details of rules, are naturally competitive, and have a strong need for competence. Modeling that involves older students and admired adults works very well at these grade levels.

General Instructional Objective

The general character development objective for third, fourth, and fifth grade students is to cultivate the seven primary virtues in a cooperative learning environment with an emphasis on (a) developing a sense of obligation to team members, (b) promoting the emergence of a rational conscience, and (c) promoting a beginning understanding of equity—all made possible by a new two-way social perspective, concrete-operational thinking, and guided practice in critical thinking, cooperative group work, and service to others.

Behavioral Objectives

1. Students will develop a rational conscience and a sense of obligation to their classmates, family members, and school personnel, and will demonstrate this sense of obligation by doing the right thing when rules do not clearly indicate what is right, and by acting in a manner that sometimes places group needs and goals above self-interest.

2. Students will expand their understanding of kindness to include showing interest in others in all interpersonal interactions and being sensitive to the needs, feelings, and circumstances of others. They will demonstrate this understanding in casual interactions, cooperative learning activities, peer mediation work, and service learning.

3. Students will learn that apologizing is honorable because it calls for courage in the form of honesty, humility, and respect for others, and they will demonstrate their understanding by apologizing with little or no prompting from adults and by exhibiting verbal and nonverbal behaviors which reflect genuine remorse.

4. Students will learn that organization, knowledge, and realism are needed to solve problems and achieve personal goals, and they will demonstrate their understanding by accepting constructive feedback about goals, plans, and self-perceptions, by showing they value knowledge through their work completion, and by assisting one another with organization during cooperative learning activities.

5. Students will learn that being studious and self-disciplined are forms of effort they should exhibit, and they will demonstrate this by making choices that reflect these virtues such as remaining on-task when others are not, beginning assignments and doing homework without reminders, bringing supplies, and continuing beyond the required study time if this is needed to succeed or do their best.

6. Students will learn about mutual support as a characteristic of true friendship and that this takes courage and integrity in situations where they may be criticized or have to deny their immediate desires to come to the aid of a friend, and they will demonstrate this quality by establishing friendships inside and outside of school and by functioning as this type of friend.

7. Students will learn that many important plans and decisions are made by groups of people who must work together and that many important accomplishments depend on the capacity of people to be good team members in terms of cooperation, productivity, responsibility, positiveness, mediational skills, and punctuality. They will show their understanding by demonstrating these skills, attitudes, and habits in cooperative learning activities, whole-class projects, and extracurricular team activities.

8. Students will add to their understanding of responsible citizenship by learning that only drug-free and physically healthy people can help themselves and their community, and that obeying the law provides order and protection. They will demonstrate their

understanding by refusing drugs and encouraging their friends to do so, by practicing healthful living, and by making and following rules in their classrooms and school.

MIDDLE SCHOOL/EARLY ADOLESCENCE

Early adolescence or the middle school years may present the toughest challenge to students, parents, and teachers during the entire developmental process due to the sudden and dramatic changes brought on by sexual maturation and the full realization of formal operational thinking (the ability to manipulate symbols in the mind and to think logically and abstractly, the capacity to assume a third-party perspective on oneself, one's peers, and one's relationships). These changes introduce unprecedented peer group activity and preoccupations and intense concern about personal and social qualities. Much of the turmoil and uncertainty of this period comes from the fact that early adolescents develop sexually and intellectually at different rates and develop natural preoccupations with personal and social matters at different ages.

Some sixth graders have entered puberty and are exhibiting at least hesitant sexual interest and experimentation. Like their age peers who have not entered puberty, however, they are still children in many ways. Most have recovered from late-elementary-school apprehensions about the future as reflected in their friendliness, openness, flightiness, extremely high energy level, lack of social criticism (which looms around the corner), and lack of cliquishness or discrimination in friendships. These characteristics continue well into the seventh grade when differences in physical maturation become more apparent.

By the middle or end of seventh grade, many students have lost their accepting, happy-go-lucky, worry-free demeanor and have become touchy, introspective, and preoccupied with being liked by their peers. This change marks the actual departure from childhood and entry into adolescence. Sometime between the middle of seventh grade and the beginning of the eighth grade, the peer group becomes the center of their world, and school becomes the stage on which the drama of friendships, rivalries, cliques, and teacher-student tensions unfolds. Perhaps because they need to convince themselves of their psychological independence, they typically feel compelled to question all rules except moral rules and are aware that rules are a changeable product of mutual consent. Their criticism of the values, beliefs, and behaviors of their parents also reflects the beginning of the process of individuation or psychological separation from their parents.

To fill the gap that they are creating between themselves and many adults in their lives, early adolescents gravitate toward same-sex cliques that satisfy many of the needs once satisfied by the family. Same-sex friendships are exclusive and characterized by mutual understanding (loyalty) and the sharing of innermost feelings and personal problems (intimacy). They begin to conceive of themselves in terms of social and personal qualities and self-evaluations that address their past and anticipated future rather than specific acts and capabilities in the present only.

With respect to moral reasoning, young adolescents continue to view what is just or "right" as that which gains approval from significant others in their lives including peers and parents, and they must deal with conflicts between what is approved by peers and what is approved by adults. They are intellectually capable of considering disparate claims to justice as well as the circumstances of a dispute or problem situation and can make decisions on the basis of equity, which reflect an understanding that the needs of some exceed those of others. Consistent with their interpersonal preoccupations, their thoughts on the value of life reflect an empathetic understanding of affectional bonds among people and the distress suffered by the friends and relatives of the deceased.

Instructional Implications and Recommendations

Interpersonal and Environmental Support

Students entering at the sixth grade level and much of the seventh are generally pretty stable and not in need of interpersonal support beyond what children in late childhood typically receive. As they truly enter puberty and become much more concerned about how they are perceived by peers, they become more needy. Teachers who recognize this need when it emerges and appreciate that students this age are distinguishing between teacher skill and likeable teacher personalities can balance their responsibilities as an authority figure with efforts to take advantage of one-on-one relationships with students who seem to like them and want to talk with them. Perhaps the most common mistake made by middle school teachers is missing the opportunity to be a big brother or big sister and friend out of fear of diminishing their power and control as an authority figure.

Unstructured Peer-Group Interaction

Middle school students need time in informal, unstructured situations in order to achieve interpersonal milestones. Some will find their way without adult efforts to provide opportunities for unstructured interaction, but school personnel can promote the normal development of early adolescents by legitimizing informal mixing during lunch periods, grade-level parties at the school that are largely student planned, and recreational activities in the community that students are made aware of through communication between school personnel and organization sponsors. Parents should be encouraged to allow their young adolescents to have get-togethers with friends in their homes under conditions that allow them a reasonable degree of privacy.

Discipline and Reinforcement

Sixth and seventh grade students are a challenge even for the best of classroom managers. This is because of their high energy level and the fact that many are still children in adolescent bodies. Eighth graders are a different type of challenge because they try to bring their cliquish preoccupations into the classroom. With these challenging student characteristics and the many classroom and teacher changes that typically take place, it is critical for middle schools to have a good school-wide discipline system that involves several levels of predictable consequences for specific types of inappropriate behavior, and a means of keeping accurate records of where each child stands as far as first, second, and third violations of particular rules are concerned. This may seem negative, but at the middle school level, it is preventive provided it includes consistent back-up from school administrators after classroom level consequences have been tried (excluding illegal behaviors of course). Greater consistency from one classroom to the next can be enhanced by establishing grade-level teacher teams of three or four and limiting each student's exposure to the teachers of one team. Teachers in each cluster should have the same rules, and student input into this single set of rules can be accomplished by having each class discuss rules followed by student representatives from each class hammering out the final list. Students should also have input into consequences for rule violations. The sequence of consequences for frequently occurring rule violations, such as tardiness and classroom disruption, should begin with some type of teacher warning, followed by a relatively minor consequence, such as being held in the room until the last minute of the passing period, followed by progressively more aversive series of consequences, such as parent notification, after-school detention, in-school suspension, and suspension.

The attention to school-wide discipline systems and classroom management is not intended to imply that various forms of positive reinforcement of individuals and groups is less important than structure and a system of negative consequences, but broadly focused management systems at this age level are viewed as a critical cornerstone for developing good character. Elaborate systems give teachers the space to develop the type of relationships with students that students need as they become more independent from their parents and anxious about peer approval. Teachers need not be overly cautious about publicly complimenting students who display virtuous behavior, but peer recognition will be more reinforcing. A student of the month for each of the seven primary virtues, selected by committees representing every classroom and announced by students over the public address system with reference to specific behaviors that resulted in this recognition, would presumably have a powerful effect and cause the entire student body to value these virtues more highly.

Observation and Modeling

Students should be encouraged in various ways to share information about same-age and older persons they admire whose lives and actions provide examples (models) of the targeted virtues. Since early adolescents look up to older adolescents, some type of effort should be made to bring model peers into the school. This should perhaps be done along the lines of drug refusal and nonviolence. Career days make more sense at this level than earlier and should be representative of the real world.

Didactic Teaching

All teachers are encouraged to visually display the targeted virtues in their classrooms with definitions for at least the seven primary virtues. They are encouraged to use these displays as a reminder to infuse these virtues into their instruction and to achieve maximum infusion through advanced planning and taking full advantage of teachable moments. Formal social skills training should probably not continue at this level, with the possible exception of refusal skills related to drugs and sex and work with deviant adolescents. If efforts at the elementary level have been adequate, didactic teaching of social-problem-solving or peer-mediation skills should not be necessary either, except for advanced training of carefully selected peer mediators. Sex education should not include both sexes and should deal more with student concerns and misunderstandings than biology. In general, what is needed at the middle school level is a course that deals with all of the life concerns and skills that are especially relevant at this age level, including concerns about peer pressure, peer approval and acceptance, friendships, drugs, sex, relationships with parents, and so forth. This could be an expanded or redesigned health course or a new course with a title such as Life Skills for the Young Adolescent.

Active Participation Within Classroom and School Communities

Cooperative learning activities may prove to be rather difficult to control at the sixth and seventh grade levels due to high energy and/or peer-acceptance concerns, but such activities should not be abandoned entirely. Long-term team projects rather than daily or weekly cooperative activities may reduce the difficulty since students would have time to get comfortable and get serious. Their use in conjunction with character building should be tied to the specific instructional objectives that identify cooperative learning as a primary strategy (e.g., teamwork). Sociodrama should be effective in life skills courses that address young adolescent concerns if the conflicts addressed are of central concern to students. Teachers should begin to have students take some responsibility for the learning of their classmates through oral reports on individual and team projects, choosing topics for in-depth study, re-teaching information to lower ability students, and so forth.

The involvement of students in making rules, sharing information about people they feel are good models for the targeted virtues, and selecting peers to recognize for their virtuous behavior are mentioned elsewhere, and these strategies clearly involve active student participation. Teachers should not ignore or stifle student criticism of school rules and procedures as long as critical students are willing to discuss possible alternative rules. Teachers should patiently try to elicit what students actually think about rules, laws, behaviors of prominent figures in the news and in history, and so forth.

Student councils/governments are useful provided these councils are actually given authority to do something meaningful, and provided representatives on the council are required to deal with real problems of collective school life just as elected officials in the real world must address real problems in their communities. All students should be involved in school-improvement and service-learning projects at the direction of school personnel. Students who have been recognized by peers for virtuous behavior should have the opportunity to serve on student disciplinary committees. Only capable, elite students should serve as peer mediators and only if they have received training above and beyond that provided within all elementary classrooms.

Experience Within the Larger Community

Teachers should work with their students to plan and carry out service to the local community. School personnel should encourage involvement in group recreation and team activities outside of school. Parents should be informed about the importance of letting their adolescents spend leisure time with their peers.

Instructional Focus

Targeted Virtues

The primary focus for sixth, seventh, and eighth grade students is *Courage* with the elaborative virtues of *independent, risk-taking, decisive, assertive, self-disclosing,* and *self-evaluating.* Another important focus is *Friendship* and the elaborative virtues of *understanding, trustworthy,* and *devoted/loyal.* Other targeted virtues include *Kindness* with the elaborative virtue of *compassionate; Ability* with the elaborative virtues of *flexible* and *objective; Effort* with the elaborative virtues of *ambitious* and *dedicated; Teamwork* and the elaborative virtues of *humble/modest* and *genuine/sincere;* and *Citizenship* with the elaborative virtue of *volunteering.*

Targeted Psychological Processes

The process focus for early adolescents is threefold and includes the development of an *early form of autonomous moral reasoning*; the development of a *social consciousness that extends beyond the peer group and family* and involves a sense of duty as a community member; and the *promotion of personal friendships* that are characterized by mutual and exclusive trust, loyalty, obligation, and the sharing of innermost feelings, all of which depend on the prior development of empathy, logical and critical thinking skills, and a rational—as opposed to authoritarian—conscience.

Primary Instructional Modes

The primary instructional mode is once again active participation in the form of volunteer work in the school, service learning, group problem solving activities, group counseling, sociodrama, class discussions about moral issues and moral dilemmas, student government, personal improvement projects, and classroom rule making. A different approach to modeling is needed at this age, one that gets students to search for and share their own models of the targeted virtues, and one where school personnel take the perspective of their students and resist criticizing persons admired by their students unless they display behavior in opposition to the targeted virtues. Group counseling should always be available during, before, and after school hours.

General Instructional Objective

The general character development objective for sixth, seventh, and eighth grade students is to promote a full understanding of the seven primary virtues from a community perspective with an emphasis on (a) courage and friendship, (b) an early form of autonomous moral reasoning, (c) social consciousness that includes a sense of obligation to the community and personal friends, and (d) an understanding of what is "right" that moves beyond that which gains approval from significant others and toward doing one's duty as a community member and friend.

Behavioral Objectives

1. Students will use their critical and logical thinking skills to take the perspective of others with feeling and understanding and will begin reasoning about moral issues in an early autonomous manner. They will expand their social consciousness and sense of obligation to the school and local community and to their close personal friends.

2. Students will learn the meaning of compassion from a community perspective and will demonstrate their understanding by participating in service learning projects, sharing these experiences in class, and studying individuals who have modeled compassion in an exemplary manner.

3. Students will expand their understanding of courage to include independence, decisiveness, assertiveness, self-disclosure, and self-evaluation, and they will demonstrate their understanding by doing the right thing when pressured to do otherwise by peers, by taking risks in establishing and honoring friendships, by pursuing opportunities for skill acquisition in areas of special interest, by being assertive but not aggressive in the classroom, by sharing their most personal feelings and thoughts with at least one good friend of similar age, and by showing in a group setting that they can evaluate themselves and self-correct.

4. Students will learn the importance of being mentally flexible and objective in their problem-solving efforts, and they will demonstrate these characteristics in class discussions, cooperative learning activities, student disciplinary committee service, peer

mediation, and other situations that require third-party perspective taking and a search for possible solution ideas.

5. Students will expand their understanding of effort to include the concepts of ambition and dedication and will demonstrate this understanding by planing and carrying out a formal self-improvement project.

6. Students will come to appreciate the nature of close interpersonal friendships between peers through direct and vicarious experience and come to appreciate and value the reciprocal understanding, trustworthiness, and loyalty that characterize such friendships. They will demonstrate this understanding by writing and talking about their close friends and those of others that they have read and heard about.

7. Students will expand their concept of effective team membership by learning about the facilitative effect of humility and genuineness, and will show this understanding by demonstrating these characteristics and critiquing them in others within the context of cooperative learning, group counseling, and other group activities where goals can only be achieved through teamwork.

8. Students will learn that responsible citizens who are concerned about their communities volunteer their time for necessary, but not necessarily pleasant, jobs and will do so without expecting thanks or appreciation.

HIGH SCHOOL/LATE ADOLESCENCE

Late adolescents are emerging from the early stages of individuation (psychological separation from the parents) and have already invested much of their time and energy trying to satisfy their interpersonal needs through their peer group. If they have survived the omnipotence and lack of caution that often accompany their newly acquired psychological independence, they have or may soon come to the point where they are less critical of their parents and more concerned about losing their love and support completely. They are emerging from same-sex cliques and spending much of their time in heterosexual cliques and groups comprised of such cliques. Many are spending increasing amounts of time in one-on-one relationships with actual or prospective life partners. They have become or will soon become secure enough to grant close friends the independence to establish other close friendships. Because of their typically fragile self-esteem and incomplete identity formation, they tend to strategically exploit social occasions and casual friendship patterns (not close friendships) to enhance the self in the minds of others and themselves. This same uncertainty about self causes them to be more clannish, intolerant, prejudiced, and cruel than they have been in the past or will be in the future.

The self-understanding or self-concepts of late adolescents are a product of much reflection, which is made possible by their recently acquired third-party perspective on themselves, their peers, and their relationships, and their self-concepts are moving away, or will soon move away, from social and personality characteristics and toward ideas, beliefs, thoughts, and philosophies. Their primary developmental task at this stage in life is to build a personal identity. This involves integrating and organizing past and present identifications, social roles, beliefs, desires, and personal attributes into an organized and unique gestalt that is acceptable to the self and that includes a commitment to an ideology or way of life and a sense of direction for the future. Successes in achieving autonomy, taking initiative, and gaining a sense of competence in childhood are necessary, but not sufficient, prerequisites for achieving the task of constructing an identity.

Late adolescents who have largely achieved this developmental task or resolved this identity crisis in ways other than a premature acceptance of parental choices (called "foreclosure"), and those who have made at least some progress in terms of occupational and ideological choices may view "right" in terms of meeting their societal obligation to participate in the making and upholding of laws and standards that protect the rights and common values of all citizens (moral maturity as defined by Kohlberg's level five), but such students are in the minority. Those who have made little progress in terms of identity formation tend to view "right" in terms of doing those things that gain approval from significant others in their lives, including peers (Kohlberg's level three), or doing one's duty by maintaining existing laws and respecting authority (Kohlberg's level four). Most have alternately viewed social conventions (as distinguished from laws and moral principles) as unnecessary and necessary, and they will soon reach the point where they view such conventions as necessary for social order but not necessarily those that conventions are presently in existence. They highly value their freedom to judge these conventions, the laws and moral principles with which they are entangled, and other people, but the moral judgments of most tend to be somewhat distorted by such things as a tendency to be overly critical (sometimes as a way of denying or repressing their own shortcomings) and an inability to recognize their experience as too limited to make the kinds of unequivocal judgments that they typically feel free to make.

Instructional Implications and Recommendations

Interpersonal and Environmental Support

More than anything else, late adolescents need the warm interpersonal support of at least one of their peers. If they are too withdrawn and insecure and too socially unskilled to find this on their own, they should be guided into counseling or into organized after-school groups and/or clubs and activities during the school day where their chances of finding this support are maximized. It would be ideal if every student could be involved in group counseling or personal-growth groups at least once a week throughout high school. If made compulsory, this would probably not work very well, but there may be ways to provide incentives for student involvement.

Unstructured Peer Group Interaction

High schools have notoriously made it difficult for teens to socialize informally during the day, and when they attempt to do so, they are too often hassled by adults. A common complaint among high school students is that they have little or no nonacademic time with their peers during the day. In an attempt to address this complaint and to promote stable identity formation and mental health, schools should provide one or both of the following: a place on the school grounds where students can gather during the day to socialize for an hour, more-or-less freely; a period during the day (called a personal development period) when students can choose from among many personal growth activities, some planned and led by their peers and some planned and led by adults. Various counseling groups and personal-growth groups, some restricted to teens and some led by various counselors, psychologists, and educational specialists, could be offered as activity choices during this personal growth hour. In contrast to this lack of relatively informal peer interaction time during the school day, most high schools have ample after- and before-school activities. If students do not feel free to socialize on school grounds during, before, or after school, they are going to do more socializing in other situations where there is no supervision at all.

Discipline and Reinforcement

School personnel should stick with logical consequences and a zero-tolerance policy for weapons possession and assault. They should be careful about publicly rewarding students for virtuous behavior and good citizenship since over-doing this could cause these students to be ostracized. Subtle and private compliments that communicate personal liking for students will produce much better results since students at this age perform for teachers that like them and are looking for adults other than parents with whom they can identify.

Observation and Modeling

High school students are going to choose their own role models and will often choose models that they know will be at least mildly objectionable to the adults in their lives. If parents and teachers choose not to control, students will at least choose models that are marginally related to the models provided by the significant adults in their lives. School personnel should consider inviting to the school at least one popular role model for students that meets minimal adult standards.

Didactic Teaching

All high school students should be encouraged to take one ethics course, one comparative cultures or comparative religions course, one personal growth course, and one parenting course so that they have a framework for exploring their identity-related uncertainties and a way of countering their natural inclination to be prejudiced and intolerant toward people who are not like themselves and fellow clique members. Such courses should include objective information about cultures and religions (approved by authorities of the various religions and cultures under study), uninhibited discussions about moral dilemmas and controversial social issues, and unequivocal didactic instruction on ethical/moral principles about which there is consensus among responsible citizens in democratic societies. With respect to ethics, the most workable model is an ethics-across-the-curriculum approach described by Lisman (see chapter 4).

Active Participation Within Classroom and School Communities

There are more ways to involve students as active participants at the high school level than any other. The problem is not finding ways to do this but finding time to use them all. Many of the methods mentioned previously, such as cooperative learning, sociodrama, class discussions, personal growth groups, participation in student government operations and elections, and disciplinary committee work, can be continued with even greater flexibility and less teacher direction at the high school level. Teen courts can be established by school systems in collaboration with the juvenile courts and other involved agencies. Discussions can be expanded to include moral dilemmas. Students are now able to do independent projects with much less guidance and direction. By this age the rules that are needed to keep classes functioning are well enough known by all students that creating rules with student involvement should not be necessary. Teachers should not ignore or stifle student criticism of school rules and procedures provided students who criticize are prepared to discuss possible alternative rules. Student councils/governments should be given as much control over the climate in the school as they will constructively take—it should be their climate *and* the staff's, not one or the other.

Experience Within the Larger Community

High school is the level where students should perhaps be required to engage in community service above and beyond service learning projects initiated at school. If school-system personnel require a minimum number of independent community service hours for graduation, they should help students to find meaningful service opportunities by providing an up-to-date list of programs in need of help and other service options. School systems should provide a school-community liaison who would work with community agencies and groups in an effort to help make character and community building experiences available, such as teen courts, exchanges of speakers among churches, late night basketball leagues, neighborhood teams to support pregnant adolescents, sports and recreational programs that fully utilize all facilities within the community, and safe zones such as parks where adolescents can interact freely knowing that drugs and weapons are absent.

Instructional Focus

Targeted Virtues

The primary focus for ninth through twelfth grade students is *Citizenship* with the elaborative virtues of *rights-respecting, educated/employed, voting/patriotic, culturally literate, historically literate,* and *family-valuing.* Other targeted virtues include *Kindness* and the elaborative virtue of *empathetic; Courage* with the elaborative virtues of *persevering* and *principled; Ability* with the elaborative virtues of *deliberate, prudent,* and *resourceful; Effort* with the elaborative virtues of *optimistic, idealistic, persistent,* and *conscientious; Friendship* and the elaborative virtues of *charitable* and *altruistic;* and *Teamwork* with the elaborative virtues of *compromising* and *temperate.*

Targeted Psychological Processes

The focus for high school or late adolescence is to (a) promote *autonomy* (being self-directed, self-governing, and principled) and the related capacity to engage in truly *autonomous critical thinking about moral issues, moral principles, and laws;* (b) the successful integration of social roles, behaviors, attributes, and values into a *personal identity* that includes a *commitment to a prosocial-ethical way of life;* (c) a view of "right" that centers on a *complete set of moral principles* and participation in making and upholding the laws and standards that protect human rights and social order; and (d) a sense of *social consciousness* that compels one to care for oneself and others.

Primary Instructional Modes

The primary instructional mode for high school students is active student participation in various forms including class discussions, student government, teen courts, cooperative learning, the use of sociodrama to analyze ethical dilemmas, therapeutic counseling groups, personal growth groups, self-improvement projects, and intercultural exchange projects. Another important mode is didactics with an emphasis on (a) ethics using an ethics-across-the-curriculum or infusional approach, (b) parenting with a focus on skills and responsibilities, and (c) world cultures and religions using an approach that compares and contrasts.

General Instructional Objective

The general character development objective for ninth through twelfth grade students is (1) to promote an understanding of the societal and global implications of the seven primary virtues within an instructional climate of open dialogue and debate, and (2) to promote the development of autonomous moral reflection, personal identity, social consciousness that compels participation, and a view of "right" that reflects a complete set of moral principles and an appreciation of the shared obligation to protect human rights.

Behavioral Objectives

1. Students will display autonomous moral reflection, form a personal identity that promises a productive future, and develop a sense of social consciousness that reflects a complete set of moral principles and a desire to contribute to and improve their world. This growth will be demonstrated through group discussions related to service learning experiences and in-class discussions about subject-specific ethical dilemmas.

2. Students will learn what it means to be empathetic and the importance of empathy in all types of relationships, and will demonstrate this understanding by engaging in group discussion about service learning activities and writing a composition about their public service experience.

3. Students will learn what it means to be courageous in terms of perseverance and adherence to moral principles, and will demonstrate their understanding by setting and achieving academic and career-planning goals, behaving in a manner consistent with their moral principles, and respectfully challenging behaviors, rules, laws, and conventions they believe violate these principles.

4. Students will develop the mental abilities of deliberation, prudence, and resourcefulness, and will demonstrate these abilities by selecting a social problem or crisis in the world for study and by writing a group or individual paper which offers creative solutions.

5. Students will recognize the type and amount of effort required to plan adequately for life after high school and demonstrate this effort by working with adult advisors to set challenging educational and career goals, by exhibiting an attitude of optimism about reaching these goals, and by being conscientious with respect to high school studies and independent work experiences that are a necessary step toward achieving these goals.

6. Students will learn the meaning of friendship—defined broadly as an unselfish regard for the welfare of others (altruism) and a willingness to give to those with needs (charity)—and will demonstrate this understanding through relatively independent participation in community service to a needy individual or group.

7. Students will further expand their capacity to be effective team members by learning the meaning of compromise and temperance in a group situation that tests their flexibility and self-restraint, and by subsequently comparing self-ratings on these teamwork behaviors with ratings made by their peers and teachers.

8. Students will finalize the process of preparing for responsible citizenship in a democratic society by coming to appreciate the importance of (a) protecting the rights of those whose beliefs and behaviors are legal but different from their own, (b) getting the training needed to realize their potential and contribute to society, (c) being conscious of social problems and being motivated to help resolve them, (d) acquiring knowledge of many cultures, (e) knowing history well enough to put current events in an historical context, and (f) working to preserve and strengthen families.

REFERENCES

Elkind, D. (1994). *A Sympathetic Understanding of the Child: Birth to Sixteen (3rd Edition)*. Boston: Allyn and Bacon.

Wood, C. (1994). *Yardsticks: Children in the Classroom age 4–12*. Greenfield, MA: Northeastern Foundation for Children.

4

Strategies and Techniques

INTRODUCTION

This chapter describes some of the strategies that promote the development of good character and community. They are grouped into six learning-mode categories based upon my assessment of which of the six is the predominant mode for each strategy. Many strategies, such as social skills training and service learning, utilize several learning modes while others are largely restricted to one.

SUPPORTIVE INTERPERSONAL/ENVIRONMENTAL CONDITIONS

Supportive Classroom and School Communities

Sergiovanni defines community as a collection of individuals who are "bonded together by natural will and who are together binded to a set of ideas and ideals" (1997:xvi). The term community implies a shared ethic, significant membership, group cohesion, and belonging. Some classrooms and schools can, therefore, be fairly described as communities while others cannot. Lickona (1991) stated that classrooms are moral communities if they are characterized by (1) teacher-student and student-student relationships that are based on respect, caring, and mutual understanding; and (2) a form of community membership that fosters feelings of personal significance and a sense of obligation to fellow class members. Sergiovanni (1997:28) stated that schools are true communities if they are places where character is built and citizenship is taught:

In the school as community, relationships are both close and informal. Individual circumstances count. Acceptance is unconditional. Relationships are cooperative. Concerns of members are unbounded, and thus considered legitimate as long as they reflect needs.

Subjectivity is okay. Emotions are legitimate. Sacrificing one's self-interest for the sake of other community members is common. Members associate with each other because doing so is valuable as an end in itself. Knowledge is valued and learned for its own sake, not just as a means to get something or get somewhere. Children are accepted and loved because that's the way one treats community members. These community characteristics emerge in part because of the ties of kinship and in part because of the sense of identity that is created by sharing a common place such as a classroom or school. But the ties that bond and bind the most are those that emerge from a compact of mutual shared obligations and commitments, a common purpose. These are the ingredients needed to create a community of the mind. (Sergiovanni, 1997:28)

Others have offered useful descriptions of school communities. Solomon and colleagues (1992) described the truly supportive school community as one in which warmly supportive interpersonal relationships and opportunities to participate in group norm setting and decision making are commonplace. They elaborated that students experience the school as a community when their needs for belonging, autonomy, and competence are met, and when they feel valued and respected (Solomon et al., 1992:629). The premise of their CDP program is that caring communities both convey a set of values and help establish the desire to abide by them. Bryk and Driscoll's (1988) school-as-community construct includes shared values, a common agenda of activities, and a pattern of caring social relations. The concept of community for McMillan and Chavis (1986) includes emotional connections, the opportunity to exert meaningful influence, and the satisfaction of psychological needs.

First and foremost, the creation of moral communities within classrooms and schools requires teachers who are models of good character and "teacherpersons" (Seeman, 1988), that is, persons who want to share of themselves and reach out to others in a warm and helpful manner, and who enjoy initiating positive and caring interactions with students. They must actively discourage selfishness and cruelty through swift intervention and must treat discipline problems as moral-educational opportunities. They must teach an ethic of interdependence that fosters empathy and the ownership of each class member's problems by all. They must help students to know one another well through activities and lessons that establish this as an objective. They must engage students in the process of making others feel important and good about themselves through techniques such as the good-deed tree, secret buddies, volunteer peer tutoring, and having students express appreciation to classmates during class meetings. They must teach a virtuous standard of conduct and encourage students to reward one another for adherence and challenge one another for nonadherence. They must allow students to participate in decision making that affects everyone in the classroom and must encourage input that takes the feelings and well being of others into consideration.

Our pilot project in Atlanta during the 1996–97 school year gave me the opportunity to do 150 structured observations in seventy-five classrooms (pre-post using the VCOF—see Appendix H) and informal observations in nearly all. It occurred to me while doing these observations that educating for character might require keeping the teachers who take pleasure in being positive and forming meaningful relationships with students, and removing those whose interactions with children are intransigently negative and hostile. Although many teachers were able to increase their percentage of positive interactions with children, the teachers who were observed to be very negative and disinclined to infuse character education in September were typically nearly as negative and disinclined to infuse in May and June. In contrast, those who were already positive and already incorporating character-related themes into their planned and unplanned instruction in September were more positive and more effective with infusion in May and June. Creating caring communities in the classrooms of teachers like the former will take close monitoring, extensive feedback, visits to model classrooms, instruction about character education and positive classroom management techniques, a strong school community, and moral leadership which makes building character the primary focus. Reluctant and negative teachers must come to believe there is a better way, must recognize the difference between their classrooms and caring-community classrooms, must develop new habits and skills, and may need to improve their character.

The orientation phase of our character education grant project in Atlanta took us to model schools outside of Atlanta, including Hazelwood in Louisville, West Point in West Point, Georgia, and Allen Classical in Dayton. Hazelwood and presumably all CDP schools have done a superb job of creating ideally supportive interpersonal and environmental conditions within nearly all classrooms, that is, true caring communities. West Point and Allen Classical were not quite as strong on this dimension, but their school climates were very positive, and most classrooms appeared to be caring, democratic communities. I concluded from these visits and my observations in Atlanta that character education provides the common purpose and ideals that bind staff and students together as a true community, but only if it is made the highest priority in the school and used as an organizing centerpiece. The "school transformation" that Bernardo in Dayton and others have described after implementing simple virtue-of-the-week programs (to which all or most staff members are highly committed) may be essentially the emergence of true community. In Atlanta where character education programs are midway through their second year (as of March 1998), I see evidence of this transformation or emergence of true community in the two schools where the principals have made character building their highest priority. School climate scores increased significantly in these two schools during the 1996–97 school year, but my conclusions about school transformation and the emergence of community come more from the changes that I have seen and felt than scores from my school climate measure.

Teacher Evaluations That Address Character Education

Character education programs are not likely to succeed if teacher evaluations continue to look only at instructional skills, classroom management skills, and academic test scores. The planners of character education programs must make it clear to all employees in the school that favorable evaluations are contingent upon relevant infusional lesson planning and the achievement of specific character educational goals, and whether or not they (1) interact with children in a way that fosters self-esteem and character growth, (2) model the virtues they teach, (3) communicate with parents in the furtherance of character goals, (4) utilize resources within the community and arrange service learning projects, (5) keep their special needs students motivated and all of their students actively involved as learners, and (6) create a climate within which students respect and enthusiastically help each other.

School Climate and Leadership Style

Sergiovanni (1992) states that the most "effective schools" possess "virtuous qualities" that largely account for their success: they are learning communities that foster self-reliance and self-management in students and teachers; they remove obstacles to learning so that all children can learn; they teach the whole child by addressing developmental, physical, social, and academic needs and by teaching an ethic of caring; they are places where teachers, students, and others treat one another with respect; they convey to parents and teachers that mutual support is a right and an obligation. Such schools expect a lot out of students, teachers, and parents and they receive a lot because they place a premium on personal growth and significant membership, and because they create an open, dynamic, and respectful climate that (1) fosters individual commitment to shared values and (2) binds people together in pursuit of a common goal.

According to Nelson (Nelson and Smith, 1976) and Sergiovanni (1992), this type of organization cannot emerge or thrive under leadership that relies primarily on (1) bureaucratic-regulative authority (which maximizes teacher and student subordination in a hierarchically arranged structure by appealing to security needs), (2) technocratic-directive authority (which presupposes superior knowledge on the part of the leader and requires respect from subordinates), or (3) idiographic-manipulative or psychological authority (which is derived from personality-based motivational and interpersonal skills and induces subordination through personal interest and concern). Both authors acknowledge the legitimacy of bureaucratic, technocratic, and idiocratic sources of leadership authority within schools but emphasize that they cannot be the primary source if the objective is to create an organization characterized by teamwork, respect, open communication, shared commitment, shared values, and the full utilization of individuals as resources.

Sergiovanni proposes that direct, high-profile, "follow me" styles of leadership draw from bureaucratic, technocratic, and idiocratic ("psychological") sources of authority, while the indirect, low-profile, facilitative styles draw from professional and moral sources. He proposes that the former are based on rationality, detachment, and the assumption that teachers are primarily motivated by self-interest, and that the latter are based on the importance of group membership, human emotion, and the assumption that teachers are primarily motivated by a sense of duty and obligation. He states that leaders who use professional authority promote high standards of professional practice by encouraging dialogue, autonomy, professional development, and an environment within which teachers hold one another accountable. He suggests that by clarifying central values and beliefs of the school community, leaders who use moral authority promote the emergence of "substitutes for [direct] leadership" including (1) norms that reflect community values and beliefs, (2) professionalism (defined as a virtue that combines competence and a commitment to exemplary practice), and (3) collegiality (defined as cooperation and mutual support among those who share values, beliefs, and commitments).

Nelson's democratic-integrative leadership style corresponds to Sergiovanni's indirect, facilitative style. He identifies group codes, standards, and norms as the source of leadership authority for democratic-integrative leadership rather than professional and moral standards, but their explanations of these sources share much in common. According to Nelson, democratic-integrative leaders organize individuals into a cooperative team that fully utilizes and develops individual competencies thereby appealing to the need for "significant membership." He makes reference to the achievement of organizational goals through creative social interaction and mutual growth, and the emergence of codes and standards from this cooperative and supportive environment, standards that guide individual action.

It is important to find and keep principals whose leadership style will promote the formation and maintenance of communities that maximize growth and build character in students and staff. Achieving this goal may require modifying principal evaluation procedures to include measures of school climate (defined as the combination of internal characteristics that reflect the unique personality of the school). In addition to measuring the level of implementation and effects of character education programs, such measures could help (1) achieve a "wider assessment of the community of players in dynamic schools," as suggested by Smylie and Crowson's (1993); (2) hold principals accountable for enabling the contributions of others within the school, as recommended by Rallis and Goldring (1993); (3) determine team effectiveness and the personality of leaders, as proposed by Hogan and colleagues (1994); (4) examine leadership style, as suggested by Nelson (1976) and Sergiovanni (1992); and (5) determine the satisfaction of consumers, as suggested by Ginsberg and Thompson (1992). Selection procedures could include direct observation of applicants in real or simulated situations, multiple-perspective appraisals (ratings by peers, superiors, subordinates), questioning of applicants about previous actions, and leadership style and personality inventories that together allow for predicting the type of climate applicants will create.

Parenting and Parent Training

Authoritative parenting combines high control with clear communication, and it balances warmth and nurturance with respectful rule enforcement and clear expectations for moral growth and maturity (Baumrind, 1988; Damon, 1988). In contrast, authoritarian parenting combines a high level of control with limited communication, high expectations, and minimal warmth and nurturance. Permissive parenting combines low control with infrequent maturity demands, clear communication, and ample warmth and nurturance. Only authoritative parenting produces in children an active sense of social responsibility, friendliness, self-control, nondisruptiveness at school, high initiative, and a willingness to cooperate with adults. Neither authoritarian nor permissive parenting produces these desirable outcomes, and, ironically, they appear to produce many of the same negative outcomes including an insensitivity toward others or blatant disregard for the rights of others.

In order for character development to progress optimally, parents must practice a predominantly authoritative approach, and such an approach requires their active participation in the academic and moral instruction of their children. Many parents practice this type of parenting without any help or encouragement from school personnel or other professionals, but many from all socioeconomic levels do not. As educators our choices are to do character education in the schools without trying to increase parental involvement or improve parenting skills where needed or to do both, that is, to work with both parents and students. If we choose to do something with respect to increasing parental involvement and improving parenting skills, the first step, particularly in impoverished communities, is to break through parental alienation from the school and school personnel, which is fairly common. Parents must feel welcome as members of the school community and must feel respected before they will accept instruction and use information they are given. This can be accomplished through such methods as home visits by teachers, home visits by parents who are involved at the school, inviting parents to assist in the classroom, involving parents in service learning activities in the community, weekly classroom newsletters, and obtaining a commitment from each parent to devote a specified amount of time to the classroom and the school each year through the use of one-on-one teacher-parent and principal-parent conferences. Bernardo in Dayton required such conferences as principal of Allen Classical-Traditional Academy and insisted that parents sign a contract. Parents can also be made to feel a part of the school community through activities such as a "family heritage museum," "grandparents day," "family movie night," involvement in preparing the "critical contract" for their child each year, and homework assignments that make them feel valued (see more detailed descriptions of these NFC and CDP strategies in subsequent sections of this chapter).

Once parents feel that they are valued members of a caring community, a variety of techniques can be used to remediate deficits or improve parenting skills. In Atlanta we borrowed the idea of a classroom news form from West Point Elementary in Troup County, Georgia and did some redesigning (see Appendix C). We included on the form a small reproduction of the visual illustration used for the virtue-of-the-week plus a few suggestions on how parents could help teach and reinforce the virtues. Other sections allowed the teacher and the class to share information about class activities and accomplishments. A third section was called "help wanted" and was used to tell parents specifically what kind of help was needed by the teacher, their child, and the class as a whole.

In schools where a significant number of parents are authoritarian, permissive, neglectful, or abusive with their children, a concerted effort must be made to teach them directly. Schools in Dayton provide workshops for all parents that are taught by specialists. I suspect that this may be a little intimidating for many parents, and I wonder if a better approach might be to periodically bring together the parents of each class to discuss parenting informally with the teacher and other respected persons with parenting knowledge such as the school psychologist, school social worker, and persons from agencies that serve the neighborhood such as Headstart and Family Connection. Since the parents have a particular classroom and teacher in common, they are more likely to participate and share than they would with traditional parent groups that are open to all and attended by those who need help the least.

Parent centers in schools need to be more elaborate than what I have observed, and they should include a variety of books, videos, and magazines plus parents with unusually good skills who volunteer their time to speak with other parents. Brookside Elementary in Binghamton, New York, has a newsletter (Brookside's Character Corner) prepared by parents that focuses on a virtue of the month (see Appendix D). This newsletter includes a definition, tips for parents, suggested readings, and scheduled activities. Some parent populations may not have the skills to do this, but all school communities can prepare a monthly newsletter which includes a section with parenting tips and principles. Parents can at least play a central role in getting input from experts, cutting and pasting, reproducing, and distributing.

The Core Essentials Program

The nonprofit Core Essentials program (a curriculum division of FamilyWise, Inc.) in Georgia was initiated by Reggie Joiner and other parents who identified the character qualities they wanted their children to acquire before leaving home and school. They selected eighteen concepts and linked these with thirty-six values words or eighteen pairs of values synonyms. These words provide for a four-school-year word-of-the-month cycle (only three of the four outlined thus far). They chose a multi-year cycle to avoid redundancy from year to year. In their package of instructional materials, they have a monthly guide for parents (see Appendix E), a small table display for the home that defines the word of the month, bookmarks that include the definition and an illustrative story from nature, and colorful "you were caught being valuable" cards. They also have teacher guides that elaborate the definition and include illustrative stories from nature and history, a list of related children's books and stories, related safety and health tips, bulletin board ideas, and instructional suggestions which include primary and intermediate lesson suggestions for weeks one through four. The four-page parent newsletter or "parent's guide for teaching values" is unique, very well written, and dovetailed with the corresponding teacher guide. The September 1997 parent guide that addresses "responsibility" elaborates the definition, gives parents guidelines for promoting responsible behavior, includes a segment about the "Respect-for-the-Aged Day" in Japan, a section on responsibility as it relates to the environment, weekly mealtime notes that focus sequentially on definition, examination, encouragement, and decisions, an illustrative story from nature about sheep dogs, safety and health tips, and family discussion ideas.

The Core Essential materials are concise, well written, and visually appealing. Their word-of-the-month idea is not unique, but most of the materials they provide are unique in the sense that they are geared toward helping parents teach values at home yet coupled with corresponding guidelines for teachers that are both simple and useful. One of their goals has been to get parents and teachers on the same page, and it is my view that the simplicity and creativity of their materials will make this possible for any school community that chooses to use them. Although they would prefer that their materials be used as written, they recognize that some schools and systems might want to borrow their format and adapt it by inserting their own values words and related information. Such an adaptation is possible, but it would be helpful if the Core Essentials group could provide parent and teacher guides for many different values or virtues besides their thirty-six, and/or a version that would collapse their thirty-six words into one school year for schools that prefer a word-of-the-week over a word-of-the-month. The authors have considered developing versions that are targeted to specific types of parent populations and will hopefully consider other adaptations or versions as well. The Core Essentials materials for parents are so good and so badly needed in my view that an effort needs to be made to develop versions that will enable all schools to use them irrespective of the type program they have in place and irrespective of any other materials they are using. For more information, contact Reggie Joiner at 770-521-4428 or by e-mail at CoreEss@aol.com.

School Restructuring That Fosters Community

School restructuring has been defined rather narrowly to include multi-grade grouping, multi-age grouping or "looping," year-round schooling, a lengthening of the school day, "schools within schools" (which largely replace subject departmentalization in secondary schools), theme schools and magnet schools, and schools that serve only one or two grades for an entire school district.

Multi-age grouping allows a team of teachers to work with a multi-age/multi-grade group of students for more than one year and to team-teach and collaborate in a more student-centered environment where teachers facilitate and coach rather than lecture. With looping, traditional classes of students remain intact for more than one year. When these intact groups of students move on to the next grade, their teacher moves with them. Proponents of year-round schooling and/or an extended school day call attention to the fact that other information-age countries keep their students in school more days each year and longer hours while demonstrating more learning. Schools within schools limit the number of teachers and students that both will have contact with in the classroom during a school year, require that teachers function as generalists to a greater degree, and, like multi-grade grouping, facilitate more teacher teamwork and a student-needs-based grouping of students. Theme schools and magnet schools bring students, teachers, administrators, and parents together who have common interests such as the arts, science, vocations, multiculturalism, and an emphasis on character growth. Finally, schools that serve only one or two grades for a district or large geographic area provide a mixing of all subcultures living within the district and allow for more school-wide projects that are developmentally appropriate. These seven forms of "school restructuring" promote the development of true communities that give members the time and opportunity to build meaningful relationships and the time to develop a shared ethic that bonds them together.

Student Committee for Welcoming/Orienting New Students

The Child Development Project includes a Welcoming Committee for new students to the school as one of many strategies for creating a caring school community. The members of these committees should be students, and they should be given some freedom to decide how they will go about making newcomers feel at home and familiarizing them with the building and routines within the school. Such plans could include a student-led tour of the building, an information packet, the assignment of a volunteer buddy, coming to visit the child at his or her home, and a welcoming gift.

Building Self-Esteem

Self-esteem results from (1) successes and acquired competencies that are valued by the self and significant others and (2) interpersonal support in the form of unconditional respect, genuine encouragement, and both positive and negative feedback. Students can acquire self-esteem or an essentially positive sense of self without being moral or concerned about others; students who are moral and concerned about others in an age-appropriate manner can lack self-esteem or an essentially positive sense of self. Many who have not succeeded in areas where society expects success (e.g., academic, social, moral) value and respect themselves anyway because they are successful in ways that are valued by a few significant others in their lives; many who are virtuous lack self-esteem because they do not receive the respect, encouragement, and positive feedback they need from people with whom they live and work and/or because they are not allowed to succeed and grow. Social environment determines if self-esteem and moral/prosocial concerns and behavior will co-exist or co-occur.

Damon (1995:70–80) contends that no matter how much adults tell children how great and special they are or how often they encourage students to say this about themselves without reference to specific behaviors, attitudes, personal characteristics, and so forth, they will only acquire self-esteem as a result of real success that can only occur within the context of relationships with significant others who provide honest feedback, both positive and negative. He stresses that holistic messages such as "you're great" have little meaning to young children because their thoughts and feelings about themselves derive concretely from how they look, how well they can do specific things, where they come from, and how they feel from moment to moment (i.e., unrelated surface characteristics). He contends that the belief that self-esteem can be directly transmitted through "abstract injunctions" and the belief that self-esteem precedes healthy development rather than derives from it effectively increases the self-centeredness of children. This self-centeredness, he says, limits character development by drawing attention away from the social realities and external demands to which children must adapt.

Damon (1995:140–42) explains that as students move from understanding the self in terms of unrelated surface characteristics (early childhood) to understanding the self in terms of comparisons with others (middle and late childhood), effects upon others of personal characteristics (early adolescence), and a personal philosophy and plans for the future (late adolescence) their capacity to integrate their sense of "essential" self around moral concerns increases.

The task for educators, therefore, is to help students develop feelings of self-esteem based upon (1) prosocial values, (2) virtuous character traits, (3) skills that will allow them to make a contribution to society, and (4) various types of success that are valued by responsible and virtuous members of society. They need to understand that many students will not value academic learning and virtuous behavior unless taught to do so, and that efforts to build self-esteem must derive from this socialization process and related success rather than direct attempts to instill self-esteem that are not tied to prosocial behaviors, attitudes, and feelings of individuals. They need to be aware that students who experience repeated failure in areas that are critical to good character development will be inclined to devalue success in these areas and will naturally try to compensate through successes in other areas (e.g., good looks, material possessions, deviant acts). They need to know that students who lack self-esteem will be inclined to disrespect others and to avoid taking the risks necessary to realize their potential. They need to set realistic expectations for each age group and each student and provide both positive and negative feedback in a respectful and supportive manner accordingly.

Specific Strategies for Building Self-Esteem

1. Make a contract with students with low self-esteem that calls for doing several things that will enhance self-esteem. Such a contract might list the following: write a recipe for the ideal friend, make a special card for a friend, write a letter to a friend, keep a list of all your friendly deeds for one week, read and report on a book about friendship.
2. Introduce a system whereby the entire class is rewarded when a student with low self-esteem makes a predetermined amount of progress in some area (e.g., academic, social,

physical). This is a technique that typically improves the social status of the person who earns the rewards for the group, and it could elicit a significant amount of encouragement from peers.

3. Set a goal of ten or more positive interactions with each student each day (e.g., praise, an affectionate touch, asking if help is needed, friendly questioning about something nonacademic). Your goal should be to have many more positive interactions than negative.

4. Praise students publicly for their successes, both academic and nonacademic, but be careful not to publicly praise only nonacademic accomplishments.

5. When offering praise, be creative and expressive. Do not limit yourself to trite phrases such as "good work" or "fine job." Say things like "wow" and "terrific" with emotion, and use statements that communicate your joy such as "it is a pleasure to teach you when you work hard like this."

6. Be friendly and affectionate toward your students and find time to interact with them one-on-one. Encourage parents to do likewise and to spend one-on-one time with their children at home and away from home.

7. Never make demeaning, derogatory, sarcastic, or harshly critical comments to students, and reprimand them privately. Low self-esteem students are much more likely than their normal peers to feel personally rejected and to interpret your comments as more negative than they were intended.

8. Before criticizing student work or offering corrective feedback, find something about the work to praise and give the child a chance to explain what she or he has done or tried to do.

9. Prevent your students from feeling disliked as persons when punished by clearly communicating in advance the negative consequences for certain types of misbehavior. Always combine negative consequences with positive reinforcement.

10. Call on low-ability students to answer in class only when you know that the information is well known. You may want to let them know in advance what the questions will be or what area the questioning will cover so that they can prepare.

11. Consider purchasing or gaining access to books that include activities for improving self-esteem or that promote self-esteem through bibliotherapy (see School Counselor Catalogs published by Paperbacks for Kids, 426 West Front Street, Washington, MO 63090; 800-227-2591).

12. Make a friendly deed tree using a tree branch, bucket, and sand or plaster. For each friendly deed observed, print the name of the child who performed this deed on a colorful card and hang it on the tree.

13. Make a "kindness" flower or ribbon that can be clipped to a shirt. Give this flower to one student and instruct him to pass it on to another child after performing an act of kindness for this child. Have your students continue passing it along until everyone has received it once.

Student Self-Discipline in the Cafeteria

School cafeterias today are typically loud places where the frequency of student conflicts and negative adult-to-student interactions are excessive. This is due, in part, to the inadequate training of cafeteria monitors in behavior management techniques, and a lack of community-mindedness on the part of teachers who are aware of the problem but choose relief time over volunteering their time to make the cafeteria a more caring and respectful place.

In Atlanta we were able to transform a few cafeterias from loud, hostile environments into much more calm and respectful environments by using a special system. We began by orienting students and cafeteria monitors. We encouraged adult monitors to reduce hostile interactions and to increase positive feedback and respectful redirection, and these techniques were modeled for them and explained. Students were oriented one class at a time with an emphasis on encouraging them to work together as a group and regulating their individual and group behavior with a minimum of adult feedback, namely, practicing some of the character traits they had been learning about. Each class selected a different class captain or two each week. Each captain wore a cap that identified them as such. Captains were asked to give respectful corrective feedback to peers and to turn the red and green cylinder on their table as needed to communicate either acceptable conduct (green on top) or the need for more control (red on top). These cylinders were made from painted four-inch plastic PVC pipe. Classes that were among the best as the system began, and classes that satisfied a predetermined criteria after the first two weeks were given gold coins that served as tokens of their successful cooperation and self-regulation. Most classes displayed these coins in a clear plastic bag, and although some backup rewards were used, students were so excited about earning them as a group that no backups were needed. Classes were asked to conduct class meetings as needed to discuss how the day went and to plan for the next, and these meetings often dealt with issues related to leader-follower conflicts. These conflicts and related discussions gave teachers opportunities to show students how to give corrective feedback without eliciting anger and resistance, and to have students practice these skills.

We found that adult monitors were the most resistant to this system and that older students were more resistant to this system than younger students and teachers. Teachers actually became more competitive than their students and began eating lunch with them so their class would be named over the P.A. in the afternoon. Many, however, commented that the atmosphere was such that they enjoyed eating with their class and interacting with their students in a more friendly and informal way. Schools that did not provide a lot of monitoring as the system was implemented had much less success, and some reverted back to the chaos they had in the beginning.

DISCIPLINE AND REINFORCEMENT

Basic Classroom Management

Broadening the curriculum to include character development goals and objectives requires that classroom management systems promote socialization and moral reasoning and not just crowd control. Nearly all teachers willingly perform the role of socializer or character educator to some degree even in the absence of formal programs, curriculums, and teacher-evaluation criteria that require this of them. Among the teachers who have good control, some are very strict, intimidating, and obsessed with student submission and silence. Others who see the value of maximizing student participation are able to develop a caring classroom, build a warm and supportive relationship with each student, and treat each discipline problem as a moral-educational opportunity.

I have learned that formal character-building programs do not convert the former type of teacher into the latter quickly even with extensive orientation, encouragement, and observation-based feedback. I have also observed at the elementary level that when strict teachers who are harsh or hostile with students leave their classrooms, all hell breaks loose unless someone is designated to take names, and when teachers who are firm with students but more caring leave their classrooms, students exhibit much more self-control. An authoritative (nurturing, firm, instructional) approach to discipline promotes the internalization of adult rules and expectations and an authoritarian (harsh, punitive) approach does not.

With the introduction of formal character education programs, control through intimidation and a reliance on external consequences should be replaced, to the extent possible, with control through the respectful and supportive treatment of students and the strategic development of an internal disposition to respect others and behave accordingly. This approach continues to require clear rules and the firm and assertive enforcement of these rules, but it also requires teachers to create a climate within which students will come to understand and strive to meet their responsibilities as members of a classroom community.

The social and moral-educational demands of a character-building approach require various types of knowledge and skill that some teachers in the past could get by without, and a level of self-awareness in terms of personality and mental ability that reflects good character and a capacity to compensate for weaknesses. In most schools today good classroom managers must be creative in their instructional planning, able to keep track of all that is going on in the classroom, and sufficiently analytical to determine the causes of disruptive behavior. In addition to these mental abilities, they need to have a personality characterized by empathy, warmth, self-control, patience, optimism, assertiveness, persistence, a strong work ethic, humility, flexibility, a high tolerance for stress, and some degree of extroversion. Those who are weak in one or more of these foundation personality characteristics can change to some degree, but they can also compensate by doing more (than the teacher with the ideal personality needs to do) in terms of (1) learning more about teaching methods, child development, behavior modification, structured classroom management systems, curriculum and teaching materials, socialization, the culture of students, individual differences, and self; and (2) skill development in terms of leadership, organization, interactive teaching, achieving active student participation, public speaking, mediating conflicts, social skills training, using routines and signals, counseling and consulting, individualizing instruction, and diagnostic discipline.

The primary focus of this book is character development; nevertheless, it indirectly presents a type of approach to classroom management that promotes character building and does so by emphasizing developmentally appropriate discipline and reinforcement, the modeling of virtuous behavior, interpersonal support, active student participation in the classroom community, and teaching that targets specific virtues. The success of the structured yet open and student-centered approach to classroom management that is implicit in this book depends heavily upon the capacity of teachers to use consistent signals and procedural routines for the many things that must occur repeatedly within the classroom, such as getting the attention of the class. The total of many procedural routines and routine signals is routine order even in a classroom with much student activity and many things going on at one time, so care must be taken when these routines are introduced to practice them extensively until they become automatic.

Charney (1992), who offered numerous management ideas, recommended that the first six weeks be spent on "reinforcin', remindin', and redirectin'" for the most part rather than "readin', writin', and rithmetic," or on teaching children how they should behave in the classroom thereby establishing a foundation for academic growth. She broke this into three stages through which she gradually opened her classrooms and gradually moved away from exclusively whole-class instruction to small-group and independent work and the introduction of new content. She identified many specific skills and routines taught in stage one and explained that she moved on to stage two when students could group up quickly, locate and replace materials, listen and make relevant comments at meetings, stay with an activity, and make simple choices.

Disruptive behavior can be largely prevented within the classroom by knowing what promotes socialization and the development of good character and acting accordingly, but even the best teachers in the best circumstances cannot prevent all student disruption. The most appropriate way to deal with disruption is to always look for the causes and to treat as discipline problems only those problematic behaviors that have actually disrupted the class or prevented the teacher from carrying out his or her responsibilities (Seeman, 1988). Too often teachers are the cause of the disruption because they (1) respond to disruptive behaviors without considering possible causes; (2) treat as discipline problems non-disruptive behaviors that are better treated as a counseling or learning problems; (3) are personally offended by behaviors that may not be disruptive to other students; and (4) have failed to realize that their inadequate relationships with students, manner of interacting with students, and other things that they do in the classroom are more likely causes for student disruption than any potential cause within the child or outside the classroom and school. The list of possible teacher causes of disruptive student behavior is several times longer than the list of possible student causes, and much longer than the lists of possible home, neighborhood, school-climate, and peer-group causes. When problematic disruptive and nondisruptive behaviors occur in the classroom, the first question asked by the best classroom managers and teachers who want to build student character ask is: "What am I doing that may be causing or contributing to this problematic behavior?"

In addition to using routines, looking for the causes of problematic student behavior, and seeking to build character through age-appropriate objectives and the seven learning modes discussed elsewhere in this book, teachers who want to be model classroom managers should strive to make their systems age-appropriate. I believe this can include one of many token systems, charting techniques, or interesting visual feedback/monitoring systems, provided social reinforcement is extensive and instances of inappropriate behavior are used as teachable opportunities. Contrary to what some have claimed on the basis of a few studies, extrinsic reinforcement does not preclude self-control unless used as the only or primary strategy. In addition to structured reward systems for desirable individual and group behavior, all systems should include a series of predetermined and progressively more restrictive consequences for persistent rule breaking since this gives students several opportunities to choose self-control, and since this depersonalizes the delivery of negative consequences. Systems should also include both group and individual contingencies. The individual component allows for dealing with individual rule breaking without penalizing the group; the group contingency can take the form of a privilege-level system for the entire class (e.g., silent seat work, interactional instruction, student choice of activity) and should be activated when there are too many rule violations for the teacher to count, and when more than a few students are breaking the rules frequently.

Once again, Charney is a good source of practical ideas for teaching discipline through the use of logical and natural consequences. She categorized three types of logical/natural consequences: reparation or "you broke it—you fix it"; breach of contract and loss of trust or "you must forfeit your rights"; and timeouts or "you must forfeit participation." She offered six steps for choosing and implementing logical consequences: stop and think or pause until your emotions have calmed and you can consider options; evaluate the options; provide a workable, realistic, specific action as a consequence; provide a time limit; emphasize the language of choice and privilege; use empathy and structure. She explained that empathy shows respect for students or faith in them even though you do not like their behavior; structure preserves the dignity of the classroom, sets limits, provides appropriate direction, and gives students ways to follow through.

Child Development Project (CDP) schools refer to their approach to classroom management as "developmental discipline." I do not share their conclusion that extrinsic reinforcers undermine intrinsic motivation and that a "growing body of research" supports this conclusion, but I gladly offer a description of their approach because it centers on character growth and because I have observed firsthand that it works well even in an urban environment. My view is that positive and negative extrinsic reinforcers are inescapably present, at least in a social or interpersonal form, and that we should adopt an approach to discipline that utilizes social reinforcers and "logical consequences" systematically and avoids an over-reliance on less natural and more gimmicky reinforcers.

CDP's Developmental Discipline rests on the assumptions that if teachers have an open, caring relationship with students, and if students are part of a caring classroom community that they have helped to create, then they will want to maintain their relationships with the teacher and the community and will respond favorably to a teaching approach to discipline without having to be treated harshly or punished. They feel that students develop social skills and moral understanding in the same way they develop academic skills and understanding: guidance and practice. Their goal is to help students internalize values and become intrinsically motivated by minimizing rewards and punishments and helping students to acquire skills and an awareness of the effect of their actions on others. They stress the use of teaching by example, treating misbehavior as a teachable opportunity with an emphasis on helping students recognize and repair the consequences of their actions, teaching social understanding and social problem solving skills by using cooperative learning and class meetings as laboratories, by involving students in the creation of class rules and norms, and by using literature as a tool for teaching social skills, prosocial values, and thinking skills.

A New Type of Grading System

Traditional grading systems do little more than compare students, thereby motivating the more capable and demoralizing the less capable. Some have argued that competitive grading should be replaced with a criterion-referenced system that focuses on the amount of grade-level material mastered. Even this is inadequate, however, if the goals are to motivate students, maximize their progress, and give them enough feedback about their standing among classmates to ensure that students and the parents of students who are retained or who fail to graduate or gain acceptance to post-secondary schooling are not surprised. The emphasis must be on rewarding progress via pre-post testing and including enough mastery teaching that the progress of each individual is known and can be communicated to students and their parents. Quizzes and individual testing for those who need remedial instruction or advanced assignments should be more common than tests that are given to everyone, but the former need not replace the latter entirely.

I recommend a report card that utilizes both number and letter grades. The number grades would reflect progress toward mastery of grade-level material required for promotion. If a scale of one-to-ten is used, students would need a grade of five by midyear and a ten by the end of the year in order to earn their way to the next grade. Letter grades, in contrast, would reflect individual progress, taking into consideration mental ability and pre-post test results. With this system even mildly retarded, slow learning, and learning disabled students could receive an A or B and be rewarded for their individual progress even if they are progressing much slower than most of their classmates. A very intelligent student could conceivably earn a ten by mid-year and F's for every grade period throughout the year if they fail to perform up to their potential. A very slow student, on the other hand, could conceivably earn A's throughout the year and never receive a ten or even a five. I believe such a system would increase the motivation and learning of students on all ability levels, while communicating whether grade level objectives are being achieved.

Hazelwood Elementary in Jefferson County, Kentucky, uses a large report card that does not include conventional letter grades. Instead, they provide detailed information about individual student growth in various areas in a strictly noncompetitive format using the following codes: RP = rapid progress, SP = steady progress, PH = progressing with help, LP = little progress, NA = not applicable. Their grade card does not clarify if they are referring to progress toward the achievement of all grade-level objectives or progress taking into consideration individual ability and pretest results, presumably the former. They acknowledge that their system creates some difficulty when the transition back to a conventional competitive grading occurs between fifth and sixth grades.

Self-Improvement Projects

Students who have reached the point where they are (1) aware of how others evaluate them, (2) sensitive to these evaluations, and (3) able to evaluate their own strengths and weaknesses on some level (second grade and beyond) are capable of doing a self-improvement project of some kind. This technique is especially appropriate for middle and high school students since they can choose a personal weakness, design a plan, carry it out, and communicate their plan and its outcome, in writing. Some structure will be needed, however, such as a discussion of various types of self-improvement projects including real examples, preliminary approval during a one-on-one conference, consultative assistance as needed during this conference, and a format for preparing the written plan, anecdotal recording requirements during the plan, and a final written report.

For elementary students the area of improvement and related improvement plan should be chosen in consultation with a teacher and/or parent and should be much more limited in length than improvement plans for children in middle and high school. With young children teachers may want to establish a verbal contract with each student on each Monday, specifying an area of needed improvement for the week. Written contracts may be more appropriate for grades three through six or seven with preliminary one-on-one consultation sessions with the teacher and a time span of six weeks or more. The area chosen for improvement should be a source of some anxiety or stress for the individual student and possibly others such as peer rejection, poor reading skills, a lack of kindness, crying too easily, shyness, poor grooming, getting off-task frequently, or a specific social skill deficit. Since many of these problems are quite personal, teachers should make parents aware in advance and encourage them to participate by discussing areas of needed improvement with their child and with the teacher. The teacher, in turn, should obtain parent approval as well as involvement when an improvement plan addresses a very personal problem or deficit.

The "Critical Contract"

Many schools have tried to use contracts with students and parents. Bernardo in Dayton, for example, had a contract that he explained to parents one-on-one and that essentially required them to commit to support the character education program. Through their "Critical Contract," the Greenfield Center School (a model school for the Northeastern Foundation for Learning) has used contracting in a manner more consistent with character development goals than any other program I have studied (Charney, 1992). This contract specifies what each student will work on during the year, and the development process involves obtaining one goal from the student, one from the parent, and one from the teacher. These goals do not target negative behaviors; rather, they address what is important to the three contributors or what they most want the child to work on during the year. Parents and teachers choose their goal for the child and the child writes them into the critical contract in his or her own words: My goal for me is ____ ; My parent's or parents' goal for me is ____ ; My teacher's or teachers' goal for me is ____. One advantage to this use of the contract is the increased communication it generates among the three contributors. Another is the trust, cooperation, and understanding that this communication typically brings.

Developing a Work Ethic

Lickona (1991) and Green (1984) have stressed the importance of building a strong work ethic or "conscience of craft" in students. A desire to work hard reflects a high level of respect for others with whom one is connected through family, friendships, and mutual membership within communities, and its absence should preclude self-respect. Just a few decades ago, people who felt good about themselves in the absence of hard work and people who felt good about unearned material comfort and status represented the minority. This type of person may now outnumber those who feel compelled by their conscience to work hard.

Educators can promote the development of a strong work ethic by using the type of grading system described, by setting high expectations and not allowing students to feel good about themselves unless they are achieving at expectancy, by modeling hard work and encouraging students to identify with hard working people, by encouraging students to set goals and emphasizing the importance of goal achievement, by providing opportunities to work in teams, and by encouraging participation in competitive individual and group activities. Team activities of all types, including cooperative team learning and competitive team sports, may do more than anything else to build a strong work ethic. Team members come to feel an obligation to one another and come to share a goal commitment. In the absence of a strong goal commitment and feelings of obligation to others, few people will discover how hard they can work and how much suffering they can endure.

Increasing Positive Interactions with Students

Positive reinforcement is a cornerstone of character building. Adults who are committed to building student character must understand the importance of frequent praise and having more positive interactions with students than negative. Behaviorists have taught for years that punishment merely suppresses unwanted behavior and that positive reinforcement teaches new behavior by identifying the new behavior, or an approximation of it, and providing incentives to repeat or improve upon this behavior. Positive reinforcement also build's self-esteem by making students feel capable and important.

Despite the benefits of positive interactions, most teacher interactions with students in most classrooms continue to be either negative in tone or to occur in response to undesirable student behavior. Few teachers consciously practice the art of "catching them being good," and few consciously strive to have more positive interactions than negative. Those who do so quickly discover the power of positive reinforcement.

As part of our pilot character education program in five elementary schools inner-city Atlanta, we endeavored to increase teacher praise and encouragement and to replace harsh or hostile criticism with respectful reprimands and redirection. The results showed slight movement in the right direction, but I was amazed at how many teachers did not reduce their hostility and/or increase their praise and other types of positive teacher-to-student interactions such as friendliness, kindness, and affection.

Teachers who wish to maximize their positive interactions with students are encouraged to place reminders around their classrooms, to expand their positive-feedback vocabulary in an effort to maximize the effect of their praise and encouragement (see subsequent list), to describe praiseworthy behaviors in detail, to highlight targeted virtues that are displayed by students, to praise students who praise peers for virtuous behavior, and to occasionally compliment students for attractive personal characteristics or for simply being who they are (e.g., "You look very nice today"; "It is so nice to have a quiet student who listens so well"; "I don't know what I would do without a strong student who can help me carry things"). They are also encouraged to consider evaluating themselves via tape recording and to consider having an objective observer come into the classroom periodically to do an event recording (e.g., recording the number of positive and negative interactions that occur during a specific time interval) or partial-interval time sampling study (e.g., recording "yes" for the entire time interval as soon as a positive interaction is observed). The latter can be facilitated through a special pre-coded observation form that includes, for example, a P for positive, N for negative, E for elaborated, U for unelaborated, and V for virtuous (see the Vessels' Classroom Observation Form in chapter 5).

Virtuous conduct can be highlighted and rewarded by having a large erasable white board in the room that lists targeted virtues down the left column and dates across the top. When a behavior is observed by a student or teacher that exemplifies a targeted virtue, the name of the student can be entered on this board by a teacher or student observer. There are many other ways that this same type of positive reinforcement can be achieved such as using a good-deed tree or a good deed jar.

100 Ways to Say "Very Good!"

1. You're on the right track.
2. You've got it!
3. SUPER!
4. That's right!
5. That's good!
6. You're working so hard.
7. You are very good at that.
8. That's coming along nicely.
9. GOOD WORK!
10. Jump back Jack!
11. I'm happy to see you working.
12. Exactly right!
13. I'm proud of you.
14. Keep it up.
15. You've just about got it.
16. That's the best you've done.
17. Are you trying to show off?
18. THAT'S IT!
19. You've figured it out.
20. You did it all by yourself.
21. GREAT!
22. I knew you could do it.
23. Congratulations.
24. Thank you for listening!
25. Keep trying. You'll get it.
26. Now you've got it.
27. You're learning fast.
28. Good for you.
29. I couldn't do it better.
30. Your giving me chicken skin.
31. You make being a teacher fun.
32. That's right!
33. You're getting better.
34. You did it that time.
35. OK. I'm impressed.
36. Nice going.
37. Looking good!
38. WOW!
39. That's the way.
40. Keep up the good work.
41. TERRIFIC!
42. Nothing can stop you now.
43. That's the way to do it.
44. SENSATIONAL!
45. That's using your noodle.
46. Show off.
47. That was first class.
48. EXCELLENT!
49. PERFECT!
50. Are you trying for an A?
51. Much better!
52. WONDERFUL!
53. You've been practicing.
54. You did that very well.
55. Fine work.
56. Way to go man!
57. Man! Look at this!
58. OUTSTANDING!
59. FANTASTIC!
60. TREMENDOUS!
61. Your mom will be pleased.
62. You should be very proud.
63. That's what I call great.
64. Right on man!
65. You are really improving.
66. You're doing beautifully.
67. SUPERB!
68. Good memory!
69. You've got that down pat.
70. You did very well today.
71. Keep it up.
72. That's using your head.
73. You did a lot today.
74. Look at you go.
75. Go girl!
76. I'm very proud of you.
77. You're a genius.
78. I really like that.
79. Way to go!
80. You've got the hang of it.
81. You need harder work.
82. Good thinking.
83. Everyone is doing well.
84. Wooo daddy!
85. No one could do better.
86. Maybe you can teach me.
87. You outdid yourselves.
88. Can I put this up?
89. Good for you.
90. Let's celebrate.
91. You finished quickly!
92. I knew you were smart.
93. OK smart guy.
94. EXACTLY RIGHT!
95. You made my day.
96. Pat yourself on the back.

97. That's your best work ever.
98. What a pro!

99. You've got it mastered.
100. I'm so pleased.

Awards for Model Citizenship and Virtuous Behavior

Many schools require that teachers choose a student of the month, and some choose this student on the basis of improvement rather than being the best at something. Few select students who have been an exemplary model of virtuous behavior. Such awards can be given for good citizenship, helpfulness, exemplary cross-grade tutoring, service learning, behavior that exemplifies a virtue such as courage or honesty, sportsmanship, independence, success as a peer mediator, patriotism, leadership, teamwork, team success, volunteer work in the school, athletic accomplishments, artistic accomplishments, academics accomplishments, and showing the most improvement in some way. From these monthly winners a committee of students and staff could choose yearly awards to be issued at a final assembly. Contrary to what some have said, rewards such as these do not preclude intrinsic motivation or group cohesion.

Awards should also be given to teachers and parents for virtuous behaviors such as helping a beginning teacher, voluntarily heading up a planning committee for a values related school assembly, recruiting parent volunteers, organizing after-school sports and recreational activities, developing the most creative and motivating lessons, welcoming and working effectively with needy students, visiting and working with parents who need help in order to be effective parents, and setting up intercultural exchange programs. Students are likely to benefit as much from seeing the value teachers place on giving and receiving these awards as they do on receiving awards themselves. Therefore, adult rewards should be given during a school assembly and not a staff meeting or PTO meeting. All awards should be given with as much fanfare as possible, and the most important awards should be reported in the newspaper or on television.

MODELING AND OBSERVATION

Adult Modeling and Mentoring

In chapter 3 it was stated that young children begin to internalize parents' views of right and wrong and begin to form a conscience if they identify with their parents. It was also stated that this identification occurs when parents are loving, supportive, and firm but not hostile. This provides a good starting point for discussing how to use modeling as a strategic instructional method. As implied by this previous analysis, the key to modeling is identification. This identification in turn depends on many factors, such as how skilled the model is (if too skilled, the observer cannot visualize being like the model), the status of the model (no person models after someone who is perceived as lower in status), how friendly and helpful the model is or has been, physical similarities such as age and sex, whether the model has control over rewards desired by the observer, whether the observer is rewarded for imitating the behavior of the model, and how effectively the behavior is modeled (clarity, repetition, no irrelevant detail, availability of multiple models).

All of this implies that teachers, parents, and other prospective models can maximize the identification process and social learning (modeling) by (1) striving to be consistently virtuous; (2) striving to be admired and liked by others; (3) developing a relationship with young observers that is characterized by love and respect; (4) openly sharing of themselves in ways that bring common feelings, thoughts, and experiences into the minds of young observers (while indirectly minimizing presumed and actual differences); (5) rewarding imitative prosocial behavior genuinely; and (6) arranging for the young people with whom they live and work to be exposed to same-age children, older children, and other adults (both living and dead) who display virtuous behaviors and with whom they are very likely to identify.

In his discussion of modeling and mentoring, Lickona (1991) emphasized the importance of showing love and respect toward students by helping them succeed, being warm and affectionate, avoiding demeaning reactions when children do not know correct answers, respecting student concerns, being open and human, following modeling with explanations that are age appropriate, showing how much they care about doing right and encouraging others to do so, using stories, avoiding favoritism and sarcasm, taking time to stop and discuss issues that have moral significance, and rewarding students in very personal and private ways for virtuous behavior, such as notes and private student-teacher conferences. Kirschenbaum (1995) emphasized that models must share of themselves genuinely but strategically with attention given to where and when beliefs, feelings, experiences, skills, and interests will be shared with students and to what extent they need to involve themselves in their students' lives. He also emphasizes that teachers must maintain their moral authority and potential to teach through modeling by being liked and respected by their students.

Exposure to Real Heroes ("Giraffes")

There are many good ways to expose children to real heroes or people who exemplify the defining characteristics of caring, courage, and taking responsibility. The staff of West Point Elementary in West Point, Georgia, wrote a biography about a local person for each of their targeted virtues and made this a part of their word-of-the-week program. Some of these people were in the school, such as the cafeteria manager who was used as a model of punctuality, and all were people the students knew.

An elementary school in Atlanta developed a "You Are My Hero" project for students in grades four through six. The initial lesson for this project involved (1) defining "role model" as a peer or older person that a student admires, looks up to, and wants to be like; (2) listing types of people that function as role models (family members, teachers, coaches, ministers, friends, neighbors, musicians, civil rights activists, politicians, adult mentors, school buddies, athletes); and (3) having students begin to identify specific persons that they admire, both living and dead. Some teachers facilitated this process by having students draw a chart that listed one or more people for each category. They used whatever research methods were available such as class discussions, reading articles and books, reading or listening to song lyrics and speeches, and conducting interviews. After completing their research they wrote a thank you letter to their hero. Students then shared their letters in class before mailing them to their hero or surviving relative. Return responses were also shared with the class. At least one hero was invited to the school to talk to students at a You Are My Hero assembly.

Two valuable resources for identifying real heroes and encouraging students to admire and emulate them are the Free Spirit Publishing (400 First Ave. North, Suite 616-61Y, Minneapolis, MN 55401; 800-735-7323) and the Giraffe Project (PO Box 759, Langley, WA 98260; 360-221-0757; email: office@giraffe.org; website: http://www.giraffe.org/giraffe/). *The Kid's Guide to Social Action, Kids With Courage,* and *Kid Stories: Biographies of 20 Young People You'd Like to Know* are available through Free Spirit Publishing. The Giraffe Project has the *Standing Tall* curriculum (Giraffe Project, 1995) which includes stories about real-life heroes drawn from a bank of over 800 stories about people from all age groups and walks of life who have "stuck their neck out" or "stood tall" for the common good. This curriculum targets the defining virtues of caring, courage, and taking responsibility. Its "hear the story, tell the story, become the story" format encourages students to model after real life heroes by combining didactic instruction and active student participation. Students first hear and read about heroes or human Giraffes and gain a deeper understanding of the virtues of caring, courage, and responsibility. After learning from these stories, they begin looking for persons with Giraffe qualities in their studies, through the media, and in their communities. Finally, they stand tall themselves by identifying needs in their school or community, planning a service project, and carrying out this project. The curriculum's teaching guides for K-2, 3-5, 6-9, 10-12 include videos and written stories about heroes, plus lesson plans that are developmentally appropriate and nicely sequenced. For schools that have access to the internet, the Giraffe Project's web page periodically feature new giraffes.

Cross-Grade Tutors, Buddies, and Adopters

Buddy programs involve older classrooms of students adopting younger classrooms of students with older-younger student partnerships that last the full year. It may be desirable for each child in your school (except kindergarten and fifth) to have a younger and an older buddy. For example, fifth graders may have second grade buddies who in turn have kindergarten buddies. Ideally, buddy classrooms should be three grades apart (e.g., kindergarten and third). In the older-buddy role, students will experience themselves as responsible and caring toward someone who needs their help, someone who appreciates it, and someone who values their experience (a form of service learning). Some may be able to make social connections they have trouble making with peers, and most will feel compelled to act more mature and responsible than they usually act and to take their older-buddy role seriously. Younger buddies benefit from the special attention they receive, become more comfortable around older children, are able to take on challenges they might otherwise avoid, and begin to model after a person with whom they can strongly identify. The school as a whole benefits because buddy activities build community and send the message that relationships are important (Developmental Studies Center, 1996).

Older students often read to their buddies in kindergarten and the first grade, but many other activities are possible including field trips, contact outside of school, buddies bulletin boards, Pen Pal letters, buddy mail (b-mail), class-to-class letters, various types of interviews, going to and participating in assemblies, school improvement projects, and writing in journals together. The *That's My Buddy* book and related video (Developmental Studies Center, 1996) include descriptions of many activities as well as guidelines on how to set up a buddy program. They give suggestions on all aspects, including how to pair and introduce buddies so that both members of each pair feel comfortable, and how teachers can plan together.

Hazelwood Elementary in Louisville, one of the DSC's model schools, uses buddy activities extensively. During our day-long visit, we observed at least four pairs of classes involved in some type of buddy activity, several class meetings devoted to preparing for a buddies activity or discussing one that had already taken place, and walls filled with visual evidence such as letters from older buddies to younger, and vise versa, and poster size b-mail letters from one class to another.

Pairings for cross-grade tutoring (as opposed to buddying) can be made on the basis of academic deficits of the younger child and the interest of older students in tutoring. These match-ups work best when tutors receive some training, when their instructional goal is made specific, when some sacrifice of free time (e.g., recess and after school) and class time on the part of the tutors effectively ensures that only committed tutors apply for the job, and when their efforts are later publicly acknowledged in some way, such as a present from the tutored student, a letter from the tutored student's parents, or an award from the principal.

Some students may need more than an ordinary buddy from a grade or two higher. Some students have serious personal, emotional, behavioral, familial, developmental, and learning problems and needs that call for very special older buddies. Special buddies should be the most intellectually capable and caring in the school as well as interested in public service professions. They should also be considerably older than their younger buddy (at least four years), and they should be referred to as big brothers/big sisters or mentors. For very needy children or those who appear to be at risk for delinquency, the mentor should come from a college, high school, or organization like 100 Black Men. Mentors or big brothers and big sisters should receive an orientation, meet and work with prospective adoptees before committing, commit to regular contact for a year or longer, and meet as a group with supervising teachers and counselors to share frustrations and experiences and to get ideas that will maximize effectiveness. A survey completed in Atlanta revealed that teachers view the adoption of younger problem students by older more capable and responsible students as a more promising strategy for improving school climate and discipline problems than any other.

"Family Heritage Museum"/"Grandpersons' Gathering"

The Developmental Studies Center published a small book entitled *At Home in Our Schools* (1994) that is loaded with ideas that will help build school communities and a healthy relationship between the school community and outside community. Their Family Heritage Museum, Family Projects Fair, and Grandpersons' Gathering are unique and fun activities that help students understand one another better and thus build a strong school community by learning about their families. The Family Heritage Museum provides a way for students and their parents to celebrate their backgrounds and proudly share them with others. Each family works together at home to choose or create pictures, clothing, stories, letters, scrapbooks, certificates, and other items that they want to use in their contribution to a school-wide display. The museum can be placed in a central location or sections within individual classrooms. When completed, the school could have an open house that could include speakers, group discussions among families, large maps on which countries of origin are identified, and so forth. *At Home in Our Schools* includes sample letters to be sent home to parents.

The Family Heritage Museum shares with Multicultural-Day programs the celebration of all cultures. During Multicultural Days schools celebrate a wide array of cultures through whole-classroom, in-costume performances at a school wide, parent-attended assembly that provides a wonderful climax to weeks of study and rehearsal. Like Family Heritage Museums, Family Project Fairs encourage families to work together on projects, but projects other than family background or heritage such as displays that reflect a special family interest. *At Home in Our Schools* lists other possible projects. Finally, Grandpersons' Gatherings provide another way for children to learn about one another and a way to encourage students to value family and respect persons with much more experience. Students who do not have a grandparent to invite can share another student's grandparent or invite an older neighbor or relative, and classroom activities might involve story-telling, giving cards, poems, and gifts, interviewing, sharing items of historical significance, and eating food items brought by the older persons.

DIDACTICS

Literature

The effective use of literature or books in moral education depends on three important factors: the quality of the books, the ease with which good books can be found, and whether teachers are able to "thoughtfully engage" students in good stories and books using the curriculum, the classroom environment, and appropriate questioning and discussion. There is a wealth of quality literature available, and this literature can be found rather easily thanks to persons and organizations who have shared the results of their search. A few have offered teacher guides and suggestions for effective use.

Leonard-Lamme and her coauthors (1992) explained that books help children learn to take the perspective of others. They explained that "as children hear how characters in books behave and why, they compare those actions to their own" and "they learn to place themselves in the role of the protagonist . . . and to predict how the protagonist might act or how they would act if they were in the story themselves." They went on to say that "children learn role-taking, which can lead to the development of empathy and the ability to reason from more than an egocentric point of view." They encouraged teachers to take full advantage of children's natural and imaginative engagement with stories by asking children authentic questions about the books they read, that is, questions that seek to find out how the book made them feel, what they learned, whether the story reminded them of something in their own lives, and so forth, rather than comprehension questions and fact questions that have a single right answer for everyone. They also provided strategies for promoting thoughtful consideration of the moral issues in children's books: story webs to help students relate stories to their lives, brainstorming possible choices the characters might make, writing about or discussing how the students would behave in situations similar to those a story character faced, writing and discussing how students feel about a character's decision, writing and discussing similar experiences of students, role playing a part of the story that involves choices and exploring alternatives, graphing and charting characters' feelings at various points in the plot, drawing pictures to make more clear what is important.

Most authors of children's books seek to promote character development, particularly those who write books for young children, but few schools have developed directories or catalogs that list the developmental level of each book in their collection, the virtues or values taught, and other useful information, such as the types of problems faced, the setting, ethnicity, and appropriate age level. This should be done as part of any character education program, and there are several publications and organizations that can speed the process along. Field and Weiss (1987) reviewed several hundred books for children and young adults centering around ten values: cooperation, courage, friendship and love of animals, friendship and love of people, humaneness, ingenuity, loyalty, maturing, responsibility, and self-respect. An even more valuable book in my opinion is *Literature-Based Moral Education* (Leonard-Lamme et al., 1992). Most of this book is devoted to reviews of three dozen or more books for each of the eleven virtues, with curricular extensions for each (follow-up activities), but their book reviews were preceded by general suggestions for promoting these eleven virtues in classrooms, suggestions that reflect the authors' understanding of the developmental characteristics of various age levels. The Utah State Office of Education has included as part of its Partnership in Character Education Homepage a list of books to be read to children and/or read with children that is subdivided into age categories and includes annotations identifying specific habits of character—hopefully this list will grow (http://www.usoe.k12.ut.us/curr/char_ed/). Another book by Kilpatrick and colleagues (1994) was written for parents but can be a valuable resource for teachers as well. Teachers must be careful not to use the "sacred texts" and "books for holidays and holy days" in a way that teaches religion rather than "about religions." Their book reviews are categorized by type (picture books, fables and fairy tales, myths, legends, and folktales, sacred texts, books for holidays and holy days, historical fiction, contemporary fiction, fantasy and science fiction, biography), and are subcategorized by developmental level (younger readers, middle readers, older readers).

Organizations such as the Developmental Studies Center (2000 Embarcadero, Suite 305, Oakland, CA 94606; 800-666-7270; e-mail: pubs@devstu.org; website: www.devstu.org), The Heartwood Institute (425 N. Craig St., Suite 302, Pittsburgh, PA 15213; 412-688-8570), and The Center for Learning (P.O. Box 910, Villa Maria, PA 16155; 800-767-9090/216-331-1404) publish values-education curriculums that use reading as a primary methodology. They find and create short stories, novels, poems, dramas, and biographies that facilitate the teaching of important universal values, and they equip teachers with a variety of instructional aids including academic and ethical objectives, teacher guides, student handouts, step-by-step lesson procedures, and recommended activities other than reading. The Heartwood Institute's *Ethics Curriculum for Children* (1995) is a multicultural collection for preschool through sixth grade students which targets seven virtues (courage, loyalty, justice, respect, hope, honesty, love). The Developmental Studies Center publishes the *Reading, Thinking, and Caring* series for K-3 and the *Reading for Real* series for grades 4-8 (1994), which includes elaborate teacher guides for each. The Center for Learning publishes *Creating a Values-Based Reading Program: Novel/Drama Curriculum Units* (1995) and four similarly structured series (English-Language Arts, Social Studies, Religion, Elementary) which target twenty-four universal values (see Part Two for a list of these values). The Center for Learning's collection includes hundreds of values-based instructional units authored by a network of three hundred teachers. Most of these units are designed for students in middle and high school; most of the Heartwood and Developmental Studies Center units are designed for elementary children. The Heartwood Institute recently extended its curriculum to preschoolers. The formats used by all three publishers provide models for categorizing and effectively using school library collections to promote character growth.

Teachers and school administrators interested in using literature to promote character growth may also find the Junior Great Books Program of the Great Books Foundation in Chicago (312-332-5870) another useful resource. This organization evaluates and lists literary works for students and adults. Their primary focus is not character education, but their emphasis on the use of interpretative and evaluative questions during teacher-led class discussions and folktales from around the world suggests that their work may be of value to character educators. With respect to their criteria for evaluating literary works, selections must (1) support extended interpretive discussion, (2) raise questions for adults and students thereby ensuring that shared-inquiry discussions will be collaborative, (3) be limited in length so that students can read and re-read closely for detail, and (4) be age-appropriate in terms of theme and style rather than reading level.

To ensure instruction and learning that corresponds to the virtues and related psychological processes targeted for each grade level in the core curriculum in chapter 3, students beginning at the second grade level could be required to read and report on one book for each targeted virtue (e.g. kindness, courage, effort, ability, teamwork, friendship, citizenship). Teachers could also assign to individual students books that address perceived individual deficits or personal problems (e.g., a lack of kindness or courage), that is, they could use independent reading for social-affective remediation and therapy. Sources for these books include published literature-based curriculums, school-library collections that have been cataloged by specific virtues, and literary works from other libraries and publishers that have categorized their books, such as Paperbacks for Educators (426 West Front St., Washington, MO 63090; 800-227-2591) and Free Spirit Publishing (400 First Avenue North, Suite 616–61Y, Minneapolis, MN 55401-1730; 800-735-7323). Free Spirit publishes many books that should be a part of your character-building collection, including *What Do You Stand For: A Kid's Guide to Building Character* (Lewis, 1997), *How Rude: The Teenagers' Guide To Good Manners, Proper Behavior, and Not Grossing People Out* (Packer, 1997), *The First Honest Book About Lies* (Kincher, 1996), *Kids with Courage* (Lewis, 1996), and *Respecting Our Differences* (Duvall, 1996).

Teaching as Storytelling

Egan (1986) contends that cognitive theories of moral development that have focused on logical-intellectual capabilities have led to an underestimate of children's abstract thinking abilities and that a more optimistic view would have emerged if the focus had been imagination rather than logic or mathematical-deductive reasoning. His argument is based more on intuition and personal observation than scientific research, but it should compel us to keep an open mind. He states that since storytelling is highly engaging and stimulates the imagination of children, teachers would be wise to incorporate the rhythm of storytelling into all of their teaching and take better advantage of the door to higher level thinking provided by children's imagination. He contends that the assumption that children's learning must progress from the concrete to the abstract is not true for all learning and that the opposite may be the case for some types of learning: "We can teach any content as long as it fits the abstract conceptual structures the child has in place." He says that stories emphasize affective meaning while most school instruction emphasizes cognitive meaning, and that we need to adopt a model for children that balances the two. He proposes a teaching model that draws upon the affectively engaging and imagination stimulating power of the story by setting up a conflict or sense of dramatic tension at the beginning of lessons that will be satisfied at the end. He suggests using binary opposites as a way of organizing and selecting content.

Egan's storytelling model for teaching begins by identifying importance: What is most important about the topic? Why should it matter to children? What is affectively engaging about it? Step two involves identifying binary opposites that best capture the importance of the topic. The remaining steps involve organizing content into story form. He offers as an example teaching a unit on communities by using the binary opposite of survival-versus-destruction or security-versus-danger, concepts the child already has in place, and beginning with an event that conveys this such as waking up with a huge steel wall around their city that cuts people off totally from the outside. He suggests that the story might be set up as a monster trying to destroy the community by setting fires that the fire fighters put out and blowing up roads which the road crews fix. Egan's ideas should be explored by character educators who wish to promote empathic understanding and critical reflection.

The Art of Storytelling

Sherry Norfolk has been a professional storyteller for fifteen years. She now specializes in finding and telling stories that promote moral growth and reflection. She believes that storytelling is the most important and effective of all character education strategies and that all teachers can develop storytelling skills. Sherry performs for students in schools and teaches teachers how to use stories and storytelling more effectively (515-A Nelson Ferry Road, Decatur, GA 30030; 404-371-8206; Shnorfolk@aol.com). Her performances as part of our Artists-for-Character Day in six elementary schools in Atlanta were so impressive that I asked her to write a section about storytelling for this book. She provided the following folktale and comments.

Truth and Story

In the beginning of time, Truth walked naked upon the earth. His skin was smooth and shining. His body was strong and well formed, and he walked tall and proud. Everywhere he went, Truth tried to share the great store of knowledge that he possessed. Each time he entered a village, he would call out: "I am Truth—come listen and learn from my teachings."

But no one listened to Truth. Oh, sometimes children came running to sit at his feet and hear him talk, but their parents dragged them away covering children's eyes with their hands. One time a young woman was drawn to Truth, looking at him with wonder and listening with awe, but her mother immediately reprimanded her and turned her aside. Young men looked at him with envy and fear and turned quickly away. Old women looked at him with fond, reminiscent smiles, and old men with a look of chagrin. No one listened. Truth wandered from village to village, town to town, always with the same reception and always alone. One day he came to the house of his sister, Story. Story lived in a fine and fancy house, surrounded by flowers and ferns, trees and blossoming vines. A wide, shady porch stretched around the house, filled with comfortable rocking chairs and hanging swings. The wide windows were hung with lace curtains and brocade drapes, and stained glass cast rainbows of light across the oriental carpets. Story herself sat in a wide wicker chair, dressed in a flowing chiffon gown that shimmered with light and color. Her curling hair tumbled about her shoulders, and was strewn with flowers and ribbons, and her fingers and throat, wrists and ankles were adorned with jewels.

When Story saw her brother approaching, she ran to him in distress: "Why Truth, you look awful. So sad and dejected. What's wrong? How can I help you."

"I don't think anyone can help me, Story. I've gone to every village and town trying to share my knowledge, and no one will listen. I have such important things to say, Story! But I can't make them listen."

"You're wrong my brother. I can help you. I know just what you need. Come with me."

Story led Truth to her bedroom where she threw open trunks and hampers and armoires full of clothes, shoes, hats and cloaks: "Dress yourself, Truth."

Truth was horrified: "Dress myself in these gaudy things? Oh, Story, I can't. I feel so silly!"

But Story insisted, and Truth obeyed. He put on purple trousers made of velvet, a fine linen shirt with flowing sleeves and a quilted vest sewn with glittering jewels. He wrapped a flowing silken scarf around his neck, and hung golden hoops from his ears. He put rings on every finger, a pair of silver shoes on his feet, and on his head he wore a hat with a long curving feather. When he thought he was finished, Story wove ribbons into his hair, poked a flower into his lapel, and hung a satin cloak around his shoulders.

At last Story was satisfied: "Now you are ready," she told him. "Back to the villages and see what happens."

Truth felt ridiculous, but he thanked Story, and set out once more to enlighten the world. After one year he returned to Story's house. "What happened, Truth? You look happier than the last time I saw you," she asked.

"I really don't understand it, Story, but these silly clothes worked! Everywhere I went, people would gather around and listen eagerly to everything I had to say! It was wonderful, but I am confused. I still have the same things to say. Why will people listen now to what they rejected before?"

Story smiled: "Don't you see? No one wants to listen to the naked Truth, but everyone will listen when its clothed in Story."   Yiddish Folktale

If we want children to hear and understand and practice the truth about the moral way to think, feel, and behave, then we need to tell stories and not preach to them. As Lickona (1991) put it, stories teach by attraction rather than compulsion, and they invite rather than impose. Smith (1986) similarly stated: "A sensitive story does not pry and badger; it gently beckons, touching children's minds here and there, inviting them to expand and reconsider their ideas about life." In order to make the task of educating for character easier and more fun, we need to use the engaging power of stories as well as their potential to capture the imagination and touch the heart.

Learning to use stories and their characters as the basis for values education is not as difficult as it may at first appear. Take, for example, a simple nursery tale such as The Ginger Bread Boy. You should begin with a character analysis, and this could include student input and a comparison of the boy's traits to a list of desirable traits or virtues: Is he patient, humble, thoughtful, courageous? This analysis of good and bad traits could lead to discussion questions such as asking whether the fox was right or wrong to do what he did. The plot, which involves the boy running away from his troubles, encountering danger along the way, and finally losing his life to the allure of promised happiness and safety, could serve as a convenient jumping off point for a discussion about the allure of drug use, the alluring promises of child abductors, and the allure of dropping out of school. The teacher should explore with children the points at which the Gingerbread Boy had to make decisions (when he ran away, when he decides to continue running, and when he decides to trust the fox) and consider alternative behaviors he could have chosen. Storytellers believe that teaching children to recognize and examine the choices and alternatives in stories helps them to do so in their own lives. Having the story as a referent for all children in a classroom gives the teacher interesting ways to respond to negative behaviors such as chanting "run, run, run as fast as you can" when a child tries to avoid or run away from a problem.

Teachers do not have to be perfect in telling a story because children appreciate the smallest kind of story and immediately relate to and respect adults who will assume the storyteller role. Reluctant teachers will find that children will not criticize. They tend to view storytelling as an act of devotion and sharing. The trick is for teachers to find stories that speak to themselves. Once this is done, the telling of stories becomes natural and necessary and a matter of following instincts and letting the story flow from the heart. If this is done, characters will delineate themselves through spontaneous body language and voice, dramatic moments will automatically be emphasized, and pacing will adjust to the demands of the story. Storytelling comes from the heart, not the head, and nothing should keep the storyteller from the sheer pleasure of telling a story.

Teachers who wish to learn more about storytelling may want to read one of the following: *Story Teller Story Teacher: Discovering the Power of Story for Teaching and Living* (Gillard, 1996), *The Storyteller Start-up Book: Finding, Learning, Performing, and Using Folktales* (MacDonald, 1993), *Tales as Tools: The Power of Story in the Classroom* (National Storytelling Association, 1994), *You Can't Say You Can't Play* (Paley, 1992), *Beyond the Beanstalk: Interdisciplinary Learning Through Storytelling* (Rubright, 1996). They may also want to obtain Bobby and Sherry Norfolk's book, *The Moral of the Story: Folktales for Building Character.* This book will be available from August House in early 1999.

Artists-for-Character Day

There are many ways to use the arts to promote character growth, and many would fit best in the Active-Student-Participation category rather than the Didactics category. Our "Artists-for-Character Day" in six elementary schools in Atlanta may fit best in the Didactics category since students were passive audience members much of the time, but it could also fit in the Active-Student-Participation category since all of our artists involved students in some way as they were asked to do.

We selected for our "Artists-for-Character Day" five performing artists: a professional dancer/actor/choreographer, a professional storyteller, a professional musician/songwriter, a creative dramatics teacher, and a master puppeteer and teacher of gifted students in Atlanta. Garry Smith, our musician, has written and recorded many songs about character. Neither he nor Sherry Norfolk, our storyteller, needed an orientation about character education since they are full-time character educators as well as performing artists. Our dancer, Leon Brown, our puppeteer, Alan Louis, and our creative dramatics teacher, Sara Moylan, were not as familiar with the concept of character education, but they came with the necessary experience and personal character and were introduced to the concept through conversation and written material. My instructions to them were simply to do a performance that would help us achieve our character education objectives and include students in some way, and to follow their performance with an instructional dialogue that would allow students to ask questions.

We scheduled the artists so that each would perform for forty-five minutes twice at one school in the morning and then rotate to a second school in the afternoon to do two more performances. This was continued for three consecutive days with two schools served each day. When the size of the school precluded having every child see every performance, we sent the youngest children to the puppet show, the middle grade students to the drama teacher or storyteller, and the oldest students to the dancer. Most of the children saw all of the artists or all but one. The most difficult challenges were finding the best location for each artist, getting the students in and out on time, and repeatedly breaking down, transporting, and setting up a large homemade puppet-show stage.

The puppet show resulted from asking Alan Louis if he thought he and his gifted students could write a play involving some of the marionettes of famous persons from history that they had already created at Lin Elementary where he taught gifted students, such as Mother Theresa, B. B. King, and Abe Lincoln, and if any of his students could help him perform the play. He and his principal graciously agreed to help. More details about the wonderful result can be found in a Puppetry Journal written by Alan Louis (1997).

Sherry Norfolk chose a variety of stories and folktales from many cultures and time periods, and her audiences were awestruck by her captivating style. One teacher asked me if she was a professional actress. My answer was "yes" because she truly becomes the characters in her stories. I highly recommend her to any system or school that wants to take advantage of her storytelling and teacher training skills.

I can also recommend Garry Smith enthusiastically. All of his songs are available on tape, and his live performances are even better and have all the kids learning the songs quickly and singing along. Although some of his songs are academically focused, most are values-related such as *Responsible-Responsibility,*

Don't Put Your Love on a Shelf, We Are Thankful, Love One Another, Great Big Sunshine, Try Again, and *Be Good, Be Generous.* One of our participating schools purchased Garry's tapes for every teacher. I recommend that you do the same and that you bring Garry to your school if funds allow. Garry is not only a creative person and superb performer but a wonderful male role model for children. Even at six feet seven inches, he fits my image of the perfect elementary teacher. Garry was a kindergarten teacher for seventeen years before starting Good Choice Music, Inc., PO Box 950084, Lake Mary, FL 32795; 407-323-2638.

Our dancer, Leon Von Brown, performed a music enhanced dance routine with a chair and himself that dramatically expressed his feelings about M. L. King, Jr. and his life. He followed this by talking to students about the character qualities Dr. King displayed, about how he has tried to do the same, and how the demands of his profession forced him to either show these qualities or give up. He was excellent at involving students cooperatively in a series of group dance movements. Leon told me that he would like to do more of what he did for us, and he has already done so in the New York City Schools. He spoke with staff at the Alliance Theater in Atlanta about joining the character education movement, and the word has apparently spread since other theaters such as Theater Gael have expressed an interest as well. I expect that there will be more Artists-for-Character Days in Atlanta with these and other new artists involved. If you choose to do something similar, I suggest using local theater people, other artists whose personal character and interest in the concept are strong, and possibly one or more of the artists who were a part of our Artists-for-Character Day.

Visual Displays

It is not possible to include in this book pictures of the many permanent and temporary wall displays produced by the teachers and students in our grant schools in Atlanta and the model schools we visited as part of our orientation in Louisville, Dayton, and West Point, Georgia, but I can describe a few and tell you that an emphasis upon visual displays creates a wonderful visual climate within the school.

Beginning with the systems outside of Atlanta that we visited, Hazelwood Elementary in Louisville had many displays that reflected its emphasis on student involvement and cross-grade buddy activities. They included poster size personal letters from one class to another and displays that focused on families. My favorite was one that resulted from children talking to their parents about their names, entitled, "the story of our names." I must have read or heard the words "our" and "our class" a thousand times during our day-long visit to Hazelwood. West Point Elementary in Georgia, was the first school to paint a colorful zigzag line with values words on the walls in all of its hallways. Blalock and Campbell did the same and used bright complementary colors. Patterns the width of a concrete block were used to draw the line, including simple curved patterns and angled patterns. These patterns were used repetitiously and in various combinations and sequences to produce creative designs. The values words were painted within the zigzag line by selecting a font style, printing the words via computer, projecting them onto oaktag cardboard using an opaque projector, cutting out the letters to form stencils, transferring them onto the wall using the stencils and a permanent laundry-type marker or grease pencil, and having a skilled sign painter brush them freehand onto the concrete blocks. Blalock painted two nine-foot circles on the walls near their entrance with "character counts" and the seven "primary virtues" (see chapter 3) on one, with the letters running in a circle, and "character first" and the seven "primary virtues" painted on the other. Campbell painted the words "We Believe In Character" in a large overhead area leading into its library. If you choose to paint a "virtue line" or choose to create other permanent displays, you need the advice and help of a sign painter and/or experienced display artist.

Blalock and two other Atlanta schools also had many temporary displays that featured character-related student writings and drawings, words of the week, and so forth. My favorites at Blalock were the "character-sauraus," "get aboard the character train," "blasting off to good character," and "nesting on good character." Like West Point, each grade cluster at Blalock chose a name such as the sunshine kids, best friends village, the get along gang, and the each-one-teach-one gang, and then created a colorful flag illustrating their name that hung on a small flag pole in the hallway outside the entrance to their cluster of classrooms.

Hope Elementary in Atlanta had a nice display that featured first grade children with their senior citizen buddies from the nursing home next door. My favorite in-class display at Rivers Elementary in Atlanta was an air balloon made out of chalk board material and hung from the ceiling. Each week the kindergarten teacher entered the virtue of the week on this chalkboard balloon. My favorite in-class display at Fain Elementary was one that featured the cartoon character Arthur and included all of the virtues that were featured as words of the week during the year. Ms. McCall, the teacher who created the display, told me that when a situation arose in the classroom that gave her the chance to use one of the virtue words, she personalized it or made it more real for her first graders by making reference to what Arthur would have done or how he would have felt or thought. A teacher at Campbell Elementary in Atlanta gradually grew a caterpillar one circle at a time around the walls of her room with a word of the week on each.

Peace Education

Peace educators are concerned with the resolution of interpersonal conflicts through peer mediation and other conflict resolution techniques, but they are also concerned with the prevention and resolution of conflicts among races, ethnic groups, religious groups, and nations. Peace education begins with self-awareness and self-understanding and extends to significant others in the family and local community and ultimately to the world community. The curricula and activities of peace education seek to instill the feelings, attitudes, skills, and knowledge that support the establishment and maintenance of peace on all levels.

Peace education addresses the human causes of inter-group conflict including prejudice, stereotyping, indoctrination, bias, racism, bigotry, ethnocentrism, inter-religious polarization, and disturbed personalities in leadership positions. It also addresses the (1) personal virtues and skills, (2) communication-facilitating processes and methods, (3) organizations, and (4) personalities/leadership styles that combine to prevent, defuse, or resolve these conflicts. With respect to personal virtues and related skills, character education programs seek to develop in students a predisposition toward peace by teaching and encouraging key virtues and related skills, including compromise, cooperation, respect, fairness, honesty, empathy, altruism, flexibility, and objectivity. Certain components of character education programs are especially important, such as inter-cultural exchange projects that provide knowledge and understanding among otherwise separated groups, and conflict resolution programs that teach and promote critical thinking, ethical reflection, perspective-taking, and creative problem-solving.

With respect to item 2 above, key processes and methods include mediation, negotiation, arbitration, diplomacy, nonviolent demonstrations, teaching about ecological and economic interdependence, the news media, and multicultural education; with respect to item 3, the most important organizations are those that deal with world hunger and disease, environmental conservation, unchecked population growth, human rights worldwide, multinational business and science ventures, and international law (the World Court and United Nations in particular); with respect to item 4, key personalities and leadership styles would include the study of Gandhi, Martin Luther King, Sadat, and other courageous peacemakers.

Many guidebooks and curricula are available for peace education including *Teaching Young Children in Violent Times: Building a Peaceable Classroom* (Levin, 1994), *Perspectives: A Teaching Guide to Concepts of Peace* (Berman, 1983), and other materials published by Educators for Social Responsibility (23 Garden Street, Cambridge, MA 02138; 617-492-1764); *The Big Book for Peace* (Durell, 1990) published by Dutton Children's Books (375 Hudson St., New York, NY 10014-3657; 212-366-2000); a journal published by the Communitarian Network (2130 H Street NM, #174, Washington, DC 20052; 202-994-7997); *100+ Peace Strategies for Conflict Resolution and the Prevention of Nuclear War* (Valett, 1983) published by Panorama West (Fresno, CA); *Teaching Peace: Skills for Living in a Global Society* (Fletcher, 1986) published by Harper and Row (800-331-3761); *Teaching Peace: A Catalog of Multimedia Resources on Peacemaking, Conflict Resolution, War Studies and War Prevention, the Soviet Union and Global Education* (1988), which can be borrowed from The Peace Education Resource Center (1515 Cherry St., Philadelphia, PA 19102; 215-241-7220); and various other materials available through The Global Classroom (P.O. Box 584, Williston, VT 05495; 800-211-5142; www.globalclassroom.com).

Social Skills Instruction

Social skills, by definition, are competencies that predict prosocial behavior and interpersonal success as well as other forms of success in various social settings.

Teaching interpersonal problem solving as a social skill using the "I Can Problem Solve" approach developed by Shure (1992) was referred to in the "Violence Prevention" subsection of this chapter. Like any good social skills training approach, ICPS involves breaking skills down into steps, teaching prerequisite skills and prerequisite vocabulary words as needed, and following the basic steps of good instruction: expert modeling, guided practice, monitored application, and independent application. The importance of good social skill training to good character education was addressed in chapter 3. Social skills training was identified as one of the primary strategies that all elementary teachers must use on a daily basis to teach the many targeted virtues that can be viewed as social skills, or as having a social skill component (e.g., being nice, being thankful, being helpful, sharing, dealing with teasing, being comforting, being brave, showing you are sorry, forgiving others, being patient, showing good sportsmanship, being assertive, taking the initiative to mediate conflicts, etc.).

The Skillstreaming approach (Goldstein et al., 1980; McGinnis and Goldstein, 1984; McGinnis and Goldstein, 1990) was recommended in chapter 3 but was not described in any detail. Other models such as Gresham and Nagle's (1982) include the same basic steps of good social-skills instruction. The Skillstreaming model lists: modeling (showing them how), role playing (letting them try it), performance feedback (talking about how well they did), and transfer training (arranging for them to practice the skill). The Structured Learning model of Gresham lists: establishing the need (in the mind of the child), identifying skill components, modeling, rehearsing behavior (corresponds to role playing in the Skillstreaming model), and generalization training. Although not listed among his four instructional steps, Goldstein also encourages initially motivating students through questions like: "Who finds it hard to wait their turn when playing a game?" He also recommends having students help in the process of thinking of real-life situations in which the skill is needed. His final "pre-teaching" step involves presenting students with the steps of the targeted skill using a Skill Steps Handout.

The first instructional step in Skillstreaming involves modeling the steps of the social skill in at least two make-believe social situations using verbal mediation as needed. The Role Play step that follows involves choosing actors, setting the stage, coaching, verbal prompts, and so forth. The Performance Feedback step focuses on how well the steps of the skill were followed. The teacher and students provide feedback and social reinforcement to the actors. The final Transfer Training step involves assigning homework by identifying situations or potential situations in which the skill will be practiced by students and using homework forms. These forms provide cues and are used to record the outcome. Goldstein recommends encouraged independent use of the skill by using reward techniques such as Skill Tickets that are handed out like money or tokens and redeemed for rewards as skills are displayed.

The Skillstreaming model is presented in three pairs of paperbacks (preschool, elementary, adolescent) that include forms that can be copied and distributed to students. Goldstein has expanded this model in his Aggression Replacement

Training (1987) and a more recent montage that appears to be conceptually related to the goals of character education. The greatest strengths of the Skillstreaming model are its detail and teacher friendly format. At the preschool level it lists forty prosocial skills categorized as follows: Beginning Social Skills (e.g. listening), School Related Skills (e.g., following directions), Friendship-Making Skills (e.g., waiting your turn), Dealing with Feelings (e.g. deciding how someone feels), Alternatives to Aggression (e.g., dealing with teasing), and Dealing with Stress (e.g., dealing with losing). The model includes sixty skills at the elementary level presented in the following categories: Classroom Survival Skills (e.g., contributing to discussions), Friendship Making Skills (e.g., offering help to a classmate), Skills for Dealing with Feelings (e.g., expressing concern for another), Skill Alternatives to Aggression (e.g., staying out of fights), and Skills for Dealing with Stress (e.g., dealing with group pressure). Finally, it lists fifty at the adolescent level, some of which repeat earlier categories and one that is exclusive to adolescence: Planning Skills (e.g., setting a goal).

Taylor (1997) presented a curriculum specifically designed for young African-American males. He shares with character educators the view that schools have become too narrow in their curricular focus, and he believes black males have been harmed the most since they lack positive social connections outside of school. His curriculum includes several general objectives, eight to ten specific objectives, and many strategies for each of these specific objectives. As a long-time urban educator, it is my impression that most of the objectives are appropriate for females as well as males and are suitable for children from all impoverished subcultures.

Multicultural Instruction

There are many good reasons for making sure students acquire knowledge about persons from cultures and subcultures other than their own and are encouraged to respect these persons. Our nation is becoming increasingly diverse and polarized along racial, ethnic, economic, and cultural lines. This polarization and related ignorance are a drain upon our democratic system and a serious threat to peace, as we have seen in Bosnia and other parts of the world. If we want all students to become responsible, contributing members of society, we must do what we can to make them feel respected and compelled to respect others.

The answer is not over-compensation by replacing one ethnocentric curriculum with another (e.g., replacing a Eurocentric curriculum with an Afrocentric or Asiocentric one); rather, it is the creation of an instructional climate that conveys respect for all cultures and celebrates all customs and traditions consistent with the values shared by citizens within democratic societies. Respect requires a tolerance for beliefs and customs with which we disagree and an adherence to laws that give others the right to believe and behave differently from ourselves, but it does not mean students should be taught that the beliefs and customs of various cultural groups are equally valid and that there is no right or wrong way to believe. The objective of multicultural teaching is not to convince anyone that one culture's or subculture's definition of morality is just as valid as any other's but to learn to treat others with the dignity they deserve as human beings. We have the responsibility to teach students that no person is superior to another by virtue of their race or culture.

There are several ways to meet this responsibility including (1) the search for an exclusion of ethnocentric textbooks and other ethnocentric curriculum materials; (2) the adoption or creation of a truly multicultural curriculum that gives special attention to racism, prejudice, and stereotyping; (3) the inclusion of specific lessons and courses that compare and contrast cultures, subcultures, and religions (Ozturk, 1991/92); (4) the creation of a special multicultural studies area in the school media center that includes books, tapes, and videos; (5) a concerted effort to go beyond carefully selected multicultural materials in day-to-day teaching by infusing lessons and additional materials about cultures and subcultures that are represented within your school or system and those that are not but that represent a significant minority or majority within the society as a whole; (6) the establishment of policies that value diversity and require sanctions for harassment and discrimination; (7) the required use of cooperative learning within multicultural schools and incentive plans to encourage English speaking students to learn the language of their immigrant classmates well enough to converse effectively; (8) the use of inter-cultural exchange programs that match students, classes, and schools from different cultures within the city, nation, and world and involve various forms of communi-cation and study; and (9) special multicultural celebrations including "We are the world" assemblies, a multicultural night that includes student and parent participation, and a multicultural week with many activities including assemblies, classroom projects, talent contests, guest speakers and performances, ethnic lunches, special morning announcements, art projects, parades, and special library activities.

Many of these strategies are elaborated in other sections of this Chapter. Teachers who wish to enhance their multicultural teaching should be aware of available materials including (1) the *Anti-Bias Curriculum* published by the National Association for the Education of Young Children (1509 16th Street, Washington, D.C. 20036-1426); (2) the *Teaching Tolerance* magazine published by the Southern Poverty Law Center (400 Washington Avenue, Montgomery, Alabama 36104); (3) the book *Celebrations Around the World: A Multicultural Handbook* by Angell (1996) published by Fulcrum Publishing (350 Indiana St., Suite 350, Golden, CO 80401-5093; 800-992-2908); (4) the article by Branch (Branch et al. 1994), which compares diversity and pluralism, reviews Bank's four levels of ethnic-content integration, and offers twenty-five lessons for each of the four levels; (5) the article by Hillis (1994) which describes the mainstream-centric, ethno-additive, multicultural, and ethno-national models; (6) Volume 51 of Educational Leadership (1994) which is devoted exclusively to multicultural teaching; (7) Harris's (1991) study of African American children's literature; (8) The Black Experience in Books published by Positive Impact (P.O. Box 1764, Ardmore, OK 73402); (9) the Developmental Studies Center books which teach respect for diversity (2000 Embarcadero, Suite 305, Oakland, CA 94606); (10) the Heartwood books about respect (425 N. Craig St., Suite 302, Pittsburgh, PA 15213; 412-688-8570); (11) the Teacher Created Materials' Multicultural Bibliography (1993); (12) the book by Jasmine (1995), which presents ways to teach about diversity and lists twenty-four publishers of multicultural children's books; and (13) other materials available from the American Ethnological Society (1703 New Hampshire Ave., Washington, D.C. 20009) and the Global Classroom (P.O. Box 584, Williston, VT 05495; 800-211-5142; www.globalclassroom.com).

Direct multicultural instruction can also be enhanced by techniques such as keeping a world map in the room and having each student place a colored pushpin in the vicinity of the country or culture studied, using games from different cultures and identifying their source, studying cultural holidays in chronological order by creating a calendar (with adjustments for the Islamic lunar calendar) and by taking care to balance attention given to religious holidays, identifying the cultural background of artists and scientists, having students keep a multicultural reading log, infusing information about world events obtained through the media, and designing lessons in keeping with Black History month (February), Asian and Pacific Islander Heritage month (May), American Indian Heritage month (September 15 to October 15), and Women's History month (March).

Virtues-of-the-Week or Month

I have observed a tendency on the part of some schools to become complacent about using important community-building strategies and reluctant to utilize all seven learning modes once they have virtue-of-the-week or virtue-of-the-month program in place, so I begin with the caution that typical virtue-of-the-week programs do not satisfy my definition of a complete or comprehensive character education program. Nevertheless, I am also convinced that this particular strategy should be a part of all elementary level character education programs. Some character education practitioners brag about not having a word-of-the-week, and they apparently assume that it is simplistic and too nonexperiential to be effective. My position is that many children do not know what the words really mean and that formally introducing them to these words places the teacher, parents, and others in the ideal position of teaching the words or virtues as concepts. This can be accomplished by calling attention to behaviors, feelings, and attitudes that serve as examples of the virtue and those that do not.

There are many ways to carry out weekly, monthly, yearly, and multi-year virtue themes within classrooms, grades, and schools. The core curriculum presented in chapter 3 identifies a primary-virtue focus for each of five developmental levels or grade clusters (*Kindness* for pre-K and K, *Friendship* for first and second, *Teamwork* for third through fifth, *Courage* for sixth through eighth, and *Citizenship* for ninth through twelfth). These virtues could be used as a yearly instructional theme for each level or cluster. The level-specific "elaborative" virtues provide enough words for a virtue-of-the-month for each developmental level. Since early elementary children like to pretend to be adults in various roles, it may be effective to use this interest plus instruction about community helpers to teach the virtues targeted for their developmental period (see chapter 3). For example, kindergarten children could be taught about many different jobs that require kindness, caring, gentleness, and friendliness, and could be encouraged to role play these jobs in their center time and free-play. Themes that extend beyond a month could be reflected in class names and mascots which are shown on flags placed outside each classroom or grade-cluster door, pledges students repeat daily, slogans on T-shirts, posters and permanent displays, and grade-specific school uniforms or hats. For schools that want to have a virtue-of-the-month and/or virtue-of-the-week for the school as a whole, the seven primary virtues could be used for the word-of-the-month (with some collapsing of short vacation months), and the "elaborative" virtues could be used for the virtue-of-the-week.

Atlanta's pilot project identified five- and six-week periods for each of the seven primary virtues. Atlanta used the elementary-level "elaborative" virtues for their virtue-of-the-week program and provided printed sheets with the word, definition, and an illustration (see Appendix F for example) to each child together with a classroom newsletter (see Appendix C) that highlighted the word and gave suggestions to parents on how to help teach the virtue. All teachers were provided with a large poster that listed the seven primary virtues and definitions. Blalock, the school that wrote songs for the primary virtues, also created elaborate wall displays, and Blalock and Campbell painted an eight-inch-wide lightening bolt on the walls throughout their buildings which included the "elaborative" virtues. The illustrated virtue-of-the-week sheets, classroom news forms, and lightening bolts were borrowed from Allen Classical-Traditional Academy in Dayton and West Point Elementary in West Point, Georgia.

Allen Classical-Traditional Academy in Dayton, schools in the Madison-Trotwood system in Dayton, and West Point Elementary in Troup County, Georgia, are other good examples of programs built around a core virtue-of-the-week idea. I recently visited Allen and West Point and found them to be similar except that West Point places more emphasis on positive reinforcement and common courtesy. Allen is more traditional in an old-fashioned but positive sense. West Point has a Character Clubhouse constructed in an abandoned double-wide trailer that children can enjoy if their behavior is good, and this clubhouse includes numerous games and activities that have been donated to the school. Allen's program includes a Monday closed-circuit television broadcast to all the classrooms in the school with older students serving as TV news reporters. Both schools do something different each day of the week with the virtue word, beginning with activities that define and use the term, moving on to talking about local and national models of the virtue and the use of illustrative stories and student writing, and culminating at the end of the week with assemblies and other activities. Bernardo, the originating principal for Allen's program, has gone on to develop writing journals, posters, coloring books and activity books, and teacher guides that can be purchased from The Institute for

Character Development, P.O. Box 520, Dublin, OH 43071; 614-761-8555.

The Core Essentials materials (parent guide, teacher guide, table display, book marks, encouragement cards, story/literature references) are designed by parents for parents and teachers (CoreEss@aol.com; 4555 Mansell Rd. Suite 300, Alpharetta, GA 30022; 770-521-4428). They are intended to help teach eighteen character concepts through the use of eighteen related pairs of values words. Twenty-seven of the thirty-six values words are assigned to a month on one of three consecutive school calendars. In contrast to Allen Classical-Traditional Academy and West Point Elementary, the authors of Core Essentials encourage teachers and parents to do something different with the word each week of the month rather than each day of the week: week 1, define the value; week 2, explain why it is important; week 3, encourage related behavior, feelings, and so forth; week 4, reflect upon personal growth and make decisions. Their materials are simple, creative, and beautifully prepared but somewhat incompatible with other materials and word lists used by schools that have chosen to use a word-of-the-week format rather than a word of the month. These two approaches could conceivably be reconciled if the Core Essentials group either "elaborates" each value with additional values words, or develops a condensed version with a value-of-the-week for one school year using all thirty-six values words.

A word-of-the-week or virtue-of-the-week might be viewed by some high school students as childish, particularly if this strategy has been used throughout elementary school and middle school. An alternative for the high school level is a "focus-of-the-week" like Lawrence Central High School in Indianapolis has been using since 1985. This "focus" is communicated in a short message or phrase communicated at the beginning of the week over the PA system or closed circuit television. Focus topics encourage students to ponder and reflect upon issues related to specific character traits their character program stresses. Students are involved in writing or choosing the focus phrase for the week, and teachers are committed to follow-up throughout the week with bonus questions on tests, discussions, writing assignments, and so forth. (Hodgin et al., 1997).

School Behavior Codes and Related Pledges

During the first two decades of the century, morality codes were encouraged by traditional character educators but not progressive educators, and for a decade or two, they were very popular. They reflected lists of virtues and were sometimes presented in the form of pledges. One of the earliest and most influential was that written by William Hutchins (1917), entitled the "Children's Morality Code." It included "ten laws of right living" that provided elaborate codes of behavior for ten virtues: self-control, good health, kindness, sportsmanship, self-reliance, duty, reliability, truth, good workmanship, teamwork. The student pledges for each were quite long and tended to stray from the targeted virtue; nevertheless, they were the most widely used at that time.

Lengthy codes of conduct and pledges such as those developed by Hutchins are not recommended, but elementary school teachers may want to develop simple, age-appropriate written codes of conduct and/or related pledges that reflect class rules and the virtues emphasized at their particular grade level. Codes and pledges make explicit what is valued and expected, foster commitment, and can be over-learned through repetition (much like class rules), thereby promoting the formation of good habits. Rather than frequently going over lists of class rules early in the year as many teachers do until habits and routines are established, teachers may want to have students repeat codes or pledges that reference class rules as well as other desirable virtues and that should be more fun to repeat if written well. Like class rules, codes of conduct and related pledges should be stated in terms of desired positive behaviors and attitudes rather than what students should not do, and for grades three through five, students and parents should be involved in their formulation.

Behavior codes and pledges for whole schools may not be as workable or effective due to differences in language proficiency among the various grades; therefore, an approach that focuses exclusively on a few core virtues and avoids extended lists of school rules and expectations is recommended (e.g., a brief pledge that addresses the seven primary virtues presented in chapter 3). A school-wide alternative to this would be narrowly focused codes such as the Code of Participation used in the Ft. Washington Elementary School in Clovis, California. It spells out the conditions and expectations for participation in extracurricular activities and includes a "no quit" provision.

Comprehensive codes of conduct and pledges are not recommended at the middle and high school levels and may even be counterproductive. A viable alternative would be pledges written by students and voluntarily signed by students, which reflect salient social problems such as drug use, interracial conflict, and sexual activity. Posters that present pledges written and signed by leaders of every faction or subcultural group in the school, and that provide enough lines for everyone in the school to sign at their leisure will prove more effective with teenagers who feel compelled to question rules and violate adult conventions than a forced or adult-driven alternative. A more confidential approach would present students with their own pledge form (with student-written statements) that they would sign and individually present to the school principal or school counselor in charge.

Teaching Parenting K-12

Most of what children learn about parenting in our culture and most other cultures comes from experiences within their own families and observations of other families in their community. Parenting style and competence can be predicted from this experience. Stories, the news media, movies, and television are secondary and presumably less influential sources. Few people have learned a lot about parenting at school, and what they have learned has been largely incidental through stories and health courses. Even at the high school level, parenting courses are typically reserved for teenage mothers who enter a special program that gives them instruction in parenting and academics.

Given the absence of good mother and father models in many homes, the high number of teenage mothers, and the use by many parents of discipline techniques that are overly punitive and/or permissive, one can reasonably argue that some type of formal parenting instruction should begin at least in middle school. The author recommends a K-12 parenting curriculum that includes core objectives that can guide infusional instruction (like the character education objectives of this book are designed to do), and specific parenting courses during high school that include units on the responsibilities of becoming a parent and related planning, stages of infant and child development, physiological considerations including pregnancy and prenatal and perinatal nutrition, and how to shape behavior with a minimum of punishment (i.e., authoritative rather than authoritarian or permissive parenting). Such a curriculum could be developed by a volunteer interprofessional team, and this team might include a pediatrician, a nurse, a nutritionist, a day-care center specialist, a developmental or school psychologist, school teachers from each grade, and select parents. Since some aspects of content and methodology may be controversial, a separate team of critics representing all segments of the community could be formed.

Those who seek to write a core parenting curriculum need not start from scratch. There are some very creative and relevant things that have been done at the elementary level, such as an eight-unit series used in Philadelphia (Lechner-Knowles and Park-Scattergood, 1989) that was built around monthly observations of a pregnant mother and her baby after it was born. Children who were developmentally ready kept various records while learning about nutritional needs, nurturance needs, early forms of communication, safety needs, and so forth. It is easy to visualize a curriculum with developmentally appropriate objectives at each grade level, and easy to visualize how this could be used in conjunction with the more general character education objectives.

High School Ethics Courses

High school ethics courses were criticized early in the century as progressive education grew in popularity. Few high schools today offer Ethics as an elective or required course. Ethics courses are certainly not the primary answer to producing more ethical and responsible citizens, but they can be a significant component of a comprehensive plan that emphasizes participation within just, caring, democratic communities at the elementary and secondary levels. High school and upper middle school students need the opportunity to think about the types of moral dilemmas they may encounter as parents, employees, and citizens, and they need to do this within a group situation that will expose them to the moral reasoning of others. The National Association of Secondary School Principals (703-860-0200) publishes a curriculum for a day-long workshop that addresses career-related ethical issues, and the Cooperating School Districts' (CSD) publication *How to PREP* (Archibald et al., 1995) includes a plan for such a workshop that involves dividing students into career-interest groups. The most valuable resource may be *Ethics: A View of Life* (Pfefferkorn and Rosenow, 1993) which explains how to construct a high school ethics course and how to use eleven traditional and progressive teaching strategies and five evaluation methods. It also includes an ethics bibliography. This publication is also available through CSD (13157 Olive Spur Road, St. Louis, MO 63141; 314-576-3535).

Teaching Ethics Across the Curriculum

Lisman (1996) proposed an "ethics-across-the-curriculum" or infusional, subject-based, case-study (dilemma discussion) approach to teaching ethics at the high school and college levels. In addition to infusion by all teachers in all subject areas, he suggested that using ethics discussions in conjunction with service learning experiences will increase the chances that service learning will bring about a greater sense of civic responsibility. He argued convincingly that the heart of moral instruction at the high school level and beyond should be "critical," that is, it should give students the opportunity to apply moral principles to concrete situations where values and principles may be in conflict, or situations where applying a single principle is difficult. He identified autonomy as one of the capacities schools must promote, and defined autonomy in terms of self-direction, self-governance in the sense of rational, responsible, principled decision making, and being insightful and respectful of one's self. He identified three types of ethics cases that teachers can present for discussion: the application of a single principle in a complicated situation, and conflicts between self-interest and the interests of others, conflicts between or among moral values and principles. His discipline-by-discipline chapters present actual dilemmas that have been discussed, and a description of how various teachers presented them. He presented seven steps for discussing cases: describe facts, describe ethical issues, identify stakeholders, present alternative decisions, discuss ethics of each, discuss practical constraints of each, and have students decide what actions they would take. He proposed three strategies for presenting and discussing cases: whole class discussion, small groups who report back to the whole group, and role playing (see the description of sociodrama in this chapter). He suggested the *Ethics in America* video series as a source for effective uses of role playing. Finally, he emphasized the importance of choosing the right cases for discussion, being a good discussion facilitator, and being careful about offering your position on the case too early or too strongly.

Although discussion of ethical problems or ethical dilemmas may not be the primary or most effective character-building strategy for elementary and middle school, it can and should be used. Critical Thinking Press published Saenger's (1993) *Exploring Ethics Through Children's Literature, Books One and Two* for middle and upper elementary grades, respectively, and Baker's (1989) *What Would You Do? Developing and Applying Ethical Standards*, booklet A-1, for grades three through seven and structured similarly to booklet B-1 for grades six through adult. Baker's booklet presents briefly described situations followed by a series of questions that can be used to stimulate discussion. Saenger's booklets present stories that include many values and ethical issues with a special focus upon truth telling, obedience, and hurting back. Each story is presented in a lesson format with objectives, story synopsis, procedure, and discussion questions. While these stories are set up conveniently to use for ethics discussions, clearly there are many stories in basal readers and in school media centers that could be used similarly. Critical Thinking Press is also a good source of material for developing thinking skills in all curricular areas.

Curricular Infusion

I share the view that character education cannot be reduced to isolated lessons about character traits and that it must infuse all aspects of school life to be effective including the core curriculum to daily lessons. Some have searched existing core curriculums for (1) content, objectives, processes, and so forth that already promote character growth in some way or which contain values and principles that can be brought out and emphasized, and (2) places in the curriculum where character education can be interwoven, such as cooperative learning and related social skill development in math instruction and an emphasis on intercultural knowledge and understanding in social studies. Such studies have produced matrices that are often ignored unless they are kept simple and combined with training that helps teachers translate them into daily lessons.

Some might argue that any teacher who understands the basic objectives of character education will readily recognize opportunities for infusion and readily utilize teachable moments including those that derive from the core curriculum and related instructional materials and procedures in specific subject areas, and those that derive from things that just happen. Having observed several teaching staffs who have not had the benefit of a core curriculum with an interwoven character focus or guidance in how to use it in the classroom, I am convinced that only a small percentage will independently infuse in their lesson planning and daily instruction. Most need structure, modeling, guidance, and encouragement, and I believe this begins by having subject-area specialists weave character education content and processes into the core curriculum, and must include training that provides guided practice in preparing lessons that promote character growth. Kristin Fink in Utah referred to the "character piece" we seek to infuse as the piece that helps give meaning to the "academic piece," and I would add that it is the piece that makes instruction more relevant to the real world and thus more interesting and valuable to students.

Utah wove character education into its state core curriculum by establishing subject-area committees that combed through the curriculum piece-by-piece and grade-by-grade, with an eye to processes, skills, and teaching strategies that would promote character growth and not just values and character traits that they wanted their students to have. Character education has also been woven into the state's

Strategic Plan and State Board of Education's Character Education Plan, and it is being woven into or linked with their (1) Prevention Dimension initiative, which focuses on building resiliency in students and creating safe schools; (2) School-to-Careers initiative, which focuses on traits students need to be effective employees and employers; (3) Life Skills document, which influences all content areas and promotes life-long learning, effective communication, employability, critical thinking, collaboration, and responsible citizenship; and (4) Service Learning, which was integrated into the Health Education Core Curriculum. In addition, character education content and processes are being used as a means of achieving the state's goal of integrating more across subject areas. Through these various programs and initiatives and with the support of government, business, and parents, the state of Utah has managed to construct a curricular model in terms of specified outcomes that promote character growth, including content or knowledge (what students should know), process/skills (what students should be able to do), and dispositions/attitudes (personal qualities or character traits).

Kristin Fink and her colleagues have not assumed that the written documents resulting from their efforts to interweave this character-building focus into the core curriculum and the endorsement of leadership will automatically result is classroom instruction characterized by full academic and nonacademic infusion. Through workshops and conferences they have shown teachers how to use the modified core curriculum in their classrooms through techniques such as text-driven and core-driven approaches to planning lessons for early-elementary level that use literature. Kristin Fink suggests that the asking of "essential questions" (e.g., What is it in this unit of study that is essential for my students to explore or discover?) can be done in a manner that considers the values implications of content and that teachers should be constantly looking for the values that underlie a particular subject or topic and the dispositions or character traits that will make success possible in professions related to the subject or topic under study. Such questions are encouraged as a means of cross-subject curricular integration, and those who keep basic character education objectives in mind will be able to ask the type of essential questions that carry character education far beyond separate lessons and isolated strategies and into the very heart of daily instruction. For additional information on infusion you can visit Utah's Partnership in Character Education Homepage: (http://www.usoe.k12.ut.us/curr/char_ed/) or contact Kristin Fink at the Utah State Office of Education (801-538-7500; e-mail: kfink@usoe.k12.ut.us).

Teaching About Religions

In *Finding Common Ground*, Haynes (1994) explains that teaching about religions is constitutional, and he argues that it is necessary since religion has always played an important role in shaping history and the arts in all cultures throughout history. He provides guidelines for teaching about religion that draw upon the principles of rights, responsibility, and respect implicit in the First Amendment to the Constitution, and he reviews resources for teaching about religions in U.S. and world history. A less elaborate set of guidelines for teaching about religion in the public schools is included in the document entitled "Religious Expression in the Public Schools" (see Appendix G). This document was sent to all school superintendents in the United States by Education Secretary Riley in 1995 in an effort to clear up a lot of misunderstanding that began when actions such as state-sponsored school prayer were ruled unconstitutional by the U.S. Supreme Court in the 1950s and 1960s. The trend in the 1990s is clearly toward instruction that does a better job of acknowledging religion as an important part of human existence.

Haynes is confident that teachers can teach about religions in a nonbiased, nonproselytizing manner. Others that I respect share his view. Nevertheless, I wonder if this might require an unnatural level of self-control and a level of First-Amendment understanding that few citizens possess. Haynes implies that teachers can avoid favoring their own religion over others, can avoid favoring the family of religions to which theirs belongs over other categories (e.g., Christianity over Buddhism), and can avoid favoring religion over no religion. But even if well-intentioned teachers cannot be totally nonbiased, the potential benefits of instruction about religion may outweigh the risks of instruction occurring that is not entirely consistent with First Amendment constraints.

The potential benefits of teaching about religion or religions are not limited to a more in-depth and contextual understanding of history, cultures, literature, art, and even science. As stated in chapter 2, religions of the world have been important carriers and originators of values that are shared by most people of the world, values upon which social order and the survival of mankind depend. Teaching about religions in an objective, comparative, academic manner that calls attention to the values taught and emphasized by each religion constitutes another useful means by which schools can contribute to the building of prosocial-moral character.

At the high school level, instruction about religion that is fair, balanced, and objective must deal openly with destructive and oppressive acts that have been carried out in the name of religion or with the endorsement of religious leaders. It must also address the fact that wars have resulted from religious differences and religious intolerance. It should include open discussions about whether members of various religions have failed to act in accordance with the values taught by their religion. In order for this type of instruction to be ethical and constitutional as well as academic and objective, it must accomplish all of this without attacking the integrity of the religions under study and without attacking the sincere beliefs of individual members of these religions.

Although school officials should not encourage or discourage students and parents to avail themselves of an excusal option, they have much discretion in granting requests to be excused from instruction that deals in any way with religion. They are advised to grant these requests when instruction about religion is infused into required courses in history, literature, fine art, philosophy, and so forth, and they should offer comparative religion courses as an elective. Multi-faith instructional materials are available from the Global Classroom (P.O. Box 584, Williston, VT 05495; 1-800-864-7626; www.globalclassroom.com).

ACTIVE PARTICIPATION WITHIN CLASSROOMS AND SCHOOLS

Rule Making

Students should be involved in rule making from kindergarten through high school, but the form and extent of their involvement should vary in accordance with developmental characteristics. Prior to grade two, the need for rules can be discussed with children in an age-appropriate way before rule establishment, and these discussions should involve dialogue with children about how they feel when treated in ways that rules could prevent. They cannot contribute a lot with respect to rule specifics (CDP school personnel would no doubt disagree) and should not be asked to memorize rules. Rules should be taught through consequences and by calling attention to the emotional and physical effects that rule-violations have on others.

Beginning at the first grade level, rules should be clearly posted and referred to when violated. In addition, teachers can facilitate the natural process of rule internalization, which begins at age six, by combining the firm application of rules and the careful modeling of rule-following behavior with enough love that students can identify with them as authority figure.

Children in the third-to-fifth-grade range have a natural interest in the specifics of game rules and an understanding of the role of rules and authority that enables them to brainstorm, discuss, evaluate, select, and over-learn class rules, and to help determine appropriate consequences for rule violations. This process should occur during the first week of school. It can occur through class meetings and/or through interactive instruction that relates class rules to rules and laws within the larger community. This process of dialogue and instruction should be used to promote a sense of student responsibility for order and fairness within the classroom community, should promote a sense of ownership of and commitment to these rules, should address the values that underlie these rules, and should be used as an opportunity to promote critical thinking and moral reasoning.

Whenever possible, the consequences for rule breaking should also be educational via some type of positive-practice or restitutional over-correction. Situations that reveal the need for rules and rule violations provide important teaching opportunities that must not be missed, but discussions and explanations should occur after and not during timeout and/or other negative consequences since combining the two (sociomoral instruction and negative consequences) diminishes the effectiveness of negative consequences.

Since middle and high school students move from teacher to teacher and are predisposed to question rules that reflect debatable social conventions, student involvement in rule making should begin within classrooms and then extend to clusters and the school as a whole via classroom representatives. Students should be encouraged to share what they actually think about rules and should be allowed to question and criticize rules if they are willing to propose alternatives and rationales for their alternatives. Order within middle schools depends on a school-wide discipline system that involves a series of consequences within the classroom, followed by a series of consequences outside, and students should be allowed enough representative input into this system each year that their influence is readily apparent to every student. The latter is true for high school as well, and this translates into real student government.

Teaching Constitutional Principles Experientially

American history is a story of how empowered citizens have slowly extended the constitutionally codified principle of respect to all persons irrespective of sex, race, religion, age, national origin, physical capability, and mental capability. This slow process of "practice being brought in line with principle" is ironic since the authors of the Constitution, and even some of the authors of constitutional Amendments, apparently had the wisdom to infuse basic moral principles into these sacred documents but were unable to see that their discrimination against various groups violated these same moral principles. Today, ignorance about the Constitution, and, in particular, ignorance about the First Amendment, appears to be so widespread that this historical extension of respect to all types of people is in danger of erosion. Many otherwise good and well-informed citizens now call for activities that would force their religious beliefs on persons from other minority faiths and nonreligious persons, and many now call for denying basic freedoms to persons whose actions they find immoral or personally offensive. It may be that only federal judges who have studied the Constitution fully understand and appreciate its moral content, and that the time has come to teach constitutional principles to middle and high school students in a way that will bring about a higher level of understanding and ultimately the preservation of basic freedoms that may be in jeopardy.

Included in Berman's (1993) edited book are descriptions of teachers who have adopted an approach to citizenship and social studies education that involves more student-initiated inquiry and discovery and guides students to a deeper level of understanding of constitutional principles. They commonly achieve this by linking personal and immediate classroom-level social needs with societal-level needs that were addressed by framers of the Constitution, and by cultivating empathy and the capacity to respectfully interact with others whose beliefs they find unacceptable. Craig Beaulieu in Brunswick, Maine, challenges his high school students to establish a democratic classroom with their own rights, rules, and responsibilities (while retaining veto power over actions that violate school guidelines), and he follows this by having students study how the founding fathers debated and constructed the U.S. Constitution. His assumption is that shared power and experiential democracy will cultivate ethical citizenship. The reduction that he has observed in disciplinary problems seems to confirm his assumption.

Kathleen Travers' approach to teaching the Constitution to eighth grade students in Cambridge, Massachusetts, is more elaborate. Her lessons reflect the conviction that the Constitution is relevant to the lives of inner-city students. She begins by piquing the interest of students by starting them on a game without clear rules and by subsequently changing the rules until chaos develops. She follows this with a discussion of different kinds of rules. She then has students translate the Preamble and parts of the first ten Amendments of the Constitution into everyday street language using a special worksheet with phrases and space for explanations. She uses two simulation games including one that places students in the position of having to get rid of all but five amendments. She also has students write a class constitution and has found that they ultimately place in these documents the rights, rules, and procedures that help them avoid using physical force. Her lessons change students' understanding of rules from externally imposed constraints to consensually derived guidelines for membership in a classroom community.

As a contributor to the February 1996 character-education issue of the *ABA Update on Law-Related Education*, I developed a lesson plan that uses sociodrama as a tool for teaching the First Amendment (Vessels, 1996). The plan calls for a socio-dramatization or skit to be preceded by reading the First Amendment, having students explain what they think it means, and highlighting its meaning in a manner consistent with U.S. SupremeCourt decisions and relevant to the lives of high school students. The teacher explains that (1) the Establishment Clause is interpreted to mean that government actions may neither advance nor inhibit religion and must have a secular or civic purpose; (2) the Free Exercise Clause is interpreted to mean that government must allow individuals to express their religious or other beliefs, even in the school, unless there is a compelling reason to prevent them such as a serious disruption of the educational process; and (3) the Free Speech Clause is interpreted to mean students can speak freely provided they do not undermine the school's responsibility to promote respect for authority and traditional social, moral, and democratic values. This lesson is just one of many in this issue that uses instruction about the Constitution and the law as a means of developing prosocial-moral character in youth.

Cooperative Learning

The term "cooperative learning" identifies a group of techniques that gives students the opportunity to work together in pursuit of a common goal and to enhance their social, ethical, and cognitive growth in ways not provided by competitive-individualistic structures and traditional recitation-presentation methods. Cooperative learning methods differ in terms of their emphasis on true collaboration and the sharing of resources and whether they endorse competition and extrinsic rewards, but they commonly provide an alternative to traditional teacher-centered approaches to teaching. They share the key elements of positive interdependence, face-to-face interaction, social skills instruction, individual accountability, and group processing, all of which strengthen group functioning through individual feedback, an analysis of group processes, and open dialogue (Johnson and Johnson, 1994a). They help to build a sense of community and foster the teaching of life skills such as listening, taking the perspective of others, communicating one's thoughts, and resolving conflicts (Lickona, 1991). They foster social consciousness when combined with the more basic strategy of creating a caring community, and they help achieve the goal of balancing an emphasis on self-realization and personal achievement with an emphasis on social-realization and collective achievement (Berman, 1990). Finally, they entail significant decentralization of decision making and require teachers to facilitate learning and expand their focus beyond academics and information transmission (Sharan, 1994).

Various forms of cooperative learning have been researched extensively during the last twenty years, and the results of this research indicate that they (1) foster the development of prosocial behaviors including respect for people from different backgrounds, risk-taking, and mutual encouragement; (2) increase intrinsic motivation; and (3) promote learning and higher-order thinking of students at all ability levels. With respect to the latter, the superiority of cooperative techniques over traditional techniques is most apparent when learning tasks require concept-ualization, problem solving, higher-level thinking, and creative solutions, and when the goals are long-term retention and the capacity to apply what has been learned (Johnson and Johnson, 1992b:122). Ellis and Feldman (1994) contend that cooperative learning promotes the highest levels of thinking and learning because students know that they may have to explain, discuss, and teach what they learn, may have to integrate information collaboratively and may have to engage in sophisticated dialogue to resolve conflicting opinions, explanations, and interpreta-tions, and because they have the opportunity to observe and benefit from the thought processes, encouragement, and feedback of peers.

With the various forms of Student Team Learning (Slavin, 1986, 1990, 1994), team success is only possible if all team members master the objectives or show improvement. Since team success depends on the individual learning of all team members, team members take each other's learning seriously and seek to prepare one another for the quizzes they must take individually. Teams are not in competition, at least in the sense that all or none of the teams may achieve an established criterion and earn rewards. The concepts of team rewards, individual accountability, and equal opportunity for success are central to Student Team Learning methods: "Equal opportunities for success means that what students contribute to their teams is based on their improvement over their own past performance" (Slavin, 1994:4).

In Student Teams-Achievement Divisions (STAD), a form of Student Team Learning, students are assigned to four-member mixed-ability/ethnicity/gender teams. Team members work together to learn material and then take quizzes individually. Team scores reflect the combined individual improvement of team members. Slavin (1994) presents a detailed description of the five components of STAD, along with information about related materials available for purchase. In Teams-Games-Tournaments the STAD procedure is followed except that quizzes are replaced with tournaments wherein students at the same ability/achievement level from different teams and compete for team points at separate tournament tables. Team-Assisted Individualization is used supplementally to teach math in grades three through six. Students on the same team work on units for which they are ready and check each other's work for accuracy.

With the Jigsaw method (Aronson et al., 1978) each student is required to learn or research one part and teach it to teammates. It was originally developed by an interdisciplinary team of people in Austin who wanted to find a way to achieve equity of participation and outcome in desegregated classrooms, and a way to reduce the competition ethos in classrooms. Step one involves the establishment of heterogeneous "home" groups and the introduction of the topic by the teacher. Step two involves dividing "home" groups into "focus" groups. Members of the focus groups work together to study their assigned part or component of the general topic under study by the class as a whole. Step three involves returning to the "home" groups and reporting or sharing what was learned in the focus groups. The final step involves integrating the information through various types of individual, small group, and whole-class activities. Slavin's (1986, 1990) version of Jigsaw essentially combines the original Jigsaw method with the principles of Student Team Learning, a combination that effectively prevents problems created by student variation in terms of motivation and ability. Many other versions have been developed as well.

The Sharans' (1994, 1992) Group Investigation method has been described by some as the most collaborative and cooperative of all cooperative learning strategies. Key elements include investigation, interaction, interpretation, and intrinsic motivation. The investigation phase begins with the posing of a challenging, multifaceted problem by the teacher, and it hinges on both the capacity of students to construct the knowledge they acquire and the capacity of teachers to facilitate student learning. Interaction occurs at all stages of the investigation and depends on basic teamwork and discussion skills. While the inquiry may involve individual efforts, pairs work, small-group work, and methods of investigation chosen by individual students, interpretation involves making sense out of what all members of the "inquiring community" have contributed. The Sharans describe this as a "social-intellectual" process. Intrinsic motivation, the fourth and final element, is apparently viewed as a natural by-product of the student empowerment central to this method.

The Johnsons (1986, 1992b, 1994b) contrast controversy with debate, concurrence seeking, no controversy, and individualistic efforts, and make the convincing case that controversy should be purposefully structured since the desirable presence of intellectual conflict is one of the major reasons cooperative learning promotes higher achievement, higher-level reasoning, greater retention, and greater creativity. They say that conflicts can only be managed constructively within a cooperative context and that it is only when participants clarify their mutual goals and see their long-term relationship as more important than the issue currently in dispute that a constructive solution to conflict is sought. By their definition, controversy exists when one student's ideas differ from another's, when they seek to reach an agreement by advocating opposing points of view through deliberate and assertive but mutually respectful discourse, and when they seek to reconcile their differences by taking the perspective of one another and carefully exploring these perspectives. They list a variety of social skills that are necessary in order for the advocates of opposing positions to reach the best decision possible. The most important of these concerns is the capacity to challenge ideas and reasoning while confirming the competence and personal worth of the person whose ideas and reasoning are being challenged. Others include perspective taking, listening and paraphrasing, maintaining enough objectivity and humility to change one's mind when the information warrants, and simply following the golden rule. They make a good case for teaching conflict resolution and encouraging conflict within caring classroom communities that can effectively allow for structured controversy.

The Child Development Project's approach to cooperative learning is uniquely designed to promote social and ethical development and to teach specific values or virtues such as fairness, respect for diversity, and personal responsibility (Watson et al., 1994). This model is based on basic "constructivist" learning assumptions. It places a high premium on intrinsic motivation and discourages the type of competition and extrinsic rewards found in the Student Team Learning methods developed by Slavin. It teaches social skills and social understanding by increasing children's understanding of and commitment to relevant values (rather than the acquisition of specific behavioral skills), and by helping children see how actions in the group relate to these values. As learning activities are introduced, teachers refer to values such as respect, fairness, and responsibility (set-up and monitoring phases), and through questions and discussion, they help students think about how they can work together in ways consistent with these values (set-up phase) and whether they succeeded in doing so (wrap-up phase) (Watson et al., 1994:143). Taking care not to undermine the students' responsibility for their own learning, teachers use small-group learning and facilitative questions and comments (monitoring phase) to help students construct their understanding of complex social concepts and ethical principles and acquire prosocial skills they will need throughout life.

During the 1996–97 school year, we had the opportunity to visit a CDP school, Hazelwood Elementary in Louisville. We witnessed more classrooms that had cooperative learning, class meetings, and buddy system activities ongoing than those that did not. The type of cooperative learning was, in fact, noncompetitive, and students were all actively engaged and feeling good enough about the experience to explain to me what they were doing. Although we encouraged cooperative learning in our pilot project in Atlanta, during my one hundred and fifty structured observations in classrooms, I saw very few instances of it being used. Apparently people talk about cooperative learning a lot more than they do it, so my suggestion to principals is to require it and to make this a part of your teacher evaluations.

Violence Prevention/Conflict Resolution/Interpersonal Problem Solving/Peer Mediation

Violence prevention, conflict resolution, interpersonal problem solving, and peer mediation identify the various types of programs that deal with intervention in situations where feelings of anger, frustration, and alienation could result in violence. These programs equip students and teachers with skills and techniques that can be used to keep conflict from escalating. They may also prevent future conflict by improved understanding and communication between disputants and by becoming an automatic alternative. Nevertheless, they can be distinguished from programs that proactively prevent conflict, such as comprehensive social skills training programs (which teach many skills other than interpersonal problem solving), intercultural studies, peace education, comparative religious studies, stress reduction, self-esteem building, the development of caring communities within classrooms and schools, and all-encompassing character education programs.

Violence prevention and conflict resolution are relatively general intervention categories that include peer mediation and various other forms of interpersonal problem solving plus many other methods that may eliminate or reduce the seriousness of conflicts without actually solving them: redirecting or distracting disputants; sending them to cooling off areas or into timeout; having them fill out fight forms; offering them choices; restructuring the environment; helping them recognize cues to anger and issue self-instructions that promote control; and seeking to discharge or calm strong feelings and underlying stress through art, physical activity, listening to music, and relaxation exercises. The narrower category of interpersonal problem solving includes conflict mediation by students and/or adults, the use of interpersonal problem solving skills by disputants without the help of mediators, interpersonal problem solving that involves input from disputants and mediators, and classroom instruction prior to or during conflicts that is designed to teach students how to resolve interpersonal conflicts. Anger management includes various forms of training that begin with the assumption that students cannot engage in interpersonal problem solving or any form of rational behavior until they are emotionally ready and can empathize with others.

I Can Problem Solve (Shure, 1992) is a cognitive interpersonal problem-solving model that teaches children how to think, rather than what to think and which teaches a pre-problem-solving vocabulary and pre-problem-solving skills. It also provides specific twenty-minute lessons, which use games, stories, puppets, and role playing, and ongoing teacher-guided interpersonal problem-solving practice within elementary classroom through a multiple-step "dialoguing" process. The Second Step Violence Prevention Curriculum (Committee for Children, 1992; Beland, 1988, 1989) targets pre-K through middle school students and uses a lesson format that addresses empathy, impulse control, and anger management. These models appear complementary in that they teach readiness for problem solving (SSVPC) and problem solving (ICPS). Emotional readiness for inter-personal problem solving and the multi-step process of interpersonal problem solving are best taught within the context of a comprehensive character education program that emphasizes self-control, an awareness of others' feelings, and social skills training in the early grades, along with teacher-led interpersonal problem solving that involves the entire class as conflicts arise, and that introduces formal peer mediation in the third or fourth grade. ICPS and SSVPC lessons are best used as part of a comprehensive approach such as this and not as isolated "add-on" lessons.

Dinwiddie (1994) discusses the use of interpersonal problem solving or teacher-led mediation with young children. She elaborates six basic steps: initiate mediation (approach conflict and make a statement, stop aggressive behavior, neutralize any object of conflict by holding it), gather data (ascertain victim's feelings and aggressor's wants, assure disputants that each will be heard), define the problem (describe disputants feelings by rephrasing; define the situation in mutual terms), generate alternative solutions (gather suggestions from disputants and observers, ask questions and allow children ample time to come up with solutions before offering your own), agree on a solution (rephrase solution when both agree, spell out how the solution will be implemented), and follow through (monitor or assign student monitors and announce successful implementation when this has occurred).

By the end of the third grade, students should understand the basics of interpersonal problem solving and should be introduced to the mediator's facilitative role. Beginning at the third or fourth grade, whole classrooms should receive basic peer mediation training, and students selected to serve as on-call mediators outside the classroom should receive more in-depth training including sociodramatic practice. Specially trained peer mediators should be on-call throughout the day or available during designated hours. Mediations should occur in a special room which is called the Mediation Center, and all mediations should be carefully documented on a contract form signed by the disputants.

The Mediation for Kids training program (Schmidt et al., 1992) provides an activity format for teaching (1) a mediation vocabulary, (2) the rules and unique characteristics of mediation, and (3) the basic steps of peer mediation. The steps are (1) introducing participants, (2) clarifying ground rules (be willing to seek a win-win solution, listen without interrupting, tell the truth, be respectful, stick to your agreement), (3) having disputants tell their story, (4) searching for solutions through questioning, (5) choosing a solution, (6) discussing how future conflicts between disputants can be prevented, and (7) closing with a summary. The Teaching Students to be Peacemakers curriculum (Johnson et al., 1993) adds confidentiality as a ground rule. The authors of this model explain that disputants enter mediation voluntarily and are guided by a neutral mediator through a basic negotiation process that involves having disputants (1) state what they want, (2) state how they feel, (3) demonstrate their understanding of the other person's wants, feelings, and reasons, (4) invent plans for resolving the problem, and (5) choose one on which they can agree.

Interpersonal problem solving and peer mediation were not identified as primary strategies for our project in Atlanta, but most schools had some familiarity because the system mandated training. In the five schools where our program was implemented, peer mediators had been trained and some whole-class instruction had occurred. In spite of this, during our numerous forty-five minute structured observations in fifty-five classrooms, I did not record a single time a student voluntarily functioned as a mediator. I observed many interpersonal conflicts, so there was ample opportunity to act as mediators. It is tempting to conclude from this that conflict resolution/peer mediation initiatives do not work apart from other efforts that give children the will to be peaceful by staying out of conflicts and keeping them from escalating into violence. We witnessed a significant drop in physical violence at the school that had the biggest problem, so perhaps this foundation is all that we need. Further research should help answer this question.

Stimulating Critical and Creative Thinking

Educators have talked for years about Bloom's (1956) taxonomy and how important it is to teach students to think critically and creatively, but few teachers make this a high priority in their lesson planning. My view is that ethical dilemmas or value conflicts are novel and complex problems that require creative and critical thinking skills, and that we cannot expect students to reason ethically and autonomously if we do not put them in situations where they must think on "higher levels" without a road map. Many social problems also demand novel solutions and thus creative and critical thought. Without attempting to become an expert on creative or critical thinking, the average teacher can facilitate ethical development by planning activities and asking questions that encourage various elements of creative thought such as flexibility, divergent thinking, originality, fluency or uninhibited brainstorming, and elaboration, and that require students to apply (apply, classify, organize, relate, transfer), analyze (analyze, categorize, compare, contrast, detect), synthesize (synthesize, combine, derive, formulate, originate, produce), and evaluate (evaluate, appraise, assess, judge, validate) and not just know and understand. For teachers who wish to do more in this area, I recommend the Critical Thinking Press as a valuable source of instructional materials for stimulating all types of higher-level thinking including creative thinking (Critical Thinking Books and Software, P.O. Box 448, Pacific Grove, CA 93950-0448; 408-393-3288/800-458-4849; ct@criticalthinking.com; www.criticalthinking.com). They have materials that are both subject specific and "across the curriculum," and materials that are appropriate for all age levels. All have been critically reviewed by educational journals and magazines.

Creative Arts Activities

Character growth can be enhanced through a variety of individual and group art projects, particularly drama where original plays on character themes offer relevant content as well as group problem solving processes that promote social growth and provide related teachable moments. I will not attempt to describe a wide range of possible uses of the arts, but I want to describe a junior high school music writing project which was brought to my attention by Kristin Fink who coordinates the statewide character education project in Utah. It was the brainchild of Michael Packham, music instructor at Syracuse Junior High School in Davis County, Utah. It occurred in response to the Values Booklet that all educators in Utah received from the Governor's Commission on Centennial Values asking them to work with values in their classrooms. Packham's general music students composed original songs inspired by social values. Students worked in cooperative groups and used software for sequencing (Mater Tracks Pro and Band-In-the-Box) and music notation (Finale), and Macintosh recording equipment. The teacher guided them through the steps of writing lyrics for the chorus; writing a rhythm to the chorus; writing pitches while remembering the importance of balance between repetition, contrast of ideas, and a climax; writing lyrics for a verse stressing the day-to-day application of the value; writing rhythm and pitch for the verse; writing chords for the melody; using the computer to sequence a recording (select accompaniment from the software library, add melody, decide on timbre from software selection); and performing the song. One product of this project is a song about integrity entitled, Picture it Purple:

Picture it purple, a promise we can keep. Picture it purple, the blessings we all reap. Purple is integrity, the flag to be unfurled. Purple is integrity; let's color all the world—color all the world. Once you make a promise, keep it to the end. You'll show integrity with nothing left to mend. So give your word, and help the world. Be the one to help the flag of promise be unfurled. (Amber Peck, Sarah Morrison, and Amy Walker, 1997).

Sociodrama

Sociodrama is a structured group role play technique that can be used within any classroom to examine conflicts and to generate possible solutions through unrehearsed skits. The problems or conflicts dramatized should be of concern to all students. This technique is recommended for use with students in grades three through twelve.

Step One: The process should begin with probing questions that will generate facts, provoke student thought, and lead to a problem definition.

Step Two: Students should then be told that you want them to participate in an unrehearsed skit to help find ways of solving the problem. No indication should be given to the direction or form the resolution should take.

Step Three: Assign characters (protagonists). These characters should be given a general idea of the scene to be enacted. For grades two or three and up, the characters should be asked to take a few minutes together to prepare.

Step Four: While the characters are away, ask the observers to look at the upcoming drama from the perspective of one of the characters, a relative of one of the characters, or any other person or type of person whose perspective is relevant and could help resolve the conflict.

Step Five: When the characters return have them briefly describe the setting and characters and then begin the skit. The skit may last five to twenty minutes and can be moved along if necessary by prompts and open-ended questions. The action should be cut when the actors fall out of role. You can use soliloquy following the initial skit and before a discussion about the skit. This involves having the characters share their inner feelings and thoughts while sitting or walking alone and thinking aloud. Each character in the skit can also be assigned a double or doubles who represent the good self, bad self, future self, past self, and so forth. Input from these doubles can be obtained (1) through brief "freezes" or "stop actions," (2) by having these doubles jump into the skit and take the place of the primary character, or (3) by having them comment on the situation after the skit. Characters can also be asked to reverse roles during the skit and repeat or continue the role-play dialogue.

Step Six: Lead a discussion beginning with the observations of students from their assigned role or perspective and then moving into the generation of solution ideas. You can use a brainstorming technique if appropriate, and it may be useful to follow the initial skit with another, depending on what the discussion yields.

Student Disciplinary Panels

Student disciplinary panels are an informal counterpart to formal teen courts (to be discussed later). Although sometimes called courts within the schools where they operate, student disciplinary panels do not accept referrals from judges, social workers, and other agency representatives outside the school as do teen courts. Referrals are made by school staff, and students have the option of going through the traditional disciplinary process of being referred to the principal or assistant principal. Students do not function as attorneys, jurors, and so forth, as they do in teen courts. They merely serve on a panel of judges after receiving the necessary training. In middle schools at least, these panels often include both students and adults, but I do not view this form of adult participation as necessary if students have the option of going through regular disciplinary channels, and if adult oversight and standards for matching sentences and offenses are provided. Proponents of student disciplinary panels contend that most office referrals can be handled by student disciplinary panels.

I recommend training all students for panel service through social studies classes coupled with in-depth follow-up training for students selected for panel service. This follow-up training should focus on learning how to match the consequences to the particular offense and familiarizing trainees with the many types of consequences that are available, such as apologies, restitution, relevant service learning, research projects, in-school suspension, detention, school maintenance work, and so forth. Care must be taken to prevent student disciplinary panels from being exclusively comprised of students from "good" cliques such as the high achievers and students who never break the rules. The best panel members are creative, intelligent, and admired students who have a history of inappropriate behavior but have made a turnaround that has lasted for at least a few months. Panel members should be taught a very formal process that includes summons forms, hearing record forms, court contracts, and a checklist for panel members to use as they evaluate the appropriateness of the sentence they are considering.

Class Meetings

Lickona's (1991) book includes a chapter on class meetings that clearly presents the rationale for class meetings as well as a detailed explanation of how it can be used and the various forms it can take. First with respect to rational, he stated that the class meeting reverses the neglected educational principle of involving students in making decisions about their lives within the classroom, a point Dewey (1968) has emphasized. Lickona further stated:

The class meeting provides an experience in democracy, making students full partners in creating the best possible classroom. It changes the dynamics and deepens the bond between teacher and class, enhances the teacher's influence as model and mentor at the same time that it enlarges the role and responsibilities of students. In the process, it fosters the moral growth of the group and its individual members. (Lickona, 1991:138)

Lickona described the class meeting as a teacher-led, student-led, or teacher/student-led meeting of the whole class that (1) emphasizes discussion among classmates, (2) occurs in a circle to promote eye-to-eye contact, and (3) occurs at regularly scheduled times and in response to special needs for ten to thirty minutes depending on age, topic, and student interest. He listed as goals for class meetings the development of (1) respectful listening and perspective taking, (2) self-esteem through self-expression that is valued by others, (3) a moral community that will support and nurture good character, and (4) skills and attitudes necessary to participate as a citizen in a democracy. He encourages beginning by using activities that help students get to know one another. He lists twenty different kinds of class meetings: good news ("Who has some good news to share?"), sentence completion go-rounds, appreciation time ("Who would you like to appreciate?"), complimenting of individuals by the group, goal setting, rule making, rule evaluating, stage setting (preparation for activities), feedback and evaluation of individual and group activities, reflections on learning, student presentations, problem solving, academic issues, classroom improvements, follow-up on changes, planning, concepts ("What is a friend?" "What is conscience?"), moral delimits, suggestion box/class business, and critique of class meetings.

Lickona offered suggestions based on the experiences of teachers who have acquired expertise with class meetings: make a good circle, signal rule violations nonverbally if possible, use a talk ticket that is passed around, model and reinforce good listening, encourage students to listen by asking them to repeat or paraphrase what others have said, encourage interaction with good questioning, use verbal structuring to help students disagree and challenge respectfully, encourage everyone to participate, use sentence starters, assign pairs and encourage them to discuss for a minute or two and then share with the whole group, assign buddies to help with rule adherence, have students who are speaking call on the next when finished, assign roles that will promote meeting success, record ideas, and evaluate meetings. Many other suggestions for using class meetings are described in *Ways We Want Our Class to Be* (Developmental Studies Center, 1996). The DSC also has an overview video and several other videos that show different types of class meetings at different age levels. The teachers that I work with in Atlanta have found them to be valuable and anxiety reducing.

Class meetings can be devoted to whole-class interpersonal problem solving that uses the ICPS dialoguing process or sociodrama, which is a more elaborate group-role-play technique which seeks to find solutions to interpersonal conflicts (see other sections of this chapter for more detail about these techniques). Teachers should use discretion in deciding what interpersonal problems to address in class meetings. If the feelings of students involved in a problem or dispute have become intense and/or if any of the students involved in the conflict are emotionally unstable, extremely aggressive, or subject to extreme psychosocial stressors, one-on-one counseling or teacher guidance, small group counseling restricted to individuals with the same problem, formal peer or teacher-led mediation, parent conferences and consultation, family counseling, and social work services may be appropriate alternatives to a class meeting. Teachers need to realize that although they are not highly trained group counselors, they are guiding a process of community building (not therapy) that is greatly enhanced if they have some familiarity with basic group leadership techniques (e.g., paraphrasing, asking open-ended questions, dealing with blocking behaviors, focusing attention back upon the highly critical person). This familiarity can be achieved through reading, taking a group counseling course, having the school counselor do an inservice, having the school counselor or another skilled teacher co-lead class meetings, or joining an adult growth group or therapy group.

Participatory Student Government and Class Captains

Student governments have been used in many ways for many years, but more often than not they do not have the power to make important decisions, and they typically include only the brightest and most popular students. Lickona listed various types of student councils, including special focus councils for cafeteria and playground management, community service, and so forth, separate councils for grades one through three and four through six, and community meetings in which all students of a grade meet with the principal to discuss issues. He emphasized the natural link between class meetings and input at council meetings.

My favorite approach to student government is the student-captain idea that Wardell Sims initiated at Campbell Elementary in Atlanta in 1996. He had each class select a captain for the week with an identifying cap, and every student eventually served in this role. Captains had specific responsibilities, including bringing their classes to order in the morning in a structured fashion and serving as monitors when their classes moved through the halls. Mr. Sims personally oriented captains on Mondays as a group and did extensive teaching about responsibility, leadership, and respect. He told me he believes students must feel empowered, must experience the leadership role, and must participate in decisions that affect their lives if they are to become responsible citizens.

Adoptions of Families by Classrooms/Schools

As described by the Child Development Project in the book *At Home in Our Schools* (1994), Adopt-A-Family programs encourage everyone within the school community to attend and respond to the special needs of others. The authors suggest having each classroom choose a needy family in collaboration with social service agencies if needed. Students within each class then develop a plan for assisting this family throughout the school year. As with all the activities described in the CDP book, they encourage communication with parents about the project and family involvement.

School-to-School and Class-to-Class Intercultural Exchanges

The "internet" has provided a vehicle through which students from different parts of the country and world can communicate. The use of this technology as a bridge between cultures will hopefully expand and become commonplace, but effective intercultural exchanges need not use computer technology. Long-distance exchanges can be just as meaningful and educational via conventional mail, particularly if art is used to overcome language barriers. The most meaningful exchanges at present are those that break down racial and/or subcultural isolation and polarization. These exchanges can even occur between schools within states, cities, and school systems.

Foster's (1989) article describes an exchange between a class in a predominantly white suburban school and a class from the same elementary grade in a predominantly black urban school. The first contact was a joint field trip followed by each class visiting the other's school. The two classes worked together on projects and activities during the year, and each student was assigned a pen pal. Even the PTOs exchanged invitations and encouraged cross-over attendance. This type of inter-cultural exchange is well suited for schools in or near large cities.

Eris Velma Morgan, a teacher at Fain Elementary in Atlanta, added greatly to the character education effort at her school by independently planning and carrying out a multi-year intercultural exchange project with students and staff from Morvant Anglican School in her native country of Trinidad, West Indies. Trinidad lies eight miles off the coast of Venezuela in the Caribbean Sea. Ms. Morgan described her elaborate intercultural exchange project as a creative/interactive teaching/learning model, and her impetus was a desire to give back to her home community and country, which provided her basic education as a child. Spanning miles of ocean and land to bring together students from very different but alike worlds became a personal mission for Ms. Morgan and, in the spirit of community and character growth, she included as many students from Fain as possible.

Many students from all grade levels were involved in the intercultural exchange during the 1996–97 school year as a pen pal for one of the students from Morvant Anglican School. The students in Ms. Morgan's classroom who had looped with her were much more deeply involved as reflected by (1) the exchange of letters, videos, poems, photographs, and gifts; (2) lessons in geography (e.g., finding Trinidad on the map), social studies and art (e.g., learning about aspects of the culture such the native cuisine, the calypso, the annual carnival, and steelband music), and math (e.g., learning about differences in currency and how to calculate mileage; (3) planning for and helping to obtain funds for the first trip for Atlanta elementary students out of the country; (4) making the trip and participating in the annual "Carnival" celebration; (5) sharing their experience with other students after their return home; and (6) preparing to host the reciprocal visit of Morvant Anglican Academy students to Fain during the 1997–98 school year. Obviously all Fain students will learn from this visit of students from Trinidad, and they will have an opportunity to display a variety of character qualities as hosts for this visit.

Ms. Morgan made a decision in 1994 to stay with her first grade students until the end of their fifth grade year, and it was when they were fourth graders in 1997 that they finally made this historic trip. She wrote and received a grant that helped with her daily instructional activities; solicited donations from several different corporations in Atlanta (including BellSouth, Kodak, Coca Cola, and IBM) that were used to finance the trip; and communicated her intentions so persuasively that many community leaders and school administrators stepped forward to give her the assistance she needed, including Congressman C.T. Martin and Congressman John Lewis. Her students certainly benefitted from the class activities and direct contact with children from another culture but also from the courage, dedication, respect, and persistence she modeled and continues to model. I have benefitted from knowing her and want to thank her for assisting me with this brief description of this elaborate intercultural exchange project.

Ceremonies and Traditions

The values of all cultures are transmitted in part through traditions, and, in particular, traditional ceremonies and rituals. Kirschenbaum (1995) describes how classroom teachers and school staffs can create their own ceremonies and rituals to help teach values and morality. With respect to classrooms, he discusses routine teacher inquiries each morning to see if students need anything; designated times for expressing appreciation to others and opinions/editorials; classroom theme songs about caring, friendship, and making the world a better place; and routine applause for when students volunteer, perform a service, accomplish a difficult task, and take a risk, speak to the group. I know a first grade teacher in Atlanta who has her students pat themselves on the back when they have done well as a group, and has them clap for one another when they have performed well individually. Jackie Woods, the Principal at Blalock Elementary in Atlanta has the students in her school routinely greeting guests who enter their classrooms by saying in chorus, "Good morning (name of guest); we're so glad to see you today."

Teachers can reduce student inhibitions during appreciation time through modeling and the use of sentence stems and preliminary activities that get students prepared. Opinion time can be facilitated through the use of a lectern, a microphone, videotaping equipment, a large cutout that makes students appear to be on television, a designated student news reporter who asks students about their opinions, and a current event or occurrence that will be of interest to students.

All schools have many traditions created through repetition and emphasis. School-wide rituals and ceremonies might include morning inspirationals on the public address system, award ceremonies for students whose behavior has provided an ideal example of the virtue of the month, homecoming days for distinguished alumni, family heritage days, grandpersons' day, drug awareness days, special fund-raisers, you are my hero projects, multicultural days, repeating pledges, school community gardens, holiday programs, Martin Luther King holiday activities that stress peace and nonviolence, field days, and cross-grade buddies programs. For schools just beginning their formal character education program, existing traditions should be studied to see if they reflect the values or virtues the school wants to teach. Additions and deletions may be needed.

Expanding Extracurricular Programs

Suburban school systems typically have a wide variety or full range of traditional extracurricular sports and clubs available to students, but this is the exception to the rule in urban school systems. Often the excuse is that it is not safe to be out in the neighborhood or even in the schools after dark, but the truth of the matter is that teachers are often too tired and demoralized to offer after-school sports and recreational activities, are not expected or encouraged to do so because such activities viewed as "extra" instead of "co-curricular," do not get the administrative and community support needed when they make an effort, assume that other providers of recreational opportunities in the community meet student needs, and often do not appreciate its importance. Schools should be places where children want to be (both during and after regular school hours) because they experience success and have a close relationship with adults and other students. Extracurricular activities greatly increase the chances that all students will perceive the school this way, particularly if all students participate and experience success.

A variety of extracurricular activities and community support for each activity will help guarantee enjoyment and success for every student. Every elementary and middle school should have several sports teams for girls and boys and a variety of arts activities such as plays, preparation for parades and shows, musical groups, dance groups, and visual arts clubs. Until recently, the Atlanta Public Schools held an arts and physical education festival each year for three days at Underground Atlanta during which every school offered performances that involved many students and were both creative and well prepared due to many months of after-school rehearsal.

School Service Projects and School Chores

Every student should bear some type of routine responsibility for the school's operation, such as classroom maintenance chores (e.g., cleaning chalkboards, washing cafeteria tables, watering plants), instructional aide chores (e.g., grading papers, passing out materials), and school operation chores (e.g., morning announcements, grounds cleanup, turning in attendance reports). Students should also be encouraged to serve others within the school in a manner that goes beyond regular chores. Individual students can be encouraged to apply or run for a limited number of positions as cross-grade tutors (as opposed to buddies), cross-grade adopters of very needy children, special teacher assistants, patrol guards, student government members, school store operators, escorts for visitors to the school, new-student welcoming committee members, school office helpers, peer mediators, teen-court staff members, staff members of the school newspaper, and gardeners for the school garden.

Classes should be expected to plan and carry out a school service project each year, such as litter pickup, mural painting on the school hallway walls, making or purchasing posters that support character building goals, fund-raising projects for the school, fund-raising for needy students in the school, landscaping outside the school, providing cross-grade tutoring after school, doing custodial chores that regular custodians do not have time for such as washing windows and doors, helping a beginning teacher, and decorating for Christmas and other holidays.

EXPERIENCES WITHIN THE LARGER COMMUNITY

Service Learning

In order for students to develop empathy, caring, and sense of social responsibility, they need experience in face-to-face helping relationships (as opposed to indirect service to others performed behind the scenes and advocacy, which are worthwhile but more limited in terms of growth potential) and need to contribute regularly to the well being of others and their community (Berman, 1990; Lickona, 1991). These experiences should be provided at all grade levels and in a developmentally appropriate sequence that emphasizes service in the classroom and school in the early grades and more and more service to the local community and society as a whole as students move into the upper elementary grades and beyond (Schine, 1997). Community service experiences should occur in conjunction with direct teaching that promotes empathy, reflection, and a clear understanding of how citizens should feel, think, and act in a various social situations; that is, it needs to be "service learning" and not merely service that may not involve learning or service which fails to promote social, ethical, and intellectual development (Kendall, 1991).

Berman (1990) encouraged this special form of community service (service learning) by recommending that opportunities for community service should be combined with other instructional components such as (1) developing the social skills, group problem-solving skills, and higher-level thinking skills needed to work effectively with others to solve serious problems; (2) giving students the opportunity to participate in meaningful decision making in classrooms and schools and to help one another; and (3) teaching students about the interdependence of people and groups of people within communities on all levels from the classroom to the world. He viewed community service as one of six components that together produce citizens who are aware of social problems and want to resolve them and can resolve them, that is, socially conscious and empowered citizens who view their membership within the community as significant.

The K-12 *Standing Tall* curriculum published by the Giraffe Project (1995–97) provides an interesting format for community service experiences, one that maximizes the educational value of such experiences for children of all ages. Students first learn about others ("Giraffes") who have "stuck their necks out" for others; next they search for Giraffes in their community and world; finally, they participate in the planning and implementation of meaningful service projects that give them the opportunity to be caring, courageous, and responsible like the Giraffes they learned about through stories or discovered through search activities. The Giraffe Project also publishes: *The Giraffe Project Handbook: A Guide to Effective Community Service and Social Action*; *The Giraffe News*; *and the Giraffe Gazette* (P.O. Box 759, Langley, WA 98260; 360-221-0757; office@giraffe.org; http://www.giraffe.org/giraffe/).

I strongly recommend *Standing Tall* for elementary and middle schools, but there are other good resource books including (1) *The Generator: National Journal of Service Leadership* (NYLC, 1910 West County Road B, Roseville, MN 55113; 612-631-3672; NYLCUSA@aol.com); (2) *Wingspread: Principles of Good Practice for Combining Service and Learning* (The Johnson Foundation, Inc., Racine, WI 53401); (3) *The Kid's Guide To Service Projects, The Kid's Guide to Social Action, Kids With Courage*, and *Kid Stories: Biographies of 20 Young People You'd Like to Know* (Free Spirit Publishing, 400 First Ave. North, Suite 616-61Y, Minneapolis, MN 55401; 800-735-7323); and others from the Global Classroom (P.O. Box 584, Williston, VT 05495; www.globalclassroom.com; 800-211-5142).

The National Service Learning Cooperative Clearinghouse (R-290 Vocational and Technical Education Bldg., 1954 Buford Ave., St. Paul, MN 55108; 800-808-SERV; serve@maroon.tc.umn.edu; http://www.nicsl.coled.umn.edu) has a list of videos that includes information about content and distributors. Several videos on the list are published by the National Youth Leadership Council (see above). The Council of Chief State School Officers also provides service learning publications including the *Service Learning Planning and Resource Guide* (One Massachusetts Ave., NW, Suite 700, Washington, D.C. 20001; 202-336-7016). The Kid's Alliance for the Protection of the Environment publishes *Hands On,* which is a newspaper written by kids (P.O. Box 307, Austin, TX 78767; 512-476-2273). Learn and Serve America, the K-12 branch of the Corporation for National Service Resources, is another useful resource in Washington, D.C. (1201 New York Avenue, NW, Washington, D.C. 20525; 202-606-5000 ext. 136). Finally, the National Helpers Network is based in the heart of New York City (245 Fifth Avenue, Suite 1705, New York, NY 10016; 212-670-2482). Resources such as these are plentiful and provide many ideas about specific types of service projects.

The type of community service you select is not as important as making sure that students see what they are doing as important, and doing what you can to help students gradually acquire the intrinsic motivation to help the less fortunate and serve their community in many ways. Many types of community service projects are possible, including waste recycling, litter pick-up, nursing home and hospital visitations, money collections for the homeless and people needing surgery they cannot afford, collecting money for organizations like the Red Cross, collecting and sending items to victims of disasters, donating clothes to the Salvation Army, working in soup kitchens and homeless shelters, donating old toys to the poor at Christmas, painting unsightly fences and walls, buying groceries for the elderly and handicapped, helping with campaigns, insulating the homes of the poor and elderly who cannot afford to heat their homes, putting up billboards which convey anti-drug or anti-violence messages, helping children in the neighborhood with homework, doing volunteer work in day-care centers and libraries, calling lonely elderly people who live alone and have little family contact, participating in protests against organizations that are harming the environment, and planting flowers and trees. The involvement of students in service-learning projects is critical to character development, and I strongly encourage their inclusion in your character education program. I also encourage principals to make them mandatory in every classroom since many teachers will not take the initiative for the first time in the absence of this type of incentive.

Teen Courts

Teen courts are real courts established by juvenile court systems, police departments, school districts, probation departments, or some combination of these four agencies. They allow teens to learn about (1) laws and legal procedures, (2) why society needs rules, and (3) good citizenship (Williamson and Knepper, 1995). Proponents believe offering adolescents who belong to delinquency-prone groups the opportunity to make contact with those who choose law-abiding behavior throws peer pressure in reverse. Teens who have been referred to the teen court by juvenile court judges, social workers, school administrators, police officers, and probation officers for minor crimes including shoplifting, drug use, and minor assault can avoid being sentenced in a regular court if they admit their offense, accept a sentence from the teen jury, and complete the sentence. In some states and communities, a referral to teen court can only be made following a finding of guilt or a guilty plea. Teen juries typically do not determine guilt or innocence, but they issue sentences that often include community service, workshop attendance, counseling, and jury duty. Teen courts are administered by an adult coordinator who recruits and trains student jurors, attorneys, clerks, bailiffs, and other participants from high schools. Only the judge is an adult. Teen courts have been established using middle and high school students, but I discourage their use at the middle school level in a form other than disciplinary panels within schools.

Support for Young Parents and Parents-To-Be

Teachers and other professionals who provide services in impoverished areas, whether urban or rural, share the view that many and perhaps most children enter preschool and kindergarten programs with social, behavioral, developmental, physical, and emotional problems that are a direct result of mothers, particularly young single mothers, not knowing how to be effective parents. Their lack of effective care begins prenatally in many cases and often involves inadequate nurturance and relevant pre-academic stimulation, disciplinary techniques that reduce empathy and caring and increase aggression, and poor models for language and social responsibility. Parenting curriculums in the schools will eventually produce results, and parenting classes for adults may reach a few, but what is really needed are significant others from within the family and neighborhood community who can convey a few very basic principles and techniques, particularly principles of behavior management.

The most common problem resulting from parental incompetence and the one that has the most direct relevance to character development is the prevalence of authoritarian as opposed to authoritative discipline (Baumrind, 1973). Sears and colleagues (1957) found that parents who were both permissive and punitive had more aggressive children than parents who were either or neither. Baldwin (1948) found that children from families that had democracy without control were often cruel and disobedient, while those with control without democracy lacked initiative and an intrinsic sense of responsibility. Authoritarian parenting as defined by Baumrind combines high control with low communication (and thus low democracy), while authoritative parenting combines high control and high expectation with clear communication and nurturance, thereby producing more kind and cooperative children. Damon (1988:58) provides a clear explanation of the high-control dimension of authoritative parenting and later contrasts this with the coercive harshness of authoritarian parents who satisfy their egocentric needs through dominance and permissive parents who avoid discipline and indulge in sentimental overprotection:

Authoritative parents produce socially responsible children for a number of reasons. First, these parents support the child's natural empathetic responses by explicitly confronting children about actions that may be harmful to others. Second, they consistently enforce their commands, thus demonstrating their decisive commitment to these commands. Third, they are direct and honest about their commands rather than indirect and manipulative. Fourth, these parents communicate to their children a general norm requiring obedience to authority, along with the sense that good behavior (and the child's identity as a "good" child) requires compliance with legitimate authority. Fifth, their consistent use of parental authority makes them attractive role models for their children. (Damon, 1988:88)

The distinctions between authoritative parenting and the other two forms is simple and can be easily communicated to all parents; however, corresponding disciplinary action may not occur due to habits, childhood models, identity problems, parenting stress, and personality problems that present formidable obstacles. One key to maximizing the number of parents who adopt the authoritative approach is to have persons with whom parents and parents-to-be can identify to make early contact, preferably by visiting them in their homes every few weeks to present and review a few basic cornerstones of effective parenting and to address problems that have emerged. It may be advisable to include a Headstart person as part of this team in communities where this program operates and to include a grandmother and mother and father who are about the same age as the parents or parents-to-be and whose baby is a little older thus guaranteeing recent, relevant experiences. If a professional is included on the visitation team, it should be someone from an organization that is established in the neighborhood, such as a church leader or an employee from National Families in Action, Families First, or a local mental health center. The role of professionals should be restricted to keeping the visitation team functional and educating them rather than being members of the visitation team.

Expanding Community Recreational and Instructional Programs

Perhaps the greatest contribution communities can make to character building programs is the provision of many different types of recreational and/or instructional activities for children and adolescence. It is no coincidence that communities that do not provide this have higher rates of crime and teen pregnancy. If necessary, schools need to make their facilities available to local governments and other groups that have the will and the personnel but not the facilities to provide the opportunities they are capable of providing. Expanding opportunities within communities should begin with structured communication among school officials, other government agencies such as police departments and recreation departments, business leaders, and church leaders. They should develop a long-term strategic plan for the community and explore the possibility of cooperative ventures. All students should be involved in some type of activity outside of school, such as little league, Girl Scouts, and midnight basketball. Their options are limited only by the skills and interest of citizens in the community.

REFERENCES

Angell, C. S. (1996). *Celebrations Around the World: A Multicultural Handbook*. Golden, CO: Fulcrum Publishing.

Archibald, G., Berg, S., Stirling, D. and McKay, L. (1995). *How to PREP*. St. Louis, MO: Cooperating School Districts.

Aronson, E., Blaney, N., Stephan, C., Sikes, J. and Snapp, M. (1978). *The Jigsaw Classroom*. Beverly Hills, CA: Sage Publications.

Baker, M. O. (1989). *What would you do? Developing and/or applying ethical standards, A1 & B1*. Pacific Grove, CA: The Critical Thinking Press.

Baldwin, A. (1948). Socialization and the parent-child relationship. *Child Development*, 19, 127–36.

Baumrind, D. (1973). The development of instrumental competence through socialization. In A. D. Pick (Ed.), *Minnesota Symposium on Child Psychology (Vol 7)*. Minneapolis: University of Minnesota Press.

Baumrind, D. (1988). Rearing competent children. In W. Damon (Ed.), *Child Development Today and Tomorrow*. San Francisco: Jossey-Bass.

Beland, K. (1988). *Second Step: Grades 1–3*. Seattle, WA: Committee for Children.

Beland, K. (1989). *Second Step: Grades 4–5*. Seattle, WA: Committee for Children.

Berman, S. (1990). Educating for social responsibility. *Educational Leadership*, November, 75–80.

Berman, S. (1983). *Perspectives: A Teaching Guide to Concepts of Peace*. Cambridge, MA: Educators for Social Responsibility.

Berman, S. and LaFarge, P. (1993). *Promising Practices in Teaching Social Responsibility*. Albany, NY: SUNY.

Bloom, B. S. and Associates (Eds) (1956). *Taxonomy of Educational Objectives I: Cognitive Domain*. New York: McKay.

Branch, R., Goodwin, Y. and Gualtieri, J. (1994). Making classroom instruction culturally pluralistic. *Educational Forum*, 58 (1), 57–70.

Bryk, A. and Driscoll, M. (1988). *The School As Community: Theoretical Foundations, Contextual Influences, and Consequences for Students and Teachers*. Madison, WI: National Center on Effective Secondary Schools.

Center for Learning (1993). *Creating A Values-Based Reading Program*. Center Ridge, OH: Center for Learning Press.

Charney, R. S. (1992). *Teaching children to care: Management in the responsive classroom*. Greenfield, MA: Northeastern Foundation for Children.

Committee for Children, (1992). *Second Step: A Violence Prevention Curriculum: Preschool-Kindergarten Teacher's Guide*. Seattle, WA: Author.

Damon, W. (1988). *The Moral Child*. New York: The Free Press.

Damon, W. (1995). *Greater Expectations*. New York: The Free Press.

Developmental Studies Center (1994). *Reading, Thinking, and Caring (K-3) and Reading for Real (4-8)*. Oakland, CA: Author.

Developmental Studies Center (1994). *At Home in Our Schools*. Oakland, CA: Author.

Developmental Studies Center (1996). *That's My Buddy*. Oakland, CA: Author.

Developmental Studies Center (1996). *Ways We Want Our Class to Be*. Oakland, CA: Author.

Dewey, J. (1968). *Problems of Men*. New York: Greenwood.

Dinwiddie, S. (1994). The saga of Sally, Sammy, and the red pen: facilitating children's social problem solving. *Young Children*, July, 13–19.

Durell, A. (1990). *The Big Book for Peace*. New York: Dutton Children's Books.

Duvall, L. (1996). *Respecting Our Differences: A Guide to Getting Along in a Changing World.* Minneapolis, MN: Free Spirit Publishing, Inc.

Egan, K. (1986). *Teaching as story telling: An alternative approach to teaching and curriculum in the elementary school.* Chicago: The University of Chicago Press.

Ellis, E. and Feldman, R. (1994). Creating "thought-full" classrooms: Fostering cognitive literacy via cooperative learning and integrated strategies instruction. In S. Sharan (Ed.), *Handbook of Cooperative Learning Methods.* Westport, CT: Greenwood Publishing Group.

Field, C. W. and Weiss, J. S. (1987). *Values in Selected Children's Books of Fiction and Fantasy.* Hamden, CT: Library Professional Publications.

Fletcher, R. (1986). *Teaching Peace: Skills for Living in a Global Society.* New York: Harper-Collins.

Foster, L. (1989). Breaking down racial isolation. *Educational Leadership*, 47 (2), 76–77.

Gillard, M. (1996). *Story Teller Story Teacher: Discovering the Power of Story for Teaching and Living.* Stenhouse Publishers.

Ginsberg, R. and Thompson, T. (1992). Dilemmas and solutions regarding principal evaluation. *Peabody Journal of Education*, 68 (1), 58–74.

Giraffe Project (1995). *Standing Tall.* Langley, WA: Author.

Goldstein, A., Sprafkin, R., Gershaw, N. and Klein, P. (1980). *Skillstreaming the Adolescent.* Champaign, IL: Research Press.

Goldstein, A. and Glick, B. (1987). *Aggression Replacement Training.* Champaign, IL: Research Press.

Green, T. (1984). The formation of conscience in an age of technology. *American Journal of Education*, Nov., 1–38.

Gresham, F. and Nagle, R. (1982). Social skills training with children: Responsiveness to modeling and coaching as a function of peer orientation. *Journal of consulting and clinical psychology*, 18, 718–29.

Harris, V. (1991). Multicultural curriculum: African American children's literature. *Young Children*, Jan., 37–44.

Haynes, C. (1994). *Finding Common Ground.* Nashville, TN: The Freedom Forum, First Amendment Center.

Heartwood Institute (1995). *An Ethics Curriculum for Children.* Pittsburgh, PA: Author.

Hillis, M. (1994). Multicultural education and curriculum transformation. *Educational Forum*, 58 (1), 50–60.

Hodgin, D. E., Holloway, L., Knoderer, L. and Mendenhall, G. (1997). School improvement planning teams initiate character education into the curriculum in metropolitan district of Lawrence Township. In P. F. Vincent (Ed.), *Promising Practices in Character Education.* Chapel Hill, NC: Character Development Group.

Hogan, R., Curphy, G. and Hogan, J. (1994). What we know about leadership: effectiveness and personality. *American Psychologist*, 49 (6), 493–504.

Hutchins, W. (1917). *Children's Code of Morals for Elementary Schools.* Washington, D.C.: Character Education Institute. (available at the Library of Congress)

Jasmine, J. (1995). *Addressing Diversity in the Classroom.* Westmister, CA: Teacher Created Materials, Inc.

Johnson, D. and Johnson, R. (1992a). *Creative Controversy: Intellectual Challenge in the Classroom.* Edina, MN: Interaction Book Company.

Johnson, D. and Johnson, R. (1992b). Encouraging thinking through constructive controversy. In N. Davidson and T Worsham (Eds.), *Enhancing Thinking Through Cooperative Learning.* New York: Teachers College Press.

Johnson, D. and Johnson, R. (1994a). Learning together. In S. Sharan (Ed.), *Handbook of*

Cooperative Learning Methods. Westport, CT: Greenwood Publishing Group.

Johnson, D. and Johnson, R. (1994b). Structuring academic controversy. In S. Sharan (Ed.), *Handbook of Cooperative Learning Methods*. Westport, CT: Greenwood Publishing Group.

Johnson, D. , Johnson, R. and Holubec, E. (1995). *Teaching Students to be Peacemakers*, 3rd Ed. Edina, MN: Interaction Book Company.

Johnson, D., Johnson, R. and Smith, K. (1986). Academic conflict among students: Controversy and learning. In R. Feldman (Ed.), *The Social Psychology of Education*. Cambridge, MA: Cambridge University Press.

Kendall, J. C. (1991). Combining service and learning: an introduction for cooperative education professionals. *The Journal of Cooperative Education*, Volume 27 (2).

Kilpatrick, W., Wolfe, G. and Wolfe, S. (1994). *Books that build character: A guide to teaching your child moral values through stories*. New York: Simon & Schuster, A Touchstone Book.

Kincher, J. (1996). *The First Honest Book About Lies*. Minneapolis, MN: Free Spirit Publishing, Inc.

Kirschenbaum, H. (1995). *100 Ways to Enhance Values and Morality in School and Youth Settings*. Needham Heights, MA: Allyn & Bacon.

Lechner-Knowles, J. and Park-Scattergood, S. (1989). Educating for parenting. *Educational Leadership*, 47 (2), 67–73.

Leonard-Lamme, L., Lowell-Krogh, S., and Yachmetz, K. A. (1992). *Literature-Based Moral Education: Children's Books and Activities for Teaching Values, Responsibility, and Good Judgment* in the Elementary School.

Levin, D. (1994). *Teaching Young Children in Violent Times: Building a Peaceable Classroom*. Cambridge, MA: Educators for Social Responsibility.

Lewis, B. A. (1997). *What Do you Stand For: A Kid's Guide to Building Character.* Minneapolis, MN: Free Spirit Publishing, Inc.

Lickona, T. (1991). *Educating for Character*. New York: Bantam Books.

Lisman, C. D. (1996). *The Curricular Integration of Ethics.* Westport, CT: Praeger Publishers.

Louis, A. (1997). Marionettes: A new medium for character education: Students puppeteers hit the road in support of Artists-for-Character Day in Atlanta Public Schools. *The Puppetry Journal*,

MacDonald, M. R. (1993). *The Storyteller Start-Up Book: Finding, Learning, Performing, and Using Folktales.* Little Rock, AR: August House.

McGinnis, E. and Goldstein, A. (1984). *Skillstreaming the Elementary School Child*. Champaign, IL: Research Press.

McGinnis, E. and Goldstein, A. (1990). *Skillstreaming in Early Childhood*. Champaign, IL: Research Press.

McMillan, D. and Chavis, D. (1986). Sense of community: A definition and theory. *Journal of Community Psychology*, 14, 6–23.

National Storytelling Association (1994). *Tales as Tools: The Power of Story in the Classroom*. Author.

Nelson, C. and Smith, E. (1976). A frame of reference for measurement of institutional leadership concepts and the analysis of system states. *Human Relations*, 29 (6), 589–606.

Ozturk, M. (1990). Education for cross-cultural communication. *Educational Leadership*, December/January, 79–81.

Packer, A. J. (1997). *How Rude: The Teenager's Guide to Good Manners, Proper Behavior, and Not Grossing People Out.* Minneapolis, MN: Free Spirit Publishing.

Paley, V. G. (1992). *You Can't Say You Can't Play*. Cambridge, MA: Harvard University Press.

Peace Education Resource Center (1988). *Teaching Peace: A Catalog of Multimedia Resources on Peacemaking, Conflict Resolution, War Studies and War Prevention, the Soviet Union and Global Education*. Philadelphia, PA: Author.

Pfefferkorn, M. and Rosenow, R. (1993). *Ethics: A View of Life*. St. Louis, MO: Cooperating School Districts.

Rallis, S. and Goldring, E. (1993). Beyond the individual assessment of principals: school-based accountability in dynamic schools. *Peabody Journal of Education*, 68 (2), 3–23.

Rubright, L. (1996). *Beyond the Beanstalk: Interdisciplinary Learning Through Story-telling*. Wolburn, MA: Heinemann.

Saenger, H.B. (1993). *Exploring ethics through children's literature, Books 1 & 2*. Pacific Grove, CA: The Critical Thinking Press.

Schine, J. (1997). Looking ahead: Issues and challenges. In J. Schine (Ed.), *Service Learning*, Chicago: National Society for the Study of Education.

Schmidt, F., Friedman, A. and Marvel, J. (1992). *Mediation for Kids: Kids in Dispute Settlement*. Miami Beach, FL: Grace Contrino Abrams Peace Education Foundation.

Sears, R., Maccoby, E. and Levin, H. (1957). *Patterns of Child Rearing*. Evanston, IL: Row-Peterson.

Seeman, H. (1988). *Preventing Classroom Discipline Problems*. Lancaster, PA: Technomic Publishing Company.

Sergiovanni, T. (1992). *Moral Leadership*. San Francisco: Jossey-Bass.

Sergiovanni, T. (1997). *Building Community in Schools*. San Francisco: Jossey-Bass.

Sharan, S. (1994). Cooperative learning and the teacher. In S. Sharan (Ed.), *Handbook of Cooperative Learning Methods*. Westport, CT: Greenwood Publishing Group.

Sharan, Y. and Sharan, S. (1992). *Expanding Cooperative Learning Through Group Investigation*. New York: Teachers College Press.

Sharan, Y. and Sharan, S. (1994). Group Investigation in the cooperative classroom. In S. Sharan (Ed.), *Handbook of Cooperative Learning Methods*. Westport, CT: Greenwood Publishing Group.

Shure, M. (1992). *I Can Problem Solve: An Interpersonal Problem-Solving Program*. Champaign, IL: Research Press.

Slavin, R. (1986). *Using Student-Team Learning, (3rd Ed.)*. Baltimore, MD: Johns-Hopkins University, Center for Social Organization of Schools.

Slavin, R. (1990). *Cooperative Learning: Theory, Research, and Practice*. Englewood Cliffs, NJ: Prentice-Hall.

Slavin, R. (1994). Student Teams-Achievement Divisions. In S. Sharan (Ed.), *Handbook of Cooperative Learning Methods*. Westport, CT: Greenwood Publishing Group.

Smith, C. A. (1986). Nurturing kindness through storytelling. *Young Children*, September Issue.

Smylie, M. and Crowson, R. (1993). Principal assessment under restructured governance. *Peabody Journal of Education*, 68 (2), 64–84.

Solomon, D, Watson, M., Battistich, V., Schaps, E. and Delucchi, K. (1992). Creating a caring community: Educational practices that promote children's prosocial development. In F. K. Oser, A. Dick and J. L. Patry (Eds.) *Effective and Responsible Teaching: The New Synthesis*. San Francisco: Jossey-Bass.

Taylor, G. R. (1997). *Curriculum strategies: Social skills intervention for African-American males*. Westport, CT: Praeger Publishers.

Teacher Created Materials (1993). *Multicultural Bibliography*. Westminster, CA: Author.

Valett, R. (1983). *100+ Peace Strategies for Conflict Resolution and the Prevention of*

Nuclear War. Fresno, CA: Panorama West.

Vessels, G. (1996). The First Amendment and character education. *ABA Update on Law-Related Education*, 20 (1), 26–28.

Watson, M., Solomon, D., Stefan, D., Shwartz, P. and Kendzior, S. (1994). CDP cooperative learning: Working together to construct social, ethical, and intellectual understanding. In S. Sharan (Ed.), *Handbook of Cooperative Learning Methods*. Westport, CT: Greenwood Publishing Group.

Williamson, D. and Knepper, P. (1995). Teen courts and violence prevention. *Update on Law-Related Education*, 19 (2), 33–35.

5

Program Planning and Evaluation

PROGRAM PLANNING

Successful character education programs have been initiated by principals and teachers at the school level (e.g., Allen Classical-Traditional Academy in Dayton, West Point Elementary in West Point, Georgia); by concerned parent groups using the PTO as an initial point of entry (e.g., Core Essentials in Georgia); by central office administrators and board members on a school-system level (e.g., Mt. Lebanon in Pennsylvania); by school-system personnel, business leaders, parent groups, churches, and so forth, on a community-wide level; by state department of education personnel, governors, legislators, and state school board members on a state-wide level (e.g., the federal grant program in Utah); and by consultants from outside the schools who have persuaded principals, teachers, and parents in schools and schools systems to choose from among alternative approaches (e.g., schools in the Atlanta Public Schools grant project sponsored by the Georgia Humanities Council) or to adopt a particular model that they feel will produce the most desirable results in any school (e.g., Hazelwood Elementary in Louisville and other Child Development Project Schools).

Programs that are planned in detail too far away from individual schools or local communities for parents and local citizens to be actively involved in program planning (e.g., state initiated) tend to encounter (1) more opposition from parents and other community members; (2) a lack of commitment on the part of local-school and/or school-system personnel who lack a sense of ownership; and (3) irrelevance in the sense that programs do not fit the unique combination of problems, clientele, and resources of a particular school. But these obstacles to success can be avoided even when program planning begins outside the school or school community if the principal, teachers, and parents of a particular school understand that their program must meet their particular needs and that only they can make this determination in a way that includes and motivates all stakeholders, particularly teachers.

The ideal in my view is a combined school/school-system/state approach with the system's and state's contributions restricted to (a) general goals and guidelines through strategic planning and core-curriculum design and (b) consultation, and the school's contribution providing specifics including supplementary or additional goals that are appropriate for the school, all behavioral objectives, and the selection of methods and materials. An acceptable alternative would be a school-initiated approach that is adequately supported by the leadership of the school system and/or state but not initiated at these levels and not required throughout the system and/or state. Schools can succeed in the absence of a state-wide or system-wide initiative or without preliminary strategic planning outside the school, as demonstrated by the Allen Classical/Traditional Academy in Dayton. However, achieving success at a particular school without significant state, central office, school board, or community support may be a uniquely low-SES/urban phenomenon. Success within suburban, rural, small-town, and high-SES/urban communities is more likely if planning occurs in a manner that fully includes parents and teachers and when most of the planning occurs at the school level. I suggest that you learn what you can from "experts" outside your school and then take control by working with other members of your school community to design a program that is right for your school. The success of the Cooperating School Districts' consultation efforts in the St. Louis area (Archibald et al., 1996; Stirling, 1997) and the Utah State Office of Education's consultation and training efforts under Kristie Fink may be largely due to the fact that they encourage grass roots innovation and ownership at the school and school-system levels and are not trying to clone a particular model.

Mt. Lebanon's System-Level Planning Experience

As Assistant Superintendent in the Mt. Lebanon School District in Pittsburgh, Huffman (1994) led an effort to initiate character education system-wide. He began with a small study group of teachers, administrators, and parents who worked for a year to educate themselves about concepts, programs, and curriculum materials. This was followed by an effort to increase staff and community awareness. This involved bringing in a nationally recognized speaker and making thorough and well written material available. He then invited all teachers to join the study group—forty joined. The school board decided at about the same time to map the system's future through a strategic plan that included three strategies that in effect endorsed character education. These strategies referred to programs for developing ethical and responsible student behavior, creating caring environments, and community service. Character education proponents used the Strategy Teams (responsible for writing action plans for achieving the three strategies) and Implementation Teams (responsible for implementing the action plans) to initiate a character education program. The teams concerned with the three strategies in the system's strategic plan worked together to design the program.

Throughout his book about the Mt. Lebanon experience, Huffman emphasized the importance of good communication with all stakeholders, including incoming school board members, concerning the why, what, and how of character education, and this advice is viewed as especially critical in nonurban communities. The system even devised an action plan specifically for communication, which was carried out in tandem with the curriculum action plan. He also stressed the importance of having a representative community group go through the process of identifying values to teach and the need to communicate these in a list of single words that can be remembered and thus used effectively as a guide for infusing character education into all facets of school life. Their curriculum plan called for all subjects and courses to reinforce the core values in ways that (1) met the developmental needs of students and (2) took advantage of the values opportunities inherent in each subject area" (Huffman, 1994:32). As they began implementing their program, they discovered the need for a developmentally adaptable concept of moral behavior that teachers could share with students and use as a general context for instruction, a concept that addressed moral knowledge, emotion, and action and placed instruction within a larger social context.

The Cumberland County System-Level Planning Experience

Like Mt. Lebanon, the Cumberland County Schools in North Carolina, one of the largest school systems in the country, managed to plan and implement a system-wide character education program. The process began with a Character Education Summit in 1994 that was attended by five hundred citizens, and was designed to answer the Superintendent's question, "Should the schools teach character?" Small groups of summit attendees were charged with reaching a consensus about what virtues should be taught. From this summit emerged a Character Education Task Force that compiled results from the Summit and developed a mission statement. The list of virtues that emerged from this compilation was nearly identical to the Character Counts Coalition's list of six pillars, so the former was eventually replaced with the latter. The Task Force also engaged in a process of studying the literature and various school programs and curriculums, and curriculum specialists studied existing programs to see how much of a foundation was already in place. These specialists also recommended strategies for implementation and integration. They recommended integrating character concepts into the existing curriculum rather than acquiring or developing a new add-on curriculum, and they specified competency goals and objectives from the existing curriculum which were related to character concepts.

Next a staff development committee prepared for training teachers by attending a workshop conducted by Philip Vincent, author of *Developing Character in Students* (1994). Lead Contact Persons from each school and many other teachers completed a ten-hour course taught by Vincent's trainees. Vincent also conducted a workshop for principals. The Task Force also established a Public Awareness Committee that coordinated a second summit, hosted a meeting of church leaders, hosted a meeting of radio program directors, produced and distributed a booklet, initiated a character-of-the-month program to promote and coordinate community involvement, and developed a campaign theme and logo. Finally, the system and community took steps to maintain the momentum and spread the word by providing a monthly newsletter message from the superintendent and a brochure with tips for parents, and by requiring regular reports from the Lead Contact Person for each school to a system coordinator.

West Point Elementary's School-Level Planning Experience

The principal and instructional staff of West Point Elementary in West Point, Georgia, (Troup County) recognized a need and took it upon themselves to plan and implement what has proven to be a successful and extensively copied character education program. Its centerpiece is a word of the week, and the words chosen were derived from a survey that asked parents to choose from a list of thirty the ten most important character qualities in their home. This was a way of using parents as a resource as well as gaining their support. West Point teachers then wrote their school-community-specific character education program (706-812-7973; fax: 706-812-7974), and this program was shared with parents during pre-planning before it was implemented. The written program or curriculum called for a somewhat different focus each day of the week beginning with a definition of the character quality for the week (Monday); looking at ways the character quality it is demonstrated in people around them (Tuesday); reading and discussing a story about a person in the school, community, or history (Wednesday); reading and discussing a story about a fictional character who demonstrates the quality (Thursday); and either reviewing or carrying out teacher-planned lessons (Friday). Teachers wrote the biographies about local models of the character qualities as well as the fictional stories which illustrate these qualities. There are many other aspects to the West Point program that were planned by the principal and teachers including their classroom news, a concerted effort to call attention to and socially reinforce virtuous behavior, and an elaborate Character Clubhouse all of which teachers have been intimately involved in planning.

In the Troup County Schools, the idea of character education spread from West Point Elementary under Bill Parsons to all schools via a mandate by the system superintendent. It is doubtful that the other schools in Troup County will be as successful as West Point Elementary unless they similarly utilize a school-level planning process which similarly brings about teacher ownership and commitment.

West Point is certainly not the only school that has succeeded with character education without special assistance from central level administrators or persons outside the school community. Allen Classical-Traditional Academy in Dayton went through a planning process very similar to West Point, and West Point, in fact, borrowed some of its ideas from Allen where Rudolpho Bernardo, the originating principal, similarly respected, trusted, and empowered his teachers. In contrast to West Point, teachers at Allen decided to have student assemblies on

Fridays as a culminating activity for the word of the week, with rotating grade level responsibility, and they now begin their week with a closed circuit television broadcast to all classrooms that introduces the word, and is conducted by upper-grade students who function as newscasters. The high energy and commitment of staff at the two schools is similar, and I attribute this to what I believe is the best approach to character education planning, "bottom-up" at the school level.

Atlanta's School-Level/School-Cluster Planning Experience

We began our orientation and planning process in Atlanta by sending representatives from our five pilot schools to a statewide character education conference that was sponsored by the Georgia Humanities Council. These representatives were exposed to a variety of materials and ideas about character education. I then wrote a grant proposal for the five schools and assigned myself the role of Project Director and Project Evaluator. This proposal called for an introductory presentation to each school staff and the exposure of select staff members to various approaches through field trips to model schools in Louisville, Dayton, and West Point, Georgia. Staffs were further oriented through written materials and videos and the creation of a resource center in each school library. The school staffs were not asked to be involved in planning the program evaluation since this was written into the grant proposal, and since I was in the process of developing program assessment instruments and guidelines.

Staffs at each of the five schools were asked to make choices about the type of program they wanted, and, for the most part, these decisions grew out of relatively open staff discussions which were co-led by teachers and principals who visited model school programs outside of the system. The five staffs commonly chose a virtue-of-the-week centerpiece and supplemented this with various other strategies such as class meetings, classroom news forms, service learning, cross-grade buddy programs, and so forth. The schools were encouraged to use both traditional-didactic and progressive-community-building strategies (or to be eclectic), but this was not required since I was convinced that exerting too much control would prevent teachers from becoming fully committed and creatively involved. By the second or third month of the second year, the two schools with the most committed staffs (Blalock and Campbell) had added additional strategies and had modified others. With the help of teachers and the volunteer group, Hands on Atlanta, they also made extensive progress on elaborate one-of-a-kind wall displays which are permanent and perhaps worth a trip to Atlanta to see.

We should have allowed more time for school-level planning and parent involvement in the planning process, and by failing to take the time, we did not achieve an ideal level of parent involvement. We may have also caused some complacent and doubting teachers to become more resistant during the first year than they might have been otherwise; nevertheless, at two of the four schools, nearly all were on board by the third month of our second year.

The principals who visited the model schools became highly committed, and this resulted in much better planning and implementation at their schools as compared with schools where principals did not avail themselves of this opportunity. I concluded very early in the process that success depends upon character education becoming the highest priority for the school principal and that teachers differ greatly in terms of the speed with which they become open to and committed to new ideas. In schools where principals did not make character education their highest priority, and in schools where too many other things were happening to allow character education to take center stage, less positive change was observed.

Curriculum-Centered Versus Problem-Centered Planning

I believe it is useful to view the character education planning process as being either curriculum-centered or problem-centered. The former begins with the assumption that your school or school system needs a comprehensive character development curriculum or a new general curriculum that more adequately addresses character development in terms of philosophy, goals, objectives, and strategies. Most states and school systems have mission statements and lists of general educational goals that address character development quite well, but these rarely receive elaboration in the form of specific curriculum goals and objectives. If you are as fortunate as educators and parents in the state of Utah, this foundation will be provided for you at the state level in various ways, including a "character-education friendly" core curriculum. Utah serves as a model or standard for curriculum-centered planning at the state level and a model in terms of their consultative facilitation of infusional curriculum-centered planning within school systems and schools.

The problem-centered approach to program design could eventually lead to a new general curriculum or add-on curriculum depending on the problems defined and the solution ideas generated, but this approach will more than likely result in definitions of specific social, interpersonal, and attitudinal problems and the selection of a few promising strategies for solving these problems. These strategies may or may not infuse the academic curriculum, supplement it with an add-on curriculum of some type, or modify the academic curriculum in some way.

I have identified a few techniques for promoting effective curriculum-centered and problem-centered planning or program design that you may find helpful in your effort to (1) promote the inclusion of all stakeholders during the program-design process, (2) foster commitment on the part of all stakeholders, and (3) produce a program that is diversified and relevant in terms of content and instructional techniques.

Techniques for Promoting Effective Curriculum-Centered Planning

It is commonly assumed that the quality of the outcome of a planning or decision-making process will be in direct proportion to the openness of this process to all interested or concerned persons, but typically very little is accomplished in situations where many people are trying to accomplish a task and are having to take turns giving input orally. While I agree with Goodlad (1984, 1976) that broad-based "bottom up" curriculum design is essential and that it will generate more personal commitment and relevant content than "top down," I do not share his assumption that "essential dialogue" (effective communication implied) and good decision making are virtually guaranteed if a "bottom up" approach is used. The "dialogue structuring" approach I propose provides this guarantee irrespective of the number of people involved and other threats to good communication and good decision making such as (1) input that is skewed in favor of the most assertive and emotional among participants, (2) disorganization and tension that typically occur when communication is primarily oral or exclusively oral, (3) authoritarian attitudes and actions that commonly stifle communication in organizational hierarchies (status/vertical communication barriers), and (4) a lack of shared knowledge, values, and language systems among participants, which makes it difficult for them to understand one another (situs/horizontal communication barriers).

"Structured dialogue" combines the Delphi technique and Nelson's "diagonally structured information exchange" technique (Nelson and Smith, 1974) with the basic idea of "bottom up" planning. The Delphi method is designed to solicit uninhibited input from any size group, and it can be described as an idea-seeking/agreement-seeking technique that overcomes the limitations of relying on experts and round-table discussions or committees. It allows for input and criticism from many teachers, parents, students, concerned citizens, and administrators at an early point through a series of four anonymous questionnaires. It also makes possible more input than would be possible through representation on traditional committees. Questionnaire number One seeks input by having respondents complete open-ended statements such as "Students should develop _____ " or add to and delete from a core list of educational goals. Questionnaire Two asks respondents to rate or judge input from Questionnaire One through some type of ranking. Questionnaire Three presents results from Questionnaire Two through a median or mode and asks respondents to re-evaluate their Questionnaire-Two input in light of the new information in Questionnaire Three. Questionnaire Four provides consensus data and a summary of dissenting opinions.

The Zengers' (1986) system for (1) determining what needs to be taught within a community through the schools (curriculum design) and (2) comparing this with what is actually being taught (curriculum evaluation) uses the Delphi technique and includes example Delphi questionnaires you may find useful, but this technique can be used on a smaller scale. For example, it could be used by those responsible for actually writing a curriculum and by school personnel and school-community representatives who are trying to design a plan to reduce violence and increase prosocial behavior in one school.

The "diagonally structured information exchange" technique developed by Charles Nelson helps to establish, improve, or re-open communication within organizations where it is poor due to fear of reprimands and the censoring of ideas by supervisors (on the vertical dimension) and specialization of language and differing norms and values (on the horizontal dimension). It puts people from different speciality areas together on special cross-departmental committees and avoids placing them on committees with their supervisors or subordinates. Within a school system, representatives from such committees would serve on a smaller number of committees or a single committee responsible for integrating information and preparing final products. This could be used within individual schools, but it appears to be most useful at the system level as part of the process of writing a new general curriculum. For example, these diagonally structured committees could begin with results from the Delphi Questionnaires (discussed previously) and work toward a general curriculum that would ultimately be passed on to individual schools in the form of general goals and general subject-specific objectives. Ideally, each school should be given the freedom to prioritize these goals and add goals and subgoals that address the unique needs of their student and parent populations.

A Technique for Promoting Effective Problem-Centered Planning

If you adopt the problem-centered approach to planning, I recommend using Parnes' (1977) Creative Problem Solving (CPS) steps. This technique helps to (1) accurately define the problem(s) in a school or community as they pertain to character and prosocial behavior, (2) maximize flexibility and fluency in the generation of ideas for resolving the problem(s) and ways to implement these ideas, and (3) evaluate these ideas and their outcome systematically in order to come up with a promising overall plan. Step one involves generating facts about the problem(s). This is followed by generating alternative problem definitions that begin with "How might we . . ." Step three involves brainstorming solution ideas with an emphasis upon quantity rather than quality. Step four involves generating criteria for evaluating these ideas. Step five involves evaluating the solution ideas using these criteria (not too many of either) by charting the ideas down the left side of a matrix and the criteria across the top, and then ranking the ideas one column at a time using the criteria which identifies each column. Step six involves a repeat of the brainstorming, criteria-generating, and evaluation steps (formally or informally) as a way of choosing ways to implement the most promising solution ideas. Step seven involves generating and selecting ideas for evaluation.

This technique can be an amazingly effective way of keeping committees focused and avoiding premature closure on unpromising ideas. When used to help a school community plan a good character program, parents should be encouraged to participate, and enough teachers must be involved to ensure a high level staff commitment to the final plan. It is a mistake to assume that teachers will become committed to or own a plan they have had little or no part in developing, particularly a character education plan which calls for a different mind set about teaching, a higher level of motivation, and a widening of the curriculum.

Suggestions for Program Planning and Implementation

I encourage classroom teachers, school administrators, parent volunteers, school counselors, school psychologists, or business partners for a particular school to prepare for the essential school-level program-planning process by first examining any planning that may have been done for your school by persons outside your school community, such as state department or central office personnel, and by subsequently joining with other interested members of your school community to investigate various models, strategies, and instructional materials. This study process could include reading, bringing in people with special knowledge and experience, such as teachers and administrators from schools that are further along, and visiting model schools.

The next step is to establish a school-wide planning committee or task force. This group should include parents, teachers who have participated enthusiastically in the preparatory study process, and other interested members of the school community. This committee should periodically report to the staff as a whole and to the PTO, and committee members should encourage input from all stakeholders and open dialogue during staff meetings and PTO meetings. The school-wide planning committee may want to seek input from staff and parents through a series of Delphi questionnaires, as described previously, and may want to use the Parnes creative problem solving technique to promote effective group problem solving. It may want to gather pre-program or formative assessment data about various aspects of the school using the CEP Eleven Principles Survey (EPS), the Vessels' School Climate Survey (VSCS), or the School Character Survey (SCS) (see reviews in the evaluation section of this chapter). The school-wide planning committee could be divided into subcommittees, with each focusing on the use of a specific learning mode and related strategies.

After a basic school plan has been developed that includes a list of about six or eight primary strategies, all staff members and interested school-community members should be assigned to subcommittees or study groups that will explore (1) how the strategies listed in the school plan will be used at each grade level and school-wide, and (2) how the school will communicate with and involve parents, business partners, churches, news networks, newspapers, and so forth, on a regular basis. This committee work will require a lot of time, dialogue, and incentives for quality work (e.g., requiring each committee to give oral and written reports to the full staff). The results of this tier of subcommittee or study-group work should be incorporated into the school plan by the school-wide committee.

With respect to implementation, it is probably unwise to attempt to implement all strategies in the school plan at once. I suggest developing a schedule for phasing strategies in over a twelve to eighteen month period. Some strategies may need to be thoroughly explained and then mandated by the school principal with follow-up monitoring (e.g., service learning projects and infusion into academic instruction) since even committed teachers may be a little reluctant to venture into unfamiliar territory. For the majority of teachers, full implementation of select strategies will not just happen because character education is a good idea, it will have to be expected and possibly even modeled for many teachers within their classrooms by other teachers who have become more skilled. The monitoring of implementation can be achieved through (1) a structured system of inter-classroom visitation among teachers, and (2) the periodic use of the Vessels' Classroom Observation Form (described in this chapter and reproduced in the Appendix H) by the principal or curriculum specialist. These structured observations should be followed by formative teacher evaluation conferences. Some teachers and administrators are slow to realize that they must relate to children differently in order to succeed with character education, and they may need to be pushed along through formative conferences and even formal plans of improvement. One of the nicest things about character education, however, is that it improves teacher morale thereby almost immediately changing the climate in the school in a way that applies peer pressure gently and respectfully. Finally, in an effort to provide optimum positive incentives for respectable implementation in each classroom, teacher successes, risk-taking, and creativity with character education strategies need to be publicly celebrated in every way possible.

PROGRAM EVALUATION

The character education literature includes no books or articles which include a thorough review and description of alternative program evaluation procedures, and few programs have been effectively evaluated because the technology and guidelines have been lacking. This is beginning to change thanks to the standard set by the Developmental Studies Center over the last decade; the recent development of a program-implementation survey by the Character Education Partnership; Leming's research and research-literature reviews; federal grants that have required formal evaluations and thus forced innovation; and prototype assessment instruments that are being developed by me and others including Leming, Jennifer Johns, who was hired to evaluate the federal grant program in Utah, and Paget who is responsible for evaluating the South Carolina grant program. Thanks to these contributors and others, I believe it is now possible for school programs to be effectively evaluated by personnel working in these schools for the most part. A significant number of school programs must be evaluated adequately if our renewed focus on social and ethical development is to survive.

The guidelines and suggestions for program evaluation presented in this chapter are for educators who know at least a little about research and evaluation and who recognize the need for some form of pre-post testing that will enable them to improve their programs and defend them against critics. These guidelines and suggestions hopefully reflect my awareness that most individual schools do not have the time, money, personnel, and technical expertise to design and carry out highly elaborate evaluations that use complex research designs, and do not have access to persons outside their school who have this expertise. A few will enjoy these advantages, so I will include descriptions of relatively complex methods such as quasi-experimental designs that use comparison groups and time-series analyses. I will also describe simpler techniques such as report forms for keeping track of the frequency of interpersonal conflicts, and questionnaires that can be administered prior to program initiation and re-administered periodically thereafter.

Your particular circumstance will dictate which evaluation techniques you should select. Ideally, evaluation plans should allow for (1) on-going monitoring that will detect immediate benefits and/or a breakdown in implementation; (2) the documentation of benefits that may emerge after a year or two as more and more of your students have multiple-year exposure to your program; and (3) an analysis of social indicators that may reflect long-term benefits such as dropout rates and rates of divorce and crime in your community. All evaluation plans should (1) be designed before program implementation; (2) be consistent with the goals and objectives of your program; (3) include a variety of measures; and (4) use all possible informants including students, teachers, parents, and trained "third-person" observers from outside the school or school system if available. Your primary objective should be to keep it as simple as possible, given the elusive target of good character, and as relevant to your goals as possible.

Very explicit goals that avoid generalities and vague terms, and objectives which state desired behavioral outcomes (see chapter 3) will greatly simplify the task of deciding "what" to measure and "where" to look for these outcomes. Decisions with respect to "what" to measure will provide guidance as you consider options with respect to "how." In response to the first of these questions, educators seeking to build character are interested in feelings and conscientiousness (affect), thinking processes and attitudes (cognition), actions and verbalizations (behavior), acquired knowledge and social skills (competence), and the instructional-interpersonal environment (school and classroom climates). The emphasis may vary somewhat depending on the type of program, its underlying theory, and the population of students being served, but some attention should be given to each in order to draw reliable and valid conclusions.

Since "moral" or "virtuous" behavior does not always justify the inference that moral feeling and thinking led to this behavior, or that the person had the necessary knowledge and social skills to behave similarly and independently in appropriate future situations without special incentives, prompting, and so forth, you cannot always draw reliable inferences about "internal" moral states and competencies from the direct evaluation or measurement of observable behavior. Even when these internal states appear to be reliably reflected in observable behaviors such as crying, a gentle touch, a smile, a considerate statement, or a complex sequence of helpful actions, an undetectable lack of genuineness or a significant amount of imitation of which you are not aware may preclude reliable and valid inferences with respect to the presence of relatively internal moral states and competencies. Conversely, moral affect, cognition, and competence do not always lead to moral action as demonstrated by the Hartshorne and May studies decades ago. People sometimes engage in "right" behavior for purely selfish reasons and sometimes imitate such behavior without feeling or understanding. They also fail to do what they know and feel to be right for selfish reasons and either suffer the moral feeling of guilt or engage in bizarre rationalizations to protect their self-esteem as a result.

It seems reasonable to assume that in most cases, however, spontaneous "moral" behaviors justify the inference that moral affect, cognition, and competence preceded the behavior or co-occurred. Therefore, the ongoing measurement of spontaneous behaviors through various forms of systematic recording by trained observers should probably be the nucleus of your evaluation plan (hereafter referred to as direct evaluation techniques), particularly for elementary school children who are not well skilled at communicating the presence of relatively internal moral states and competencies through oral or written language. Your evaluation plan could include elicited or contrived behaviors as well. Both elicited/contrived and spontaneous behaviors can be verbal (oral or written expression), nonverbal, or a combination of both. It seems reasonable to assume that the most reliable way to get at moral affect, cognition, and knowledge is indirectly through elicited verbalization. It also seems reasonable to assume that the best way to measure the social skills necessary for moral behavior is directly through the observation of spontaneous behaviors and behaviors in contrived situations designed to elicit the combinations of verbal and nonverbal behaviors that occur naturally in social situations.

Ideally, therefore, your evaluation plan should include a combination of (1) *direct observations* of behaviors with a primary emphasis on naturally occurring or spontaneous behaviors, and (2) *indirect observations* of internal states (feeling, thoughts, knowledge) through elicited verbal responses that essentially ask the student to tell what is going on inside. Results from the latter will be invalid if the instruments or questions used are poor or the person fails to communicate the truth due to a lack of skill or will; therefore, you should use tested instruments, if available, and should take care to adapt to the limitations of the various age groups you are evaluating. Results from direct measures will be invalid if there is an inadequate sampling of behavior, if the recording devices are faulty, or if the observers are incompetent due to a lack of ability or training. The elusiveness of morality or virtuousness demands a diversified approach, and this is thought to be possible without sacrificing simplicity and manageability.

Direct Evaluation Techniques

Time Sampling/Event Recording/Pre-Coded Observation Forms

Most direct measures involve observing and recording specific behaviors. This can be done as behaviors occur or later via (1) tape recording (video and/or audio), (2) the review of anecdotal notes, or (3) the recall of past experiences and observations. Decisions to be made include what to observe and record (e.g., conflicts, prosocial acts, suspensions, absences), who will do the observing and recording (e.g., students, teachers, third persons), and how the observing and recording will be done. The most structured and reliable approach, particularly if trained third-person observers are used, involves the use of pre-coded observation forms that facilitate the recording of behaviors that are operationally defined in advance. Like the Developmental Studies Center (1993), I have developed such a form for use in evaluating character building programs (see subsequent description). Pre-coded observation forms limit the amount of writing that must be done by using various combinations of letters, numbers, pluses, and minuses.

For some behaviors such as interpersonal conflicts and other types of student-to-student, teacher-to-student, and student-to-teacher interactions, it may be possible to record every instance of the behavior as well as related reactions and outcomes during specified time periods. This is called event recording. A partial-interval time-sampling system may be more appropriate for other things that you want to record, such as whether students are actively involved. This recording method requires only a single occurrence of the behavior during the designated time interval (e.g., five minute or one-half hour intervals). In other words, the observer/recorder would record "yes" or "no" for each interval, depending on whether the behavior was observed at least once during this interval. This can be combined with the recording of a response, such as whether the teacher attended to or reinforced the behavior. Other time-sampling options include "whole-interval," in which the behavior or type of behavior is recorded if it occurs throughout the chosen time interval (e.g., social harmony in the classroom), and "momentary," in which the behavior or type of behavior is recorded if it is occurring at the end of each time interval (e.g., at least one student in the room voluntarily assisting another).

The Developmental Studies Center's Observation Form

The classroom observation form created by the Developmental Studies Center in Oakland (1993a) uses a partial-interval time-sampling design that focuses alternately on the (1) teacher and whole class and (2) small student groups. It calls for recording the presence or absence of specified behaviors and conditions (frequencies) and intensity or salience of other behaviors and conditions (qualities).

Leming's Classroom Observation Form

Leming developed an observational rating instrument, the Classroom Character Rating Form, to assess the character-related dimensions of classroom climate (Leming et al. 1997). In his evaluation of the Heartwood curriculum, it was used independently by two observers who completed several observations in each classroom. The instrument requires ratings on nine well-defined dimensions: Curricular Substructure (Seriousness of Academic Environment, Teacher Competence, Classroom Discipline), Teacher Characteristics (Moral Character of Teacher, Spontaneous Moral Expressiveness), Curricular Emphasis (Character Inclusive Curriculum, Student Engagement), Interpersonal Relations (Reciprocal Regard, Character-Related Classroom Climate).

Vessels' Classroom Observation Form

My observation instrument, the Vessels' Classroom Observation Form (VCOF; see Appendix H) uses a combination of event recording for interpersonal interactions, quality ratings (made at the end of the forty-five minute observation period), and whole-interval time sampling using nine five-minute time periods and recording at the end of each. For the event recording section, the observer simply enters a tally mark in one of thirty-two pre-coded interpersonal-interaction categories (e.g., HC for hostile/critical teacher-to-student; RR for respectful reprimand/redirection; see Appendix H for all 32 codes). For the time sampling component, minutes or percentages are entered for four of the eight categories: minutes of active teaching, minutes of nonteaching discipline, minutes of teacher inactivity, and percent of students on task. Letter codes are entered for four remaining items: type of student activity (T=active, I=interactive, P=passive, N=none), type of student relations (C=cooperative, X=competitive, L=independent, N=none), instructional content (A=academic, V=values-related, N=none), and character infusion (Y=yes, N=no). The quality ratings are made using a scale of one to nine for each of the following: teacher kind and respectful, students kind and respectful, teacher motivated and responsible, students motivated and responsible, preventive/moral discipline, caring community/character education.

The statistical significance of differences between the school-wide pretest and school-wide post-test totals for each of the coded categories can be determined using a paired-samples *t*-test for each. For the interpersonal-interaction categories, it is possible to combine or collapse them into total student-to-student negative, total student-to-student positive, total teacher-to-student negative, total teacher-to-student positive, and so forth, and to run *t*-tests using these totals or proportions derived from them. For further detail about data interpretation, see the VCOF instruction sheet in Appendix H).

The field testing of the VCOF included 150 class observations of forty-five minutes each. Since an inter-rater reliability study has not been completed, and since procedures for training multiple observers has not been developed, I recommend that it be used in a given school by just one observer for all classroom observations (see instructions in Appendix H). I expect that it will eventually be used widely with good inter-rater reliability provided training is thorough and includes observed practice with corrective feedback. The VCOF reflects my view of what principals should be looking for if their goal is to have a school filled with classrooms that build character.

Counting Interpersonal Conflicts and Good Deeds

Field testing of my Interpersonal Conflict Report Form was not as successful since most teachers failed to get the cards filled out and turned in following each conflict, but one of five schools had some success when it simplified the card and had a staff member go to each classroom near the end of the day to pick them up.

A positive counterpart to this would be the use of good deed jars. Each time a caring or helpful deed occurs in the class, the teacher or a student writes the name of the virtuous student on a card and puts it in the jar. If you use either the jars or conflict report forms to help evaluate your program, you will need to keep the positive consequences for good deeds and negative consequences for conflicts as constant as possible throughout the year.

Whether or not my observation instrument is used, school personnel are encouraged to do some type of baseline count, and then subsequent counts, of specific behaviors that may help to demonstrate the effectiveness of their program, including interpersonal conflicts, acts of caring and helpfulness, frequency of classroom rule violations, number of suspensions and detentions, number of absences, number of nonretainees who score within certain percentile ranges on standardized group achievement test scores, number of nonretainees whose percentile scores increase by a specified amount, the average number of minutes that the teacher is able to spend teaching rather than disciplining each day, and the average number of minutes students spend in participatory versus didactic instruction.

School-Climate and Classroom-Climate Measures

School climate and classroom climate can be defined as the readily perceptible personality or atmosphere within a classroom or school that is created by its unique combination of organizational characteristics. Measures of school and classroom climate can help determine if your independent variable is in place as intended (the various components of your character education program) and whether your program is producing enough responsible, respectful, and caring behavior on the part of students, teachers, and administrators to change the total atmosphere. School climate instruments are available that could conceivably be used to assess character education programs even though they were not designed for this purpose. The Comprehensive Assessment of School Environments (NASSP, 1986/1987) solicits input from teachers, students, and parents about relationships, values, academics, and management, but its content validity is suspect in my opinion, and the authors' conceptual distinction between "shared perceptions of climate" and "personal satisfaction within the organization" is puzzling.

Bernardo (1995) developed the School Character Survey to help school personnel "diagnose the character of the school" and the impact of staff on this character, and to help them plan for improvement. The face validity or content validity of this instrument appears to be fairly good as suggested by its subscales: motivation, openness/trust, innovation/improvement, involvement, service to students, vision, recognition, leadership, teamwork, and learning/development. It needs to be scrutinized statistically to determine its reliability, construct validity, ability to discriminate between good and bad school climates as reflected by other measures, and the quality of individual items.

A high percentage of items on the Developmental Studies Center's student questionnaires (Deer and Mason, 1995; DSC, 1995b, 1993b, 1993c) focuses on the presence or absence of a caring classroom community (climate) that fosters student autonomy and prosocial behavior. One section of the DSC teacher questionnaire (1995a)—the section labeled "school climate"—seeks the impressions of teachers about the attitudes, behaviors, and relationships of students, teachers, and administrators within the school as a whole. But like the student questionnaires, as a whole, it is largely a school-climate and classroom-climate measure or measure of community as reflected by the names given to the primary sections: classroom activities and practices, classroom management and relations with students, teacher goals, teacher beliefs and attitudes, relations with other adults in the school, feelings about self as a teacher, and school climate.

Like all of the DSC questionnaires, the DSC teacher questionnaire was designed to help the DSC determine if the various components of the Child Development Project model are in place and whether things that are in conflict with their philosophy are in evidence, such as a heavy reliance on punishment and external rewards and controls. These various components are reflected in the names of the subsections of their teacher questionnaire (e.g., student collaborative work, class meetings, student autonomy and participation in decision making, teacher goals with respect to prosocial and moral development, teacher use of praise). The DSC has provided internal consistency and item-total score coefficients and factor analytic loadings for the various subsections using samples of four hundred or more from 1991–92 and 1992–93, and these numbers suggest good reliability and good construct or factorial validity. The internal consistency coefficients range from .60 to .91 for the various subsections.

The DSC teacher questionnaire is essentially a program evaluation tool that reflects the Child Development Project philosophy, but it covers many relevant domains and could be used to assess any character building program. The DSC leadership has been willing to let other programs use it for research and evaluation purposes free of charge.

Lickona and his colleagues from the Center for the 4th and 5th Rs recently developed the Eleven Principles Survey (EPS) based on the document *Eleven Principles of Effective Character Education,* which was prepared by the national Character Education Partnership in 1997. Like the DSC questionnaires it is designed to assess whether, and to what degree, various critical elements of a "quality program" are in place, namely, implementation of a specific concept of character education. It is not designed to assess whether schools with or without these "quality programs" are effectively developing or improving students' moral thinking, feeling, and behaving, but one subsection describes this type of evaluation as part of a complete program.

One subsection of the EPS survey, "the school is a caring community," could be viewed as a potential measure of program effect in terms of school climate if the survey is used as a pre-post assessment tool. The other subsections assess the extent to which a school has (1) taught specific virtues; (2) promoted moral feeling, thinking; (3) designed a program that is proactive and comprehensive; (4) given students opportunities for moral action; (5) infused character education into the academic curriculum; (6) promoted intrinsic student motivation; (7) motivated staff to model good character and share ownership of the program; (8) found and shaped moral leadership that is committed to character education; (9) involved and informed parents; and (10) assessed the character of the school and its students. Respondents are asked to rate on a one-to-five scale the level of implementation of several specific aspects of each of the eleven principles, and this yields total-scale and subscale scores. These scores could be analyzed statistically. Schools could eventually be provided with representative pre-program, early program, and full implementation norms or comparison-group means and standard deviations for urban, suburban, low SES, and high SES populations. Although the EPS is designed for formative assessment and should provide valuable information to program planners, it could be used to assess success with program implementation using conventional within-subject, pre-post designs.

Cletus Bulach at West Georgia College near Atlanta has developed two questionnaires that reflect his operational definition of sixteen character values: honesty, self-discipline, kindness, responsibility, integrity/fairness, perseverance, cooperation, compassion/empathy, forgiveness, citizenship, tolerance/diversity, courtesy, generosity, sportsmanship, humility, and respect. He essentially defined each of these values in terms of observable behaviors and designed two instruments that ask students to rate their fellow students on these behaviors. He is attempting to assess the character of students within classrooms and/or schools, and the moral climate that their character or lack thereof creates, by asking students what their fellow students do and do not do, an interesting and ostensibly useful approach to assessing student character and school/classroom climate. One of his two surveys is for elementary and middle school students but does not identify the specific ages that can be administered the questionnaire. The second version is for high school and college. For additional information contact Bulach at 770-836-4460 or by e-mail at CBulach@westGA.edu.

Jennifer S. Johns developed the Character Development Survey (CDS) as part of her effort to evaluate schools participating in the Utah Community Partnership for Character Education, one of the first four statewide initiatives to receive federal funds to implement character education (directed by Kristin Fink in the Utah State Office of Education at 801-538-7948). The CDS consists of a core of twenty-six items measuring kindness/caring, respect/responsibility, fairness/honesty, and school expectations regarding behavior. The parent and staff forms of the CDS contain additional items pertaining to parent-staff relationships and school climate. It has been administered in more than sixty-five schools in six school districts. As the contracted evaluator of the Utah program, Jennifer is in the process of examining reliability and validity. Anyone interested in obtaining a copy of the copyrighted Character Development Survey should contact the author at 505-812-8468. The following is a sampling of items from the forty-six item staff form of the Character Development Survey:

> The Students in this school are nice to each other.
> The Students at this school try to include everyone.

The adults at this school are kind to the students.
The adults at this school let students know they care about them.
The Students at this school take responsibility for their actions.
Our school expects everyone to get along even if they are different.
The school staff cares about the students' families.
The school staff models the behaviors they expect of students.
The administration at our school demonstrates moral leadership.
The school staff makes a conscious effort to develop students' character.
The students at this school can work out problems without insults or fights.
The students at this school get along well together even if they are different.
Our school is a great place to work.
Our school involves parents as full partners in the character-building effort.
Our school expects everyone to obey the rules.
Children get an excellent education at this school.

Vessels' School Climate Survey

My school climate survey (the Vessels' School Climate Survey or VSCS; see Appendix I) is specifically designed to assess the social-environmental effects of character education programs and whether critical elements of a character-building community are present. There is an emphasis on leadership and relationships among members of the school community that reflects my thinking about what must be occurring interactively in order for character growth to be maximized. Thus far, the VSCS has been field tested in five Atlanta elementary schools, one elementary school in the urban midwest, and one small-town elementary school in southwest Georgia (all collected between September 1996 and September 1997). It was used in the five Atlanta schools as a pre-post measure.

VSCS scores from the five Atlanta schools yielded a test-retest or stability coefficient of .67 over a nine-month period. The final 100-item scale yielded a pretest mean of 290, with a standard deviation of 39; it produced a post-test mean of 309 (out of a possible 400) and a standard deviation of 53 (scores from the two comparison schools were included in the post-test category, even though students completed the survey only once, because they have established character education programs). The post-test mean for the five-school Atlanta subsample was 292 with a SD of 48; the mean for the two comparison schools combined was 359 with a SD of 32. Crombach's alpha (internal consistency) was .99 for the June 1997 data and .97 for the September 1996 data.

The internal consistency (alpha) coefficients for the VSCS subscales ranged from .93 to .98, with the exception of the four-item Physical Climate subscale where the coefficient was .87. The individual-item to total-survey correlational coefficients ranged from .50 to .87; the individual-item to total-survey correlations ranged from .52 to .77 using Atlanta post-test and comparison school scores and .32 to .69 using Atlanta pretest scores. The subscale to total-survey correlations using Atlanta post-test and comparison school scores ranged from .87 to .96 with the exception of the four-item Physical Climate subscale where the coefficient was .67; corresponding figures for the Atlanta pretest scores ranged from .73 to .97 with a Physical Climate coefficient of .33.

The factor analysis results supported the subscales well enough that all were retained in the scoring procedures. These results suggest good factorial or construct validity. A general subscale called "Quality of Relationships" was added based on the factor analysis results. The factor analysis was used in conjunction with individual-item to total-score correlations and a study of item wording to identify and eliminate or improve poor survey items (fifteen were eliminated).

Results from the within-subject or pre-post *t*-tests using Atlanta scores, and between-subject or between-school comparisons using scores from all seven schools allowed for drawing some provisional conclusions about criterion validity or the extent to which the VSCS is sensitive to the presence and effects of character-building programs. The pre-post *t*-test results (hereafter referred to as within-subject) showed a difference for all five Atlanta schools combined that was not significant at the conventional .05 level but was significant at the .09 level. There was a similar finding for the General Quality of Relationships subscale (.08). Finally, there was a significant mean score difference in the predicted direction for Student-Teacher Relations (.025) and Character-Building Activities (.007).

When examined by school, the school with the best program implementation and staff commitment (as observed by the project director and confirmed by the VCOF) showed a statistically significant increase in the total VSCS mean score and all subscale scores; the school with the second best implementation showed a statistically significant increase on all subscales except Leadership; the two schools with less commitment and more ambivalent principals showed no significant improvement in total score or any subscale score even though many of the teachers were committed and some strategies were carried out; the fifth and final school showed a significant increase in the total score and three of the eight subscales.

Looking next at between-school comparisons, the total-survey mean for the two non-Atlanta comparison schools was significantly higher than the Atlanta pretest and post-test means at the .000 level (presumed variability due to pretest scores and SES not removed via covariance). The ANOVA results showed a total-survey mean score for the southwest Georgia school that was significantly higher than the Atlanta pretest and post-test mean scores but not the mean score for the midwest urban school. The midwest school, which was well matched with four of the Atlanta schools on SES and racially matched with the fifth, had a mean score that was higher than all five of the Atlanta schools on the pretest but only three on the post-test. After removing score variability due to pretest scores and school SES (using an analysis of covariance and Atlanta post-test scores as the dependent variable), a significant difference related to levels of school-wide program implementation was found with high-implementing schools scoring higher.

The VSCS Leadership subscale mean scores for the midwest school and southwest Georgia school were not significantly different and were significantly higher than any of the Atlanta pretest mean scores and all but one of the Atlanta post-test mean scores: the school with the most committed principal and most conducive personality and leadership style. With respect to Student Discipline, the southwest Georgia school was unmatched in all comparisons, and the midwest school had a significantly higher mean score than all the Atlanta schools on the pretest, but only the two Atlanta schools with the poorest program implementation on the post-test. A similar pattern was found with Student-Student Relationships, Student-Teacher Relationships, School Community, Character-Building Activities, and General Quality of Relationships scores, with the number one and number two ranking Atlanta schools comparing more favorably on the post-test with the midwest school and the most middle class of the Atlanta schools.

These beginning statistical results are encouraging enough that I recommend using the VSCS as part of your program evaluation. I ask you to share the data with me or another researcher in order to further judge the reliability and validity of the VSCS. Its usefulness in measuring the effects of character education in general and for a particular school has not been fully demonstrated.

Vessels' Classroom Climate Surveys

My classroom climate instruments (the Vessels' Classroom Climate Survey-Late Elementary [VCCS-LE] and Vessels' Classroom Climate Survey-Early Elementary [VCCS-EE]) may prove to be useful as well, but they should only be used for the near future as research tools and as part of a program evaluation plan that includes other measures (see Appendix J). These instruments were field tested in five urban Atlanta schools, a small-town school in southwest Georgia,, and an urban school in the midwest. The midwest school is fairly well matched with four of the five Atlanta schools in terms of SES but not race. Only one of the Atlanta schools is racially and socioeconomically diverse, and this school matched the southwest Georgia school fairly well on SES and the proportion of black and white students. The remaining four Atlanta schools serve disadvantaged African-American populations. In all seven schools, 65 percent or more of the students were on free and reduced lunch when the data was collected.

The VCCS-EE data collected in September from first and second grade students from six urban schools yielded a total-sample mean of 11.5, with and a standard deviation of 2.5. The pretest mean for the Atlanta subgroup was 11.5, with a standard deviation of 2.5. The mean for the much smaller midwest subgroup was 11.9 with a standard deviation of 2.3. The June VCCS-EE data yielded a total six-school mean of 11.5 with a larger standard deviation of 2.7. Most of the students in the Atlanta subgroup completed the survey earlier in the year as a pretest and again in June as a post-test, and the post-test yielded a mean of 11.4, with a standard deviation of 2.7. The much smaller southwestern Georgia subgroup answered the questions for the first time in June, and this yielded a mean of 13.1, with a standard deviation of 2.7.

With respect to reliability, the VCCS-EE produced an alpha of .73 for the post-test data and .65 for the pretest data. Coefficients for first and second grade students were quite different with numbers for second graders being about .10 higher. The alpha for the beginning-first-grade students was .56; the alpha for the end-of-first-grade students was .67. This difference and the difficulties we encountered keeping first graders on the right question and listening attentively, particularly beginning-first-grade students, suggest that the VCCS-EE should be administered individually or in small groups at this age. The test-retest or stability coefficient was .40 with comparable numbers for first and second grade students.

With respect to validity, the urban midwestern mean of 11.9 was not significantly higher than the total Atlanta mean of 11.5 for the September administration, but the small N for the former and correspondingly high standard error of the mean (.45) suggests that a larger sample may have produced a statistically significant difference. This was essentially a comparison of first graders who had been in a progressive program one year with first graders who were just beginning a character building program. A similarly small N for the southwestern Georgia school yielded a mean of 13.1 that was significantly higher than the mean for Atlanta students. This was a comparison of first graders who had been in a traditional program for two years in a small-town, racially mixed school in south Georgia with first and second grade students in the five Atlanta schools where a program had been in place for nine months and where most of the students were poor and black. When broken down by school, the only significant difference was between first graders at the southwestern Georgia school and first graders at the fairly well-matched multicultural Atlanta school in favor of the former.

With respect to pre-post testing using the VCCS-EE in Atlanta, the post-test mean was larger than the pretest mean for the two schools (Blalock and Campbell) that implemented the character education program the most thoroughly, but the increase was not statistically significant. Means went down in the other three schools, but they went down significantly at only one of the three. The school that implemented the program the most thoroughly at the first grade level had three of four classrooms with a higher VCCS-EE mean at the end of the year; however, only one had a significantly higher mean. Two of the three teachers who were the least committed to the program in the program director's opinion and whose behavior was contrary to the program had statistically significant pre-post decreases.

The VCCS-LE data collected from second, third, fourth, and fifth grade students in September yielded a total-sample mean of 20.8, with a standard deviation of 5.9. The mean for the Atlanta subgroup was 20.36, with a standard deviation of 5.8. The mean for the urban midwest subgroup was 24.63, with a standard deviation 5.7. The June data yielded a total-sample mean of 20.5, with a standard deviation of 6.5. The mean for the Atlanta subgroup was 19.0, with a standard deviation of 5.7. The mean for the southwest Georgia subgroup was 28.9 (29.6 excluding second graders), with a relatively small standard deviation of 3.4.

With respect to reliability, the VCCS-LE data yielded a Crombach's Alpha coefficient of .82 for the September data (first administration for all subjects) and .85 for the June 1997 data (second administration for most subjects). The test-retest or stability coefficient was .52 over a nine-month period and with varied levels of program implementation among the schools.

With respect to validity, the factor analysis produced a Teacher Support factor and a Caring Community factor for the LE form, and these were included in the scoring procedures for the final 34-item scale. The means scores from the southwest Georgia (28.9) and urban midwest (24.6) schools were significantly higher than the means obtained from each of the five Atlanta schools (which ranged from 16.33 to 21.66) and all five schools combined (September and June data). The mean for the southwest Georgia school was significantly higher than the means for the other six schools. The Atlanta school with the best program implementation had a significantly higher mean for the post-test than three of the remaining four Atlanta schools, and this was not true for the pretest. Variability due to pretest scores and SES could not be removed for these comparisons via covariance.

A grade-by-grade comparison of schools revealed that for third through fifth grade, the southwest Georgia school had a significantly higher mean than each of the five Atlanta schools and the urban midwest school. The urban midwest school (established character education program) did not have a higher mean than the Atlanta schools at the third grade level but did have a higher mean than two of three schools at the fourth grade level and all three schools at the fifth grade level. Their mean compared better using Atlanta pretest scores: significantly higher than all but one school at third and fourth and all at fifth. They did not score better at third and fourth grade levels than the one Atlanta school that had the best program using Atlanta post-test scores (no control for pretest scores or SES differences).

One very interesting finding was that the two comparison schools that have had programs for a few years had mean VCCS-LE scores at each grade that were essentially equal (not significantly different), whereas the Atlanta schools that did not begin programs until September 1996 showed a drop in mean scores from third grade to fourth, and from fourth grade to fifth using pretest and post-test scores. It appears that character education programs may help prevent classroom climates from getting worse as the years pass but may not create better climates at higher grades than they do at lower grades.

The paired-samples or pre-post comparisons revealed a statistically significant drop in scores overall and a significant drop for three of the five schools including the two schools with the best implementation. There was also a significant drop at grades three and five but not four. Only one of nineteen teachers showed a significant mean score increase. This drop may reflect increased honesty in responding, but the fact that the means did not increase suggests that if character education changes classroom climates, they do so in the second year or sometime thereafter.

Behavioral Observations During Contrived Small Group Tasks

One way of judging whether students will behave prosocially in real world situations is to involve them with one another in contrived small-group tasks which seek to elicit the same array of interpersonal behaviors that occur naturally as they play and work with one another. This technique is used outside the classroom under controlled experimental conditions that allow investigators to evaluate the extent to which specific prosocial behaviors have generalized beyond the classroom. This technique is not an appropriate way of evaluating every type of virtuous or prosocial behavior, but it is well suited for some types, such as cooperation, helping, and sharing. Unfortunately, it is an option only for schools and systems that have the considerable resources that will be needed, including videotaping equipment and persons who have the time and expertise to administer these tasks and interpret the results.

If used to evaluate a character education program, the task-creation process would begin with the selection of specific virtues or character traits from among those your program is seeking to develop, and to operationalize these so that behavioral indicators can be counted and/or rated. Behavioral objectives provide a starting point for brainstorming possible tasks that will conceivably elicit prosocial behaviors from students who are so disposed. These tasks must be interesting to students, sufficiently unique to do more than elicit well-rehearsed behaviors, and sufficiently open or ambiguous in terms of instructions (semistructured rather than structured) that behaviors other than prosocial behaviors and various forms and degrees of prosocial behavior can occur (Tauber et al., 1989). Care must be taken to use administration procedures that will not inadvertently cause students to act differently than they would ordinarily. It may be necessary to leave students in the room alone, to place video cameras out of sight, or to place observers/recorders behind a one-way window/mirror.

As with questionnaires and direct observation forms and procedures, the Developmental Studies Center (Battistich et al., 1989) has led the way in developing small-group tasks. After extensive piloting they developed several two- and four-person tasks. Although more complex in terms of number of tasks, administration procedures, and scoring/rating procedures than most evaluators would want to use, simplified versions may be possible.

The four-person tasks developed by the Developmental Studies Center (Battistich et al. 1987; Battistich et al., 1985; Tauber et al., 1989) include Pep-Board I, which allows children to play with blocks either independently or together; Pep-Board II, which asks participants to work together to make one design; Unequal Resources, in which each participant is asked to make a chain but is given only a partial set of necessary materials; Chain Building in which the group is asked to make one chain from the materials placed in the center of the table; and Reward Distribution, which allows the group to divide up extra reward stickers in any way that they choose. The two-person tasks (Stone et al., 1989) include Catastrophe, in which one child is asked to bring to the table a box of blocks that has a loose bottom and the other child is free to help or not help with the spilled blocks; Helping/Scarce Resource, in which one person is given a more time-consuming task than the other and the early finisher is given a choice between helping or playing with a toy; and Trucking Game and Bridge Building Game, which are designed so that maximum individual gain can only occur through communication and cooperation.

The scoring of these two- and four-person tasks includes counting specific acts and rating the quality of various types of interaction. Included among the counted acts for the four-person tasks are referring to fairness, exchanging resources, helping, comforting, imitating, calling attention to self, calling attention to other, evaluating self, arguing, and suggesting a strategy; included among the interaction ratings are equality of participation, equality of access to resources, equality of distribution, behavioral coordination, extent of collaboration, group cohesiveness, competitiveness, individual versus group orientation, and planfulness. Two-person tasks are scored for affiliativeness, equality of participation, collaborativeness, turn-taking, helping, willingness to share, supportiveness, competitiveness, and equality of outcome and intent.

Teacher Anecdotals, Journals, and Diaries

Teachers' anecdotal notes can be used to help evaluate the effectiveness of a character education program if they are done consistently, and if they routinely include detailed descriptions of relevant interpersonal events. Of course, it would be easy for teachers who do not like the program to over-report the negative and for those who support it to over-report the positive and under-report the negative, but with guidelines to ensure routine entries and the option of excluding from subsequent review teachers whose objectivity is suspect, anecdotals provide a useful data base. Having teachers make their entries while students are working in their journals, and requiring them to submit them weekly with lesson plans might guarantee regular entries. They will also need examples of what to record and how detailed and descriptive to be. Guidelines such as asking teachers to record the three most significant interpersonal events each day, positive and/or negative, and to avoid referring to any one child more than once each week might make these notes a more reliable and valid indicator of program effectiveness. Those responsible for interpretation could count specific types of negative and positive behavioral entries, or count negative and positive entries irrespective of type, and describe significant increases and decreases over time as one way of assessing program effectiveness. True job-related diaries that teachers know will not be seen by administrators but will be reviewed by independent program evaluators provide another measure of program effectiveness, at least in the sense that they would reflect teacher morale and school climate.

Portfolios with Follow-Up Visits by Outside Evaluation Teams

The traditional "Values and Character Recognition Program" in the Fresno area initiated a voluntary evaluation program in 1988 that required each school to complete an application. This application included five categories of questions about the school's character education program: school planning; instructional activities; school goals, standards, and procedures; opportunities for student involvement; and student recognition. A select committee from outside the participating schools and school systems evaluated the responses to these questions along with supportive documents including handbooks, school newspapers, and announcements for special activities, that is, a portfolio of information. They chose finalist schools and then made site visits to validate what was described in the portfolio. This method, therefore, involved two levels of direct observation: observations by those who had prepared the portfolio and validating observations by the select committee from outside the schools. This evaluation method also resulted in special recognition for schools that were determined to have the strongest programs.

With respect to the application and in particular the "school planning" question, the application instructed the school staff to "describe the kind of student [the] school wanted to develop and to provide evidence of [the] planning and organization of [the] school's programs and/or activities as they relate to character and values education" (Benninga et al., 1991:268). With respect to instructional activities, the application further instructed the school staff to "cite specific activities that offered evidence that instruction in the area of character and values education was part of the school/classroom curriculum." The "school goals, standards, and procedures" category focused heavily on school rules and expectations for students, teachers, and parents; the "opportunities for student involvement" category asked for the percentage of students involved in various curricular, extracurricular, and community services projects, and how students were involved in school government; the student-recognition category simply asked how students were recognized for virtuous behavior.

Curriculum-Based Assessment of Social Skills Acquisition

Many moral virtues or traits of good character, particularly those targeted in chapter 3 (e.g., being thankful, being helpful, sharing, dealing with teasing, being comforting, being brave, showing you are sorry, forgiving others, being patient) have a social skill component or can be viewed as social skills. These virtuous social skills must be taught via the basic steps of good instruction: (1) establishing the need in the minds of students, (2) identifying skill components and modeling them (showing them how), (3) guided practice or role playing with feedback (letting them try it), (4) monitored application or transfer training (arranging for skill practice), and (5) independent application. Teachers who use these steps on their own or in the ICPS or Skillstreaming mode are in a position to actually witness when the skill has been mastered well enough to be used outside the social skill training sessions, and they can observe first-hand the independent use of this skill within the classroom and school. They are also in a position to monitor the use of the skill outside the classroom and outside the school through the use of homework forms (see Skillstreaming model of Goldstein). To provide data for purposes of program evaluation, teachers could simply list the students who have acquired the prerequisite skill and rate the degree to which each student uses the skill virtuously and when appropriate.

Teacher and Parent Ratings of Student Virtues

One of the most direct but presumably not the most objective or reliable type of measurement instrument is a scale that lists the virtues targeted at each developmental level (see chapter 3) and asks both teachers and parents to rate the extent to which the student demonstrates each virtue and related skill(s). The problems with this are a lack of objectivity on the part of parents, a lack of teacher objectivity at the end of the year when they want to see positive results, and a lack of teacher familiarity with each student early in the year when pre-instruction ratings are completed. Possible alternatives are (1) to have the post-instruction ratings from the previous year serve as the pre-instruction ratings for the next, or (2) to have the teacher from the previous year do the pre-instruction ratings for the first program year; however, the pre- and post-ratings will have been done by different people who may differ in terms of their tendency to over- or under-report. Another approach would be to have teachers get to know students a few weeks before pre-instruction ratings and to assure teachers that their pre-post comparisons will only be seen by outside program evaluators and will not affect their yearly evaluations. This may not solve the issue of bias completely, but it could limit it enough to justify including such ratings in the total evaluation plan.

Leming developed a Behavior Rating Scale which was used as a pre-post measure and completed by teachers on all students using a one-to-five response format (Leming et al., 1997). The items present examples of character-related behaviors. He reported a strong internal consistency coefficient of .95.

Indirect Evaluation Techniques

Hypothetical Problem Situations Presented by Interview or Essay

Constructed statements that present students with hypothetical conflict situations, dilemmas, and other problems have been used extensively. With this technique, students are presented with a hypothetical problem and asked what they would and/or should do if they were near or involved, and/or what others who are directly involved in the situation should do. These hypothetical situations have been presented orally through interviews and in writing through essays. Whether students are asked to respond in writing or speech, the advantage of this technique is that they can convey their inner thoughts, feelings, needs, knowledge, opinions, and beliefs freely and honestly, provided they see no need to hide what they really think, feel, need, and know. Even young children will sometimes avoid being honest and open if they think their parents or teacher will find out how they have responded, and it is rather natural for students of all ages to say or write what they believe others want to hear or read, particularly if they anticipate a very favorable response to an untruth and/or an unfavorable response to the truth. The key to reliability, therefore, is to make students believe there will be no reward for lying or distorting the truth, and no punishment for telling the truth. Someone other than significant adults in their lives should do the interview or administer the essay, and verbal assurances should be given that no one who knows them will listen to or read their answers.

The disadvantage of this technique is that someone must review, interpret, and classify the responses so that results for the group can be summarized and interpreted. This is time consuming and will inevitably involve some distortion of what students were trying to convey. Some investigators have attempted to deal with this by having students respond in just one sentence, or by having them furnish the ending to a sentence stem, but these techniques may prevent students from fully and freely expressing themselves.

In the Measure of Moral Values (MMV) (Hogan and Dickstein, 1972), respondents are presented with fifteen brief statements such as they might hear in everyday conversation and are asked to write one-line reactions to each. These reactions are scored for (1) concern for the sanctity of the individual, (2) judgments based on the spirit rather than the letter of the law, (3) concern for the welfare of society as a whole, and (4) the capacity to see both sides of an issue. The Moral Judgment Interview (MJI) (Kohlberg, 1979) presents dilemmas in either written or oral form followed by a series of open-ended questions that are actually not very open-ended. Hoffman's (1970) approach presents students with story beginnings and asks them to write endings, but the scoring of these is as difficult and prohibitive as scoring for the MMV and MJI.

The MJI and MMV were designed for secondary and college students, but this constructed statement or hypothetical situation technique can be used at any age if the content and delivery are developmentally appropriate. Battistich and colleagues (1989) used an interview approach and pictures to present three conflict situations to kindergarten, second, and fourth grade children. These conflicts involved a focal child whose use of an object was interfered with by another child. The conflicts were described in the second person and audiotaped. The oral presentation was followed by a standard set of open-ended questions, and were later coded for (1) the type resolution strategy offered (aggression or take it back, appeal to authority, do nothing or give up, ask for it back or discuss the problem, cooperate or share), (2) who was favored by the strategy (self, other, both), and (3) whose needs were considered (only one's own, only the other's, both).

This same research team used two other hypothetical situations with first and third grade students. One involved attempting to acquire an object from a peer, and the other involved entering into play with a group of peers. Both situations were taken from the Social Problem Solving Analysis Measure (Elias et al., 1978), and the presentation was again aided by pictures and followed with open-ended questions. The responses were scored for variables including (1) the interviewee's understanding of the thoughts and feelings of the conflict participants, (2) the child's belief that his or her actions will solve the problem, (3) means-ends thinking (planning, considering alternatives, anticipating consequences and obstacles), (4) the type of strategies suggested, and (5) the proportion of prosocial and antisocial strategies offered.

Hypothetical situations need not be restricted to dilemmas and need not be scored according to cognitive theories of moral development. The creation process should be guided by behavioral objectives such as those presented in chapter 3 (particularly those dealing with kindness, courage, friendship, and teamwork) and an awareness that very young children must be presented with situations that are almost identical to situations they have actually experienced. They should be modeled after actual problematic interpersonal situations that commonly occur at various age levels such as students fighting over a toy or struggling to be first in line. Through the third grade, an interview approach combined with a standard set of open-ended questions or incomplete sentences about the conflict or problem should yield "scoreable" detail. For grades three through five, presenting the hypothetical situation(s) in essay form and asking students to write their responses can be effective provided oral clarification is available, and provided student responses are guided by one or more questions. An approach that relies exclusively on essays and written responses without oral clarification is not recommended until middle school. Scoring should not be a major concern during the creation process since there will always be a way to determine and compare the prosocial quality of student responses.

Presented Statements: Choosing from Ready-Made Responses

Cline and Feldmesser (1983) refer to the preceding technique as "constructed statements" and the technique that presents pre-formulated alternative responses as "presented statements." The latter essentially involves the presentation of questions that have ready-made responses much like teacher-made and standardized academic tests that use a multiple-choice format. Students can be asked to designate the response that corresponds most closely to their views, or they can be asked to respond in one of several other ways, such as ranking responses from most to least desirable. It is difficult to construct such instruments in a way that prevents students from recognizing the socially desirable alternative, that is, the alternative they feel their teachers and parents would want them to choose. As with constructed statements, students can be assured that neither parents nor teachers will see the results, but the temptation to choose an obviously "right" or "good" alternative, and the natural inclination for students to deceive themselves into thinking they would act prosocially rather than selfishly in a given situation may pose an insurmountable threat to the validity of obtained results. Another potential threat to reliability and validity is the language level of the questions and ready-made responses. Care must be taken to use language that is suited for slow learning students and students who are intellectually capable but underachieving in reading and writing, otherwise the instrument will assess intelligence or verbal ability rather than moral or prosocial inclinations.

Several instruments have been developed using presented statements including the Kohlbergian Defining Issues Test (Rest, 1974). The student questionnaires developed by the Developmental Studies Center (1995b, 1994, 1993b, 1993c) include good examples of presented statements including the following:

Suppose you put your pencil down for a minute and a boy in your class comes along and takes it. You ask him to give it back, but he says "no." What would you do next?

A. Take the pencil away from him.
B. Tell him that you really need your pencil to finish your work.
C. Ask the teacher to make him give it back.
D. Help him try to find another pencil, or tell him he can use yours after you are finished with it.
E. Tell him that you will hit him or take something of his if he doesn't give back your pencil.

Leming used both incomplete sentences and ready-made responses to complete sentences to measure students' understanding of the virtue vocabulary of the Heartwood curriculum (Leming et al., 1997). For grades one through three students were asked to circle one of two virtue terms after each complete sentence was read to them. For grades four through six students were asked to complete sentence stems such as "A person is loyal when" and "A person shows courage when." Responses were scored as "no understanding," "partial understanding," or "full understanding" using detailed scoring rubrics and example responses for each of the three levels of understanding.

Introspective Questionnaires

Questionnaires that use students as respondents often include questions about classroom and school environments and questions that try to get at the various internal aspects of morality. Following the model provided by the Developmental Studies Center, I originally included both types of questions in my elementary student questionnaires, but after analyzing the results, I decided to separate the two and to refer to the classroom climate instruments as surveys and the more personal introspective instruments as questionnaires. This section addresses only the questionnaires.

Introspective questionnaires may provide the best tool for determining the existence and degree of moral feeling, thinking, and knowing. There are, in fact, no good alternatives since these "internal predictors" of moral behavior can only be determined indirectly through observational inferences or indirectly by asking students questions about what is going on "inside." But will enough students answer questions about right and wrong honestly under group administration conditions to make the results reliable and valid for program evaluation purposes? This is the big unanswered question. I have learned through my use of personality assessment instruments one-on-one that nearly all children will provide honest and thus reliable and valid answers to very personal questions if they are (1) asked to be honest, and (2) asked to choose from just two descriptive statements. They seem to find being honest easier when neither of the choices sound so good that normal children delude themselves into believing they are more virtuous than they actually are in order to protect their self-image, or so good that they cannot resist selecting the statement that reflects what they know adults want from them regardless of what is true. Students who are into being the best at being bad will do the opposite if baited with very negative items. The data from our Atlanta project suggest that students may answer very personal questions more honestly the second time asked (nine months later in this project), and the data suggest that offering socially desirable (as opposed to true) answers may peak at third grade and then drop back. The process of repeatedly asking such questions may stimulate a natural phase of values acknowledgment and clarification that precedes real change. Future research will hopefully answer some of these questions.

The student questionnaires developed by the Developmental Studies Center (1995b, 1994, 1993b, 1993c) include questions that concern individual character traits and related social skills, and questions that concern classroom and/or school climate. The questionnaires include questions that probe children's feelings about their school and classroom, trust in and respect for teachers, intrinsic and extrinsic motivation, feelings of belonging, perceptions about the classroom and school as supportive communities, helpfulness and caring toward others who are in need, feelings of self-confidence, self-esteem and efficacy, sense of autonomy, social competence and prosocial motivation, critical thinking and conflict resolution skills, democratic values (assertion responsibility, willingness to compromise, equal participation), social consciousness, and altruism. The questionnaires include many questions in each of these subsections that are grouped within several primary sections: School and Classroom Practices, School Attitudes and Learning Orientations, Feelings of Belonging, Sense of Efficacy and Autonomy, Intellectual and Social Competencies, Social/Moral Orientations. These questionnaires are comprehensive, and administration procedures are thoroughly standardized. The problem is that they are too complex and lengthy and thus not very user friendly or easy to analyze through factor analysis and validity studies. DSC has provided information about reliability which looks quite good including internal consistency coefficients for the subsections in the .60 to .87 range and item-total correlations. In reviewing these questionnaires, I was impressed by their face validity or content validity and comprehensiveness, but I was also convinced that the average school could not use them independently.

Leming developed an introspective questionnaire to measure the extent to which students possessed "ethical sensibility," which was defined as a positive mental or emotional responsiveness toward actions consistent with the Heartwood Institute's seven attributes of character (Leming et al., 1997). It consists of twenty "I" statements (e.g., "If I see someone being mean I will tell the to stop."). Students in grades one through three were asked to respond after the reading of each item by affixing a red, yellow, or green circle on a black-line drawing of a stoplight; students in grades four through six were asked to respond to the same statements by circling a number from one to five. Leming and colleagues reported internal consistency coefficients of .80 for the younger group and .83 for the older.

Vessels' Student Character Questionnaires

The early elementary (VSCQ-EE), late elementary (VSCQ-LE), and middle-high school (VSCQ-MH) student character questionnaires (see Appendices J, K, L) reflect my attempt to assess all aspects of individual moral functioning including moral feeling, moral thinking, moral skills, and moral behavior. The factor analysis of the EE, LE, and MH versions partially supported this four-part concept of morality and produced three additional factors for each form that were incorporated into the scoring: Socialization/Self-Control/Non-Aggression (LE & EE), Teamwork/Social Maturity (EE only), Honesty/Exaggerated Responses (LE only), Moral Initiative/Moral Courage (EE, LE, HS), Moral Maturity (HS), Social Consciousness/Responsibility (HS). Empathy/Caring and Conscience/Moral Obligation were added as subscales to the final scoring procedures simply because the items were easy to extract and promised to be useful. Questionnaire items were eliminated if they did not (1) load well on any of the factors, (2) correlate adequately with the total score, and (3) enhance overall reliability.

I found it interesting that all three versions of the VSCQ produced a clear and distinct Moral Initiative/Moral Courage factor. I also found it interesting that there was no factor-analytic support for a separate moral reasoning/thinking component or subscale. The moral thinking items were distributed among all the factors (more on some than others) with behavior and thinking items typically loading on separate factors for the most part. I considered the possibility that the thinking items were not well conceived or well written, and I tried to improve many of these items, but I suspect the next round of factor analysis will not produce a thinking factor either since it appears that the ability to reason independently in novel situations is either not the essence of moral functioning for children, particularly young children, or varies so much from situation to situation that item clustering is precluded.

The VSCQ-EE (see Appendix K) is designed for use with first and second grade students and under administration conditions that offer at least a one-to-five adult-to-child ratio. The September VSCQ-EE data yielded a total-sample mean of 19.7, with a standard deviation of 3.4. The mean for the small urban midwest subgroup was 19.5, with a standard deviation of 3.4; the mean for the Atlanta subgroup was 19.7, with a standard deviation of 3.4. The June data yielded a total-sample mean of 19.6, with a standard deviation of 3.8. The southwest Georgia subgroup had a mean of 21.9, with a standard deviation of 2.5; the urban Atlanta subgroup had a mean of 19.5, with a standard deviation of 3.8.

With respect to reliability, the September VSCQ-EE data yielded an alpha coefficient of .68, and the June data yielded an alpha of .74. For both sets of data, the alpha was much higher for first graders than second graders. Alphas for the subscales (eight to fourteen questions each) ranged from .40 to .68. The VSCQ-EE stability or test-retest reliability coefficient for the total score was .38—the coefficient was higher for first grade than second grade. Most of the stability coefficients for the subscales were similar. With respect to practice effects, the second-administration mean for students who completed the questionnaire twice was nearly identical to the mean for those who completed it just once—the latter was actually higher but not significantly higher.

The VSCQ-EE mean difference between the southwest Georgia first graders (end of their second program year) and Atlanta first graders (end of their first year) was found to be statistically significant at the .005 level using the independent-samples t-test (populations poorly matched and no control for pretest scores). The mean difference between the urban midwest first graders (beginning of second program year) and Atlanta first graders (beginning of first program year) was not significant and nearly zero (populations well matched on SES but no control for pretest scores). With respect to the September data, none of the four schools (three from Atlanta and one from the midwest) that provided first grade scores had a significantly higher mean score than any other. The June data (five Atlanta schools and one southwest Georgia school) revealed statistically significant differences between the southwest Georgia school and the three least committed Atlanta schools (pretest scores not controlled through covariance).

The pre-post paired-samples t-test for the VSCQ-EE (five Atlanta schools) showed an increase at the first-grade level at the school with the best school-wide program implementation and a first-grade teaching staff that was highly committed to the program. The difference was significant at the .07 level for the total score and significant at the .03 level or better for four of the nine subscales: Moral Behavior, Conscience, Socialization/Non-Aggression, and Moral Thinking. The four other schools showed no significant improvement in their total-scale or subscale mean scores. Across all five schools, the mean difference for high-program-implementing versus low-program-implementing teachers was significant for both the September and June data. There was no significant difference between the means for boys and girls. First graders had a higher mean than second graders on the pretest and post-test, but the difference was only statistically significant on the post-test. An analysis of covariance with pretest scores and school SES as covariates and levels of implementation for school, grade, and class varied as factors revealed differences in favor of first grade and high-implementing teachers.

For the VSCQ-LE (see Appendix L), which was designed to be read to or read by third, fourth, and fifth grade students, the data collected from the urban midwest school in September and the data collected from the southwest Georgia school in June were entered with both the Atlanta pretest and Atlanta post-test data to allow for all possible between-subject or between-school comparisons. The "pretest" data yielded a total-sample mean of 28.9, with a standard deviation of 7.8. The large Atlanta subsample had a mean of 26.9, with a standard deviation of 7.3; the small urban midwest subsample had a mean of 29.8, with a standard deviation of 6.1 (data collected September); the southwest Georgia subsample had a mean of 37.4, with a standard deviation of 4.4 (data collected in June). The post-test data yielded a total-sample mean of 28.0, with a standard deviation of 7.7. The large Atlanta subsample had a mean of 26.3, with a standard deviation of 7.0. The third-, fourth-, and fifth-grade means for the pretest data were 30.2, 28.1, and 28.0 respectively; corresponding means for the post-test data were 27.8, 27.4, and 28.7.

The pretest mean was 28.5 for boys and 29.3 for girls; the post-test mean was 27.5 for boys and 28.5 for girls. Means for classrooms ranged from 21 to 38.

With respect to reliability, the pretest data produced an alpha coefficient of .83; the post-test data produced an alpha of .86. The test-retest or stability coefficient using only Atlanta students who took the questionnaire in September and June was a respectable .49. The fact that third graders scored significantly higher than fourth and fifth graders on the "pretest" suggests a stronger tendency at this age to give socially desirable rather than honest answers.

With respect to validity other than factorial validity, which was discussed earlier, the southwest Georgia school with an established traditional character education program scored higher than the other six schools using both September and June data (variability due to pretest scores not controlled via covariance). The urban midwest school with an established progressive program scored significantly higher than two of the five Atlanta schools using Atlanta pretest scores, and two of these schools using post-test scores (no pretest control). At each grade level, the southwest Georgia mean was significantly higher than the means for all the other schools using data gathered in September and June. The urban midwest mean was significantly higher than that of the Atlanta schools at the fifth grade only, and to a greater extent on the post-test than pretest. This was also true for the Atlanta school that implemented the program the best (no pretest control via covariance).

Like the VCCS-LE, the two comparison schools with established programs had means for all grades that were not significantly different. For the Atlanta schools combined, the pretest mean for grade three was significantly higher than the mean for grade four, and the pretest mean for grade four was significantly higher than the mean for grade five. Differences in favor of higher grades were only evident when pretest scores and school SES were covaried and differences related to school implementation and teacher character were factored into the analysis.

Looking next at the Atlanta pre-post data, the mean for the post-test was significantly lower than the pretest for the total sample, but when examined by school, three of the five schools showed a statistically significant drop. Only five of the nineteen teachers involved had a significant drop in their class mean, but the small sample sizes largely precluded statistical significance. There were no pre-to-post mean increases, statistically significantly or otherwise. I suspect that these within-subject results indicate no improvement during the first nine months of the character education program or a tendency on the part of students to answer more honestly the second time around. This could conceivably be a paradoxical indicator of improved character if children answer more honestly the second time around because of the program's influence. I suspect, however, that we see in this drop, or lack of increase, and the corresponding drop from grade-to-grade in the between-subject comparisons in Atlanta (but not schools with more established programs where scores were the same from grade to grade) how overwhelming the task of building good character will be and that our initial sights should perhaps be realistically set on stopping a steady loss of character during the elementary years.

With respect to the VSCQ-LE subscales, the subscale-to-total scale correlations ranged from .74 to .91, and the test-retest or stability coefficients ranged from a low of .31 for Socialization to a high of .49 for Moral Courage and Moral Skill. The internal consistency (alpha) coefficients ranged from a high of .73 for Moral Behavior and Moral Conscience and lows of .43 for Moral Thinking and .51 for Moral Courage. All others were in the .60 to .65 range. For the within-subject, pre-post *t*-tests, pretest scores were all significantly higher than the post-test scores except for Moral Courage where the pretest score was still higher but not significantly.

The between-subject or between-school Oneway ANOVA results (using Atlanta post-test scores and scores from the comparison schools), showed the southwest Georgia school to be higher than the other six schools on every subscale (variability due to pretest scores not controlled through covariance). The urban midwest school (established progressive program) scored significantly better than only one of the Atlanta schools on the Moral Behavior subscale, three on the Conscience subscale, only one on the Moral Courage subscale, two on the Socialization subscale, one on the Moral Thinking subscale, and two on the Moral Skill subscale. The urban midwest school was not significantly higher on any subscale than the fairly well matched Atlanta school with the best first-year program. All of this could mean that the VSCQ-LE may not be sensitive to real differences between children in schools that have had programs for years and those that have not, but students in the southwest Georgia school scored consistently higher on all subscales for some reason (no control for pretest scores or SES through covariance).

Data for the VSCQ-HS (see Appendix M) is limited to a single administration to 155 sixteen- to eighteen-year-old students in south Georgia. It remains to be seen if the revised, item-reduced and item-improved version that appears in Appendix M can be used with children fourteen or fifteen. If they are language or reading deficient, I suspect not. The data produced a mean of 219, with a standard deviation of 18. With respect to reliability or internal consistency, the obtained alpha was .86 for the final 62-item version. Since many of the thinking items were reworded, this statistic and its value as a program evaluation tool will hopefully increase. Alphas for the nine subscales ranged from an unacceptably low .46 for the Moral Thinking subscale (many items reworded on the final version which has not been used) to .85 for the Moral Maturity subscale (22 items) and .81 for the Moral Feeling subscale (19 items). The other alphas were Empathy .67, Conscience .73, Social Consciousness/Responsibility .62, Moral Courage/Initiative .68, Moral Skill .62, Moral Behavior .62. With the exception of the Moral Thinking subscale, the subscale totals correlated well with each other and with the scale total (range from .67 to .89). Results from the other versions of the VSCQ also suggested that moral thinking is something very different than the other aspects of moral functioning and that students may be inconsistent in their moral reasoning from situation to situation. It may also be that truly autonomous moral reasoning comes much later in development than some have recently suggested.

Unstructured/Semi-Structured Interviews and Related Rating Scales

Interviews were previously discussed as one of two ways to present hypothetical problems to students, but interviews can also be used in a less structured way to indirectly assess the degree of moral emotion that students experience (e.g., empathy, guilt, obligation to share), the extent of their sociomoral knowledge (e.g., what is considered morally right in a given situation), and the moral reasoning or thinking in which they engage (e.g., their conceptions of fairness) as they deal with everyday situations that have moral implications. Such interviews could be conducted one-on-one or with groups of students as problems arise, and they can be combined with interactive instruction that encourages empathetic understanding, and higher level of moral reasoning than is typically demonstrated at a particular age level. Interviews can be semi-structured, which implies that questioning is conversational but intended to elicit information that will allow for answering a few basic questions following the interview.

One-on-one interviews that probe for internal affect, cognition, and knowledge can be aided by projective devices such as those used by clinical and school psychologists (e.g., Sentence Completion Tests and the Thematic Apperception Test). Projective pictures and sentence stems could conceivably be created that help students focus on certain types of feeling and thinking that have been taught at a given age level. Unlike the use of pictures to present hypothetical conflicts as previously described, these pictures might suggest the same social situation to many students, but students would be able to interpret them freely and to freely create stories about them. The interviewer would do nothing more than prompt them with who, what, when, where, and why questions that include the words "feel," "think," and "know" whenever possible.

Perhaps the best way to quantify the information gleaned from interviews such as this is to have interviewers complete a rating scale on each child that focuses specifically on internal moral states (affect, cognition, knowledge). I know of no rating scale in existence that is specifically designed for this purpose. If teachers do the interviewing and complete the rating scales, they would logically draw as well from many months of day-to-day observations that similarly provide insights about individual students.

Student Diaries and Journals

By the third or fourth grade, most students have developed writing skills to the point where they can convey their thoughts and feelings to others fairly well. Additionally, journal writing has become a rather common practice in elementary schools. Journals and diaries, therefore, provide a convenient and valuable source of information about moral affect, cognition, and knowledge, particularly if students are encouraged to recount and reflect upon interpersonal and moral problems they have encountered incidentally or by instructional design each day. Most elementary children will need considerable prompting in order to convey their feelings and thoughts fully. Journals and diaries become a more workable data source for program evaluation at the middle school level, but the older students get, the more concerned they become about privacy. The key to using journals and diaries as a data source is to devise a system for collection and review that will effectively assure students that their privacy will be honored and that neither teachers nor parents will ever see the content (this may necessitate parent permission since parents will not have access and a strange adult will). I have never used journals and dairies as a data source but can imagine that (1) the proportion of prosocial and antisocial entries, (2) the proportion of positive and negative feelings toward others, (3) the proportion of selfish and unselfish acts, (4) the number of positive and negative feeling words used, and (5) the apparent degree to which friendship and positive relationships with peers and teachers are valued might be ways to categorize the information so that it can be summarized.

Research Design

Evaluating character education programs using pure experimental designs with experimental and control groups is not possible in education. This is because (1) it is not possible to randomly assign students to different schools or to keep school populations essentially intact for more than a few months due to transfers, and (2) the random assignment of students to classrooms within schools and the use of character building curricula with some classes and not others (a) precludes critical school-wide components of character education programs and (b) offers no assurance that classes will remain intact without cross-contamination. Another obvious barrier is the difficulty of holding extraneous variables constant, particularly those that might have a significant positive or negative effect upon various potential indicators of program effectiveness.

Some have claimed and others have acted upon the related assumption that *quasi-experimental* designs, which use the terms *treatment group* and *comparison group* rather than *experimental* and *control*, are the next best thing to a true experiment. But *quasi-experimental* designs that match schools and carry out character education programs in one but not the other can be criticized for never achieving adequate matching of student populations, leadership styles, and quality of teaching staffs. There is nothing inherently wrong with making a *quasi-experimental* design a part of your evaluation plan, or at least including a *between subject* component, but in most situations the benefits do not justify the cost of carrying out direct and/or indirect pre-post measures in both *treatment* and *comparison* schools, and the cost of demonstrating that adequate matching of schools (and thus students, teachers, principals, and so forth) has been achieved.

An attractive alternative to *quasi-experimental* and other less elaborate *between subject* designs is the *within subject* design. The advantage of this design is that matching is functionally the same as matching two or more separate groups on all subject variables. This is achieved by exposing each subject to each independent variable (in this case a character education program or additions to one) and measuring the effects of these independent variables through successive measures following each. With character education programs, this essentially involves *pre-post measurement* of each student in a single treatment or program school. To control for any effects that pre-measurements might have upon similar post-measurements, pre-measurements can be carried out with only part of your students. Controlling for the confounding effects of sequencing or the ordering of treatments will not be a problem as you move from no character program to a fully implemented program. This will become more difficult as you introduce changes and additions to your program over the years, but as long as your measures reflect character growth and no digression, you need not be concerned.

Not all measures lend themselves to pre-post usage; therefore, you need to select those that do, such as school-climate questionnaires, introspective-projective questionnaires (Appendices K, L, M), the number of suspensions and detentions, the number, type, and outcome of interpersonal conflicts, the percentage of students scoring within each quartile on standardized achievement tests, possibly a presented statement measure of student responses to hypothetical problem situations, and the targeting of a few operationalized behaviors within classrooms using objective observers, time-sampling, event recording, and both frequency counting and rating depending on the targeted behaviors. After the first year, of course, all of the post-measures or periodical measures carried out during the first year can be used as pre-measures for the second year.

Ongoing monitoring that involves frequent curriculum-based assessment and various pre-post measurement may do little to prove that your program is better than another school's or that it produces better results than nonprogram schools in terms of academic progress and sociomoral behavior, but it will allow you to demonstrate that you have achieved your goals and objectives. You are therefore advised to keep your evaluation in-house, simple, and manageable and to leave *quasi-experimental* designs and other designs with *between-subject* components to researchers whose purposes go beyond the goals and objectives for your school.

No program should be initiated until goals and objectives have been translated into specific research hypotheses, and to the extent possible, these hypotheses should make reference to the measures you have selected just as instructional objectives specify in behavioral terms how the child will demonstrate mastery. Instructional objectives, including those presented in chapter 3 are research hypotheses. I encourage you to develop other more global hypotheses to complement these, however, since you want to know the effects of your program on such things as instructional time, academic learning, required disciplinary action, school climate, volunteerism, and various internal aspects of morality. These should be very straightforward. For example, the character program as planned for this year will reduce the number of serious interpersonal conflicts that occur, as reflected in such measures as the number of Interpersonal-Conflict Report Forms submitted to the office. Another might state that the character education program will result in classroom and school climates that are more comfortable and pleasant for students and teachers and that this will be reflected in increased attendance and classroom/school climate questionnaires. A third might be that the character education program as a whole will increase the amount of instructional time in the classroom and student achievement and that this will be evidenced in teaching time as measured through a classroom observation form and standardized group achievement test scores. Another might be that the multicultural teaching component of the character building program or the program as a whole will improve inter-racial relationships within the school as evidenced by observed increases in in-school and out-of-school contact among students of different races.

Recent Character-Education Research

In my opening paragraphs about program evaluation, I distinguished between practical program evaluation procedures that can be used by personnel within schools, and more complex research designs that can be used to effectively evaluate programs but are typically used by research specialists and not school-based educators. In this final section I will mention and in some cases describe a few published or to-be-published studies of character education or related topics which used more complex research designs.

In chapter 3 I identified seven learning modes that are available to educators. Each of these learning modes has been studied in isolation, and some of this research has been related to the goals of character education, including studies of (1) the relationship between community or sense of community and various attitudinal, motivational, and behavioral outcomes (Battistich et al., 1995); (2) values clarification and Kohlbergian moral development (for reviews see Leming, 1981); (3) direct inculcative methods employed in the second decade of this century (Hartshorne and May, 1928, 1929, 1930); and (4) cognitive social problem solving (for reviews see Greenberg and Kusche, 1988; Durlak, 1983). Few studies have compared the effectiveness with which these learning modes have achieved character education objectives (Benninga et al., 1991) or the effectiveness with which combinations of these seven learning modes have achieved the goals of character education (Leming, 1993). Research findings seem to contraindicate the use of a single mode or methodology and suggest that the modes preferred by traditionalists are probably no more effective than those preferred by progressivists, and vice versa (Benninga and Tracz, 1988; Tracz and Benninga, 1989).

The study by Battistich and colleagues (1995) showed that a relatively progressive approach that emphasized the development of a caring community benefited all students irrespective of SES but benefited the poorest students the most. This suggests that such an approach may be better than more traditional methods for disadvantaged children if it were not for the successes of the traditional approach with impoverished populations, such as that at Allen Elementary in Dayton and West Point Elementary in West Point, Georgia. These findings yield the reasonable hypothesis that any type of character building program will be more effective with children living in poverty since they tend to live in homes and neighborhoods where parental warmth and support (Dodge et al., 1994; Garrett et al., 1994) and an emphasis on educational and personal goal attainment (Ogbu, 1987; Tharp, 1989) are low.

The SMILE program, which was initiated in Weber County, Utah, a few years ago and was recently reformulated (Weed, 1995), is one of just two programs that Leming (1993) credited with demonstrating its effectiveness through controlled research. Weed (1993) reported a two-and-one-half-times reduction in problem behaviors among program students and an increase in problem behaviors within the control schools. This K-6 program combines stimulating interest in moral principle (S), modeling them (M), integrating them with prior knowledge (In), linking with parents through homework (L), and extending the principle learned into real-life situations (E). This model attempts to infuse character education into various specific components of the academic curriculum using special lesson plans written for this purpose and an emphasis on a few core values.

Leming also credited the Child Development Project (CDP) with demonstrating its success through controlled research (Benninga et al., 1991; Developmental Studies Center, 1993, 1994, 1995; Battistich et al., 1989; Solomon et al., 1988, 1990). The CDP schools in these studies used a combination of (1) exposing students to prosocial values; (2) providing opportunities to help others; (3) cooperative learning activities; (4) helping children to be sensitive to, understand, and respect others through various means; and (5) using developmental discipline which combines a caring classroom community with instructional socialization (Watson et al., 1989).

In the CDP studies students were followed over periods of three to six years using observational measures, questionnaires, and hypothetical-reflective interview methods. CDP students scored higher than comparison students on interpersonal sensitivity, consideration of others' needs, and means-ends thinking (Battistich et al., 1989), helpfulness, cooperation, and giving of support (Solomon et al., 1988), and perceptions of the classroom as a caring community (Solomon et al., 1990). They found no difference in with regard to the incidence of negative behaviors and "harmoniousness" (Solomon et al., 1988). Significant reductions in drug use and delinquency have also been found in CDP schools (Battistich et al., 1996).

Benninga's comparison of a more "traditional" extrinsic-motivational school (EXC) with more "progressive" intrinsic-motivational schools (CDP) revealed greater self-esteem for the former and greater helpfulness for the latter, no differences between students in the two programs with respect to social problem solving, and overall improvement for students in both programs when compared to control students (Benninga et al., 1991).

Leming's evaluation of the Heartwood Institute's "Ethics Curriculum for Children" (Leming et al., 1997) assessed students' (1) undersanding of specific character attributes, (2) their "ethical sensibility," and (3) their ethical conduct. The quasi-experimental design involved pre-post testing in program and comparison schools: two from a western Pennsylvania school system and two from a southern Illinois school system. The study used several new assessment instruments developed by Leming. The results showed a significant increase in favor of the program or treatment schools in ethical understanding (understanding of the Heartwood character vocabulary) but not ethical sensibility (defined as a positive mental or emotional responsiveness toward actions consistent with Heartwood's seven attributes of character). The results were mixed for student conduct: only program students in grades four through six showed significantly improved conduct when compared to comparison school students. The Pennsylvania program school reported a fifty percent reduction in discipline referrals; the corresponding comparison school reported a ten percent increase. The Heartwood curriculum in combination with the observed moral character of the teacher appeared to have a positive effect on student behavior; the curriculum in combination with an emphasis upon character-related topics and activities reduced the ethnocentricism of caucasian students.

The Atlanta Pilot Project

The pilot project in five elementary schools in inner city Atlanta (Vessels, 1998) is being evaluated at the end of the first year using a design that includes within-subject (pre-post) and between-subject components. Seven schools were involved in the project: five treatment schools in the Atlanta system and two comparison schools with well-established programs. The study did not include pre-post testing in a program-free comparison school and did not include pre-post testing in the two comparison schools (i.e., questionnaires and surveys were completed only once during the year). The goal of the project was to implement an eclectic program in the five elementary schools in Atlanta. The result was a predominantly traditional approach in all five due to the strong influence of a successful traditional school program in southwest Georgia. Four of the five schools used a few progressive strategies in an effort to build community.

The research hypotheses for the project focused upon change in terms of school and classroom climate, relational behavior, instructional time, learning rate, inner moral character, and program implementation. A variety of evaluation instruments were used in September (pretest) and June (post-test) including the VSCS, VCCS-EE, VCCS-LE, VSCQ-EE, VSCQ-LE, and VCOF (see Appendix), and 1997 ITBS scores for two high-implementing schools were compared with scores from previous years. A variety of statistical tests are being used to analyze the data including the paired-samples t-test for the within-subject or pre-post comparisons, and the independent-samples t-test, analysis of variance (ANOVA), and analysis of covariance (ANCOVA) for the between-subject comparisons.

With respect to program implementation, schools were rated on a ten-point scale with ten representing a complete, comprehensive program. Among the five Atlanta schools, the best school program was rated a six. The weakest was rated a two for grades three through four and a three for grades one and two. Two of the remaining three schools were given a rating of four and the third a rating of five. The comparison schools were given a rating of eight. Teachers were identified as high-program-implementing or low-program-implementing. They were also rated based upon the project director's observation of their ability and willingness to establish meaningful relationships with students and model targeted virtues.

Although the data from this project are still being analyzed, the results thus far suggest some movement in the right direction, particularly in the two Atlanta schools that have very committed principals and the best program implementation. In general, the results suggest that school and classroom climates and student behavior may change for the better as a result of a well-implemented first-year program and that character education may at least prevent children from losing ground in terms of moral character as they move through elementary school. Programs may not improve the inner moral character of students, at least not during the first year, unless schools provide an ideal mix of effective school-wide, grade-level, and class-level implementation and make available teachers who can establish meaningful relationships with children and model good character.

The within-subject analyses revealed no significant increase in student-character-questionnaire scores between September and June. Only the first grade at the school with the best school-wide program and the best first-grade program showed a statistically significant pre-post increase. Mean increases for the first grade at this school were significant for four of the nine VSCQ-EE subscales: moral behavior, conscience, socialization, and moral thinking. The two schools with the best programs and most committed principals, and a third school that had about ten highly committed teachers showed significant pre-post gains on the Vessels' School Climate Survey (VSCS), which was completed by teachers and paraprofessionals. The within-subject analysis of ITBS (achievement) scores at the two highest-implementing schools revealed a significant drop in scores at Blalock, which doubled in student population during the school year, and a significant increase in scores at Campbell, which had a stable population. The drop at Blalock was largely due to a drop at the second grade level where there was a lack of good instruction and a chaotic climate.

Results from the Vessels' Classroom Observation Form (VCOF) showed a significant pre-post decrease in physical aggression (due to a dramatic drop at the school with the strongest program and a high beginning level), hostile student-to-student interactions, hostile teacher-to-student interactions, student and teacher motivation, and the amount of time spent teaching and learning. The pre-post comparisons showed a significant increase in student-to-student kindness, negative student-to-student interactions, student-to-student off-task interactions, student-to-student provocation, teacher-to-student friendliness and courteousness, character education infusion, caring/respectful community, and preventive/moral discipline.

The between-subject analyses that did not control for differences in pretest scores or school differences in terms of the average socioeconomic or social-class level of students suggested that student-character, school-climate, and classroom-climate scores were higher in the southwest Georgia school than each of the other six schools, higher at the fifth grade level *only* in the urban midwest school when compared to each of the Atlanta schools, sometimes higher in the two highest-implementing schools in Atlanta when compared to the other three, and not significantly higher at higher grades (when compared to lower) either at the end of the first-year program in Atlanta or at the end of several years in the two comparison schools. After controlling for initial differences in pretest scores and school SES (Atlanta schools only) and factoring in differences related to other variables, such as teacher character/modeling and relative levels of program implementation by schools, grades, and teachers, a few significant post-test differences were found in favor of lower grades for class climate (VCCS-EE and VCCS-LE), high-implementing schools for school climate (VSCS), grade one and high-implementing teachers and schools for the first- and second-grade student-character measure (VSCQ-EE), and higher grades and high-implementing schools (only the four impoverished schools for the latter) for the third-through-fifth-grade student-character measure (VSCQ-LE).

Federal Grant Evaluations

A few of the federal grant programs have been evaluated using interesting and elaborate designs and techniques. Jennifer John's evaluation efforts in Utah included formative and summative components with the former focusing on implementation and the latter on student and climate change using pre-post testing of students, parents, and staff using her Character Development Survey, pre-post testing of student's knowledge of character education concepts, and the collection of pre-post student discipline data. She was a participant observer in all major training activities and conducted several workshops on action research that provided inservice to all forty of the participating schools during the 1996–97 school year. Her approach combined qualitative and quantitative research and trained school personnel to assist with the evaluation effort. Her plan for 1997–98 is to use a more tightly controlled study using all fourth grade students.

Kathleen Paget in South Carolina worked with representatives from four participating school districts to develop an Indicators Report Form that requires districts to submit data every forty-five days for each of its schools. Most of the requested data concerns disciplinary action and attendance, but districts were also asked to report the number of service learning projects, the number of awards given for citizenship/service, the number of volunteers from the community, and the number of volunteer episodes. Her evaluation model also includes a process component to monitor implementation. In the near future focus groups in each district will begin gathering data from various affected groups, including students, faculty, and parents. Her design includes data collection from demographically matched school districts that do not have character education programs. The South Carolina federal grant project is in its first year, and, like Utah, it allows schools and districts to use any character education model. Therefore, future evaluation results should be interesting and should shed some light on which models work best with which populations and how much implementation is enough. Their state plan is to extend character education statewide in four years.

The Iowa project, which is being evaluated by Troyce Fisher (1997), involves twenty-four rural districts in north-central Iowa that have been involved in a reform initiation related to character education. In contrast to Utah and South Carolina, which have left decisions about program content to individual districts and schools, the Iowa program has avoided "values word" elements and has included service learning, conflict resolution, more active student involvement, writing infusion, instruction designed to enhance higher-level thinking, and collaboration with clergy. The desired outcomes include effective communication and problem solving skills and work place readiness skills. Their evaluation involves collecting survey data from all fifth, eighth, and eleventh grade students using the Resiliency Survey (presumably completed periodically) and teacher interviews. Troyce Fisher emphasized to me that they do not expect significant change immediately and that she expects meaningful change to take twelve to fifteen years.

The Search Institute's Research

The Search Institute has not endeavored to measure the effects of "character education" per se, but the results of its survey research with over a half million sixth through twelfth grade students since 1989 (Benson, 1997) suggests that various community-building and relationship-building efforts which provide support, boundaries, and expectations for students may be causally related to success in school and responsible citizenship thereafter, or may even prevent involvement in various at-risk behaviors that could prevent success. Benson's concept of "developmental assets" (important internal and external building blocks needed to thrive) is a conceptual relative of the progressive approach to character education and perhaps e eclectic approaches as well. His list of twenty internal assets and related categories of Commitment to Learning, Positive Values, Social Competence, and Positive Identity correspond to my categories of Personal and Social Integrity and associated primary virtues of Kindness, Courage, Ability, Effort, Friendship, Teamwork, and Citizenship. His list of twenty external assets and categories of Support (school, family, neighborhood), Empowerment, Boundaries/Expectations, and Constructive Use of Time correspond to several of my learning modes, namely, those that emphasize community building within classrooms and schools and relationship building within the home, school, and community at large. The Search Institute's research shows that most students possess only about half of the forty necessary internal and external assets and that only students who possess most of the forty appear to be effectively "inoculated" against at-risk behaviors and predisposed to school success and responsible citizenship. Though not experimental, the Search Institute's research appears to support the focus of progressive character educators upon other aspects of development besides academic (social, ethical, intellectual, personal) and appears to validate the emphasis of progressive and eclectic character educators upon experiential community-building and relationship-building strategies without precluding the possibility that direct instructional strategies may contribute significantly to character growth and ultimate success in life as well.

REFERENCES

Archibald, G., Berg, S., Stirling, D. and McKay, L. (1996). *How to Prep: Using Character Education in Schools, Homes and the Community.* St. Louis, MI: PREP, Cooperating School Districts.

Battistich, V., Schaps, E., Watson, M. and Solomon, D. (1996). Prevention effects of the Child Development Project: Early findings from an ongoing multisite demonstration trial, *Journal of Adolescent Research,* 11 (1), 12–35.

Battistich, V., Solomon, D., Dong-il, K., Watson, M. and Schaps, E. (1995). Schools as communities, poverty levels of student populations, and students' attitudes, motives, and performance: A multilevel analysis. *American Educational Research Journal,* 32 (3), 627–58.

Battistich, V., Solomon, D., Watson, M., Solomon, J. and Schaps, E. (1989). Effects of an elementary school program to enhance prosocial behavior on children's cognitive-social problem-solving skills and strategies. *Journal of Applied Developmental Psychology,* 10, 147–69.

Battistich, V., Tauber, M. and Rosenberg, M. (1987). *Administration Manual: Four Person Task Assessments.* Oakland, CA: Child Development Project, Developmental Studies Center.

Battistich, V., Tauber, M. and Solomon, J. (1985). *Scoring Manual: Four-Person Task Assessments.* Oakland, CA: Child Development Project, Developmental Studies Center.

Benninga, J. and Tracz, S. (1988). The effects of a competitive program on the prosocial attitudes and behaviors of elementary school children. Paper presented to the American Educational Research Association, New Orleans.

Benninga, J., Tracz, S., Sparks, R., Solomon, D., Battistich, V., Delucchi, K. and Stanley, B. (1991). Effects of two contrasting school task and incentive structures on children's' social development. *The Elementary School Journal,* 92 (2), 149–67.

Benson, P. L. (1997). *All Kids Are Our Kids.* San Francisco: Jossey-Bass.

Bernardo, R. (1995). *School Character Survey.* Dayton, OH: Human Systems Development.

Cline, H. and Feldmesser, R. (1983). *Program Evaluation in Moral Education.* Princeton, NJ: Educational Testing Service.

Deer, J. and Mason, E. (1995). *Questionnaire Administration Manual.* Oakland, CA: Developmental Studies Center.

Developmental Studies Center (1993). *The Child Development Project: Description of Findings in Two Initial Districts and the First Phase of a Further Extension.* Oakland, CA: Author.

Developmental Studies Center (1993a). *Classroom Observation Form.* Oakland, CA: Author.

Developmental Studies Center (1993b, 1993c). *Student Questionnaire: Spring 1993, Part II, Grade 5; Student Questionnaire: Spring, 1993, Part II, Grade 4.* Oakland, CA: Author.

Developmental Studies Center (1994). *Student Questionnaire: Spring 1994, Part II, Grade 6.* Oakland, CA: Author.

Developmental Studies Center (1994). *The Child Development Project: Summary of Findings in Two Initial Districts and the First Phase of an Expansion to Six Additional Districts Nationally.* Oakland, CA: Author.

Developmental Studies Center (1995a). *Teacher Questionnaire.* Oakland, CA: Author.

Developmental Studies Center (1995b). *Student Questionnaire: Spring, 1995, Part I.* Oakland, CA: Author.

Dodge, K., Pettit, G. and Bates, J. (1994). Socialization mediators of the relation between socioeconomic status and child conduct problems. *Child Development*, 65, 649–65.

Durlak, J. (1983). Social problem solving as a primary prevention strategy. In R. Felner, L. Jason, J. Moritsugo and S. Farber (Eds.), *Preventive Psychology*. New York: Pergamon.

Elias, M., Larcen, S., Zlotow, S. and Chinsky, J. (1978). An innovative measure of children's cognition in problematic interpersonal situations. Paper presented at APA Toronto.

Garrett, P., Ng'andu, N. and Ferron, J. (1994). Poverty experiences of young children and the quality of their home environments. *Child Development*, 65, 331–45.

Goodlad, J. (1976). *Facing the Future*. New York: McGraw-Hill.

Goodlad, J. (1984). *A Place Called School*. Highstown, NJ: McGraw-Hill.

Greenberg, M. and Kusche, C. (1988). Preventing pathology and promoting social competence: A developmental model. Paper presented at the annual meeting of the American Association of Orthopsychiatry, San Francisco.

Hartshorne, H. and May, A. (1928–30). *Studies in the Nature of Character: Volume 1. Studies in Deceit; Volume 2. Studies in Self-Control; Volume 3. Studies in the Organization of Character*. New York: Macmillan.

Hoffman, M. (1970). Moral development. In P. Mussen (Ed.), *Charmichael's Manual of Child Psychology (3rd Ed.)*, 261–359. New York: Wiley.

Hogan, R. and Dickstein, E. (1972). A measure of moral values. *Journal of Consulting and Clinical Psychology*, 39 (2), 210–14.

Huffman, H. (1994). *Developing a Character Education Program: One School District's Experience*. Alexandria, VA: ASCD & CEP.

Kohlberg, L. (1979). The meaning and measurement of moral development. Heinz Werner Memorial Lecture.

Leming, J., Hendricks-Smith, A. and Antis, J. (1997). An evaluation of the Heartwood Institute's "An Ethics Curriculum for Children," A paper presented at the annual meeting of the American Educational Research Association, March 28, 1997 in Chicago.

Leming, J. (1993). In search of effective character education. *Educational Leadership*, 51 (3), 63–71.

Leming, J. (1981). Curricular effectiveness in moral/values education: A review of research. *Journal of Moral Education*, 10, 147–64.

National Association of Secondary School Principals (1986/1987). *Comprehensive Assessment of School Environments*. Reston, VA: Author.

Nelson, C. and Smith, E. (1974). Achieving institutional adaptation using diagonally structured information exchange. *Human Relations*, 27 (2), 101–19.

Ogbu, J. (1987). Variability in minority school performance: A problem in search of an explanation. *Anthropology and Education Quarterly*, 18, 312–34.

Parnes, S., Noller, R. and Biondi, A. (1977). *Guide to Creative Action & Creative Actionbook (revised edition)*. New York: Scribners.

Rest, J. (1974). *Manual for the Defining Issues Test: An Objective Test of Moral Judgment Development*. Minneapolis: Author.

Rosenberg, M. and Tauber, M. (1985). *Videotape Coding Manual: Individual Child Behavior: Four Person Tasks*. Oakland: Developmental Studies Center.

Solomon, D., Watson, S., Delucchi, K., Schaps, E. and Battistich, V. (1988). Enhancing children's prosocial behavior in the classroom. *American Educational Research Journal*, 25 (4), 527–54.

Solomon, D., Watson, M., Battistich, V. Schaps, E. and Delucchi, K. (1990). Creating a caring community: A school-based program to promote children's sociomoral development. Invited presentation at the International Symposium on Research on Effective and Responsible Teaching, Fribourg, Switzerland.

Stirling, D. (1997). An active partnership between school, home, and community defines the personal responsibility education process—The largest community experiment in character education. In P. F. Vincent (1997), *Promising Practices in Character Education: Nine Success Stories From Around the Country.* Chapel Hill, NC: Character Development Group.

Stone, C., Solomon, J., Tauber, M. and Watson, M. (1989). Procedures for assessing children's social behavior: dyadic tasks. *Moral Education Forum*, 14 (1), 12–21.

Tauber, M., Rosenberg, M., Battistich, V. and Stone, C. (1989). Procedures for assessing children's social behavior: Four-person tasks. *Moral Education Forum*, 14 (1), 1–11.

Tharp, R. (1989). Psychocultural variables and constants: Effects on teaching and learning in schools. *American Psychologist*, 44, 349–59.

Tracz, S. and Benninga, J. (1989). Effects of the accountability model on the prosocial attitudes and behaviors of elementary school children. Paper presented to the American Educational Research Association in San Francisco.

Vessels, G. (1998). First year effects of a character education program in inner-city Atlanta, (unpublished research report).

Vincent, P. F. (1994). *Developing Character in Students*. Chapel Hill, NC: New View Publications.

Watson, M., Solomon, D., Battistich, V., Schaps, E. and Solomon, J. (1989). The child development project: combining traditional and developmental approaches to values education. In L. Nucci (Ed.), *Moral Development and Character Education*. Berkley, CA: McCutchan.

Weed, S. (1993). *Character Education—Weber Project Summary*. Salt Lake City: Institute for Research and Evaluation.

Weed, S. (1995). *Weber School District Character Education Evaluation, Summary Report*. Salt Lake City: The Institute for Research and Evaluation.

Zenger, W. and Zenger, S. (1986). *Curriculum Development Accountability): At the Local Level*. Saratoga, CA: R & E.

Appendix A

Public Law 103-301

Public Law 103-301

[S.J. Res. 178]
108 Stat. 1558-1559

"National Character Counts Week" Proclamation of 1994
October 16 through October 22

Whereas young people will be the stewards of our communities, Nation, and world in critical times, and the present and future well-being of our society requires an involved, caring citizenry with good character;

Whereas concerns about the character training of children have taken on a new sense of urgency as violence by and against youth threatens the physical and psychological well-being of the Nation;

Whereas more than ever, children need strong and constructive guidance from their families and their communities, including schools, youth organizations, religious institutions and civic groups;

Whereas the character of a Nation is only as strong as the character of its individual citizens;

Whereas the public good is advanced when young people are taught the importance of good character, and that character counts in personal relationships, in school, and in the workplace;

Whereas scholars and educators agree that people do not automatically develop good character and, therefore, conscientious efforts must be made by youth-influencing institutions and individuals to help young people develop the essential traits and characteristics that comprise good character;

Whereas character development is first and foremost, an obligation of families, efforts by faith communities, schools, and youth, civic, and human service organizations also play a very important role in supporting family efforts by fostering and promoting good character;

Whereas the Congress encourages students, teachers, parents, youth and community leaders to recognize the valuable role our youth play in the present and future of our Nation, and to recognize that character is an important part of that future;

Whereas in July 1992, the Aspen Declaration was written by an eminent group of educators, youth leaders and ethics scholars for the purpose of articulating a coherent framework for character education appropriate to a diverse and pluralistic society;

Whereas the Aspen Declaration states that "Effective character education is based on ethical values which form the foundation of democratic society";

Whereas the core ethical values identified by the Aspen Declaration constitutes the Six Core Elements of Character;

Whereas these Six Core Elements of Character are—
(1) trustworthiness
(2) respect;
(3) responsibility;
(4) justice and fairness;
(5) caring; and
(6) civic virtue and citizenship;

Whereas these Six Core Elements of Character transcend cultural, religious, and socioeconomic differences;

Whereas the Aspen Declaration states that "The character and conduct of our youth reflect the character and conduct of our society; therefore, every adult has the responsibility to teach and model the core ethical values and every social institution has the responsibility to promote the development of good character";

Whereas the Congress encourages individuals and organizations, especially those who have an interest in the education and training of our youth, to adopt these Six Core Elements of Character as intrinsic to the well-being of individuals, communities, and society as a whole; and

Whereas the Congress encourages communities, especially schools and youth organizations, to integrate these Six Core Elements of Character into programs serving students and children: Now, therefore, be it

1 Resolved by the Senate and House of Representatives
2 of the United States of America in Congress assembled,
3 That the week of October 16 through October 22, 1994,
4 is designated as "National Character Counts Week," and
5 the President is authorized and requested to issue a
6 proclamation calling upon the people of the United States
7 and interested groups to embrace these Six Core Elements
8 of Character and to observe the week with appropriate
9 ceremonies and activities

Appendix B

Developmental Theories

Juxtaposition of Relevant Developmental Theories See second half of chart on the next page	Piaget Cognitive Development	Piaget Moral Development	Kohlberg Moral Development
Preschool Early Childhood Kindergarten Pre-Kindergarten	- They cannot decenter or take the perspective of others. - They can sense and perceive but not symbolically manipulate. - They cannot comprehend classes and subclasses. - They cannot relate to adult reasoning. - They cannot reflect on or think about their own thinking. - They assume you know what they know and are imitative.	- They are subject to the morality of constraint or heteronomy. - They exhibit social play but do not try to win. - Justice is viewed as that which is commanded by authority. - Attitude about rules is casual. - Authority maintains egocentrism. - Egocentrism is an intermediate step between individual play of younger children and socialized play of children six and older.	(Preconventional 1) - They display heteronomous or adult-dependent morality. - They think in terms of absolutes of right and wrong. - They have an egocentric viewpoint. - They are good to avoid punishment and/or to gain rewards. - They view the value of life the way they do the value of objects.
Early Elementary Middle Childhood First and Second Grades	Concrete Operations - They move from perceptual or preoperational to conceptual or concrete operational thought, i.e., they begin to solve problems in their heads because they can manipulate objects symbolically. - They cannot imagine events that are not real events, need real things to think about, and cannot think abstractly. - They can take the perspective of others. - They are becoming more and more interested in peers. - They willfully engage in social cooperation.	- They display instrumental cooperation. - They are subject to the morality of constraint for the most part. - They want to win by age seven but have only a vague notion of the rules of games. - They view rules as sacred and unchangeable. - They view justice as that which is commanded by authority.	(Preconventional 2) - They view right as that which satisfies their own needs. - They have a concrete, pleasure-seeking, reward-seeking, individualistic perspective. - Their cooperation is instrumental, and they will exchange favors to satisfy needs. - The value of life is viewed as instrumental to need satisfaction.
Late Elementary Late Childhood Grades Three Through Five		- They are in transition between heteronomy and autonomy or the morality of cooperation. - They come to know codified game rules well and show an intense interest in them. - They continue to view rules as unchangeable. - They view justice in terms of equality that comes about from solidarity and mutual respect.	(Conventional 3) - They view right as that which gains approval. - They have an interpersonal, Golden Rule, good-child/bad-child perspective. - They gain approval by being caring and accommodating toward significant others. - They view the value of life in terms of affectional bonds.
Middle School Early Adolescence Grades Six Through Eight	Formal Operations - They move from concrete-operational to formal-operational thought, think logically and abstractly, and begin to manipulate symbols in their heads. - They can imagine hypothetical as well as real events.	- They are subject to principled moral autonomy or the morality of cooperation. - Their rule mastery and codification of rules in games that began at about age ten continues. - They view justice in terms of equity rather than equality. - Rules are viewed as a changeable product of mutual consent.	(Conventional 4) - They view right as doing one's duty, showing respect to authority, and maintaining social order. - They have an organizational-need, societal-need, law-maintaining perspective. - They view life as sacred within the context of a scheme or moral rights.
High School Late Adolescence Grades Nine Through Twelve	- They can introspect, reflect, and think about their own thinking. - They can consider many viewpoints and take the perspective of others fully. - They are much more self-conscious than previously.	unexplained	(Post-conventional) - They view right as upholding basic rights, values, and legal contracts or in terms of meeting mutual obligations within the context of societally established rights and standards. - They have a law-creating, moral-legal view that obligates them to honor social commitments. - They show principled moral reasoning.

Selman & Youniss Friendship Development	Damon Moral Development	Erikson & Havighurst & Hoffman Moral-Affective Development	Juxtaposition of Relevant Developmental Theories See second half of chart on the previous page
(Level 0) - Children have an egocentric understanding of friendship that involves sharing toys and enjoyable activities with incidental playmates. They are becoming more selective and selfish with their prosocial behavior. They cannot distinguish between their own perspective and others'.	- 0-A (4 years old) : They make no attempt to justify choices and feel they should get more because they want more; they are inclined to distort the commands of authority to fit their own wishes. - 0-B (5 years old): They justify choices in a selfish, after-the-fact way; they view authority as an obstacle to satisfying desires and do not relate to authority function.	(Erikson/Hoffman) - They must take initiative and will experience excessive guilt and fail to realize their potential in life if they fail. - They are at the dawn of conscience but have not internalized adult expectations. - They have emotional empathy or feelings of concern that limit aggression.	Preschool Early Childhood Kindergarten Pre-Kindergarten
(Level 1) - Friendship is defined by unevenhanded reciprocity that derives from a subjective, unilateral, or one-way social perspective. Friends begin to realize that feelings and intentions and not just actions keep them together. They know others have a different perspective but can focus only on one.	(Egalitarianism) - 1-A : They view fairness in terms of equality; authority is confused with the power to enforce, i.e. might makes right. - 1-B: They view fairness in terms of merit and reciprocal obligation. Fairness emerges as a value in its own right. Children see obedience as a legitimate trade for adult favors and help.	(Havighurst) - Authoritarian conscience becomes an inner guide; the child takes in the controlling voice of parents as a result of discipline and parental love. (Erikson) - They must gain a sense of industry and competency and will suffer a sense of inferiority and relationship problems if they fail.	Early Elementary Middle Childhood First and Second Grades
(Level 2) - Friendship is defined by twoway, cooperative, even-handed reciprocity or mutual helping. Fair-weather friendships may not withstand conflicts. They can self reflect and realize that people have an outer and inner self. They realize that people have varying viewpoints and are aware of their mixed feelings.	(Equity/Benevolence) - 2-A: They view fairness as a right of all persons, especially the needy; they view leaders with knowledge as more legitimate. - 2-B: They view justice (by 10) as context dependent and can make reasoned decisions based on claims and conditions, but their perspective is limited to the situation.	(Havighurst) - A rational conscience gradually replaces the authoritarian conscience during elementary school through peer-group identification, cooperation among peers, and a growing understanding of the function of rules.	Late Elementary Late Childhood Grades Three Through Five
(Level 3) - Friendship is defined by mutual and exclusive trust, loyalty, and intimacy that involves sharing inner-most feelings with a trusted few. This is built on the ability to take a third-party perspective with respect to self, others, and relationships, i.e., they can step outside a social situation and view its complexities.	(general) - Self-understanding is based on social and personality characteristics rather than capabilities of childhood or the beliefs and thoughts of late adolescence. - They will gain the ability to view a situation involving disparate claims to justice from a wider perspective than the situation and can apply moral principles.	(Havighurst) - They begin to form a complete set of moral principles that they use to judge self and others. (Erikson) - They are seeking to consolidate or integrate their social roles and identifications into an ego identity that is a unique gestalt. - They tend to over-identify with individuals and groups and tend to be clannish and intolerant.	Middle School Early Adolescence Grades Nine Through Twelve
(Level 4) - Friendship is defined by autonomous interdependence whereby friends are close and intimate yet grant each other the independence to establish other close friendships. Words, glances, and gestures can have deeper shared meanings that are unknown to others.	- Self understanding or selfconcept is based on beliefs, philosophies, and thoughts rather than personality qualities as in early adolescence.	- They are driven by a concern for how they are perceived by peers. - The resolution of this crisis allows for moving on in terms of moral development and the capacity for sexual intimacy. - Failure can be due to unresolved earlier crises or the failure to commit to an ideology and way of life.	High School Late Adolescence Grades Nine Through Twelve

Appendix C

Classroom News Form

Blalock Elementary
Our Weekly Classroom News

Teacher _____ Date _____

Current Events

Reminders

Character Education

GENTLE
WORD OF THE WEEK
Using a soft and sweet touch and voice and being kind
when a person or animal might be more upset if you don't.

Talk to your child about the difference between being gentle and rough and about when being gentle is right thing to do.

Explain to your child that animals are often afraid of children because children move too fast and don't notice when animals are afraid of them.

Explain that the word "gentleman" means that a man has manners and is gentle and considerate of women and others who are not as strong.

Keep your child from exposure to excessive roughness and violence by controlling what they watch on television and what they listen to on the radio.

Appendix D

Brookside's Character Corner

**BROOKSIDE
CHARACTER
EDUCATION**

3849 Saddlemire Road, Binghamton, New York 13903   (607) 669-4105   Fax: (607) 669-4811

Brookside's Character Corner

The school and the community working
together for our children...our future

Every month Brookside will be featuring a different attribute as a building block in the foundation of teaching our children how to become good citizens. At Brookside Elementary we will be incorporating activities and discussion around our "Attribute of the month." We would like the community to get involved and support our efforts. When we see elementary students around town and at home, teach them, talk to them, and show them.

Responsibility

September's Attribute of the month

Responsible people are reliable, accept the consequences of their words and/or
actions, can be trusted, take care of themselves as well as others, and are
accountable for all that they say and do.

* Talk to your child about what responsibilities you have at home and work
* Help children follow through on commitments they have made to a team or group by
reminding and explaining their responsibilities
* Setting limits helps children understand responsibility for their behavior
* Give children age-appropriate household chores to help teach the concept of family responsibility
* Brainstorm a list of how a child is already responsible (such as brushing their teeth, setting
the table) and show how much you appreciate their responsibility
* Teach children to own up to their mistakes
* Read *Teaching Your Child Values* by Linda and Richard Eyre

Suggested Reading:

Rice, Eve. *Sam Who Never Forgets.* (grades PS-1)
Delton, Judy. *Backyard Angel.* (grades 3-5)
Blos, Joan W. *A Gathering of Days.* (grades 5-6)
Barton, Byron. *The Little Red Hen.* (grades K-2)
Seuss, Dr. *Horton Hatches the Egg.* (grades K-3)
Gardiner, John Reynolds. *Stone Fox.* (grades 3-6)
Bernstain, Stan and Jan. *The Bernstain Bears - The Messy Room.* (grades PS-2)
Bernstain, Stan and Jan. *The Bernstain Bear - Telling the Truth.* (grades PS-2)
Arnold, Tedd. *The Signmaker's Assistant.* (grades 2-3)

Good Character is...what you feel in your heart, what you think in your head, and what you do with your hands.

Appendix E

Core Essentials Parent Guide

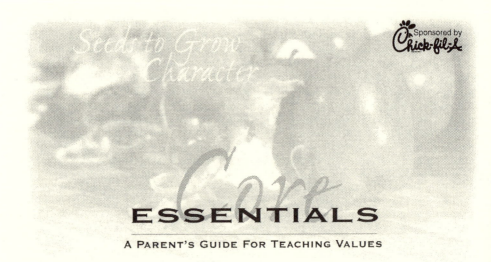

ESSENTIALS

A PARENT'S GUIDE FOR TEACHING VALUES

VALUE OF THE MONTH *Cooperation*

Our children start life completely dependent upon us. We care for them and watch them as they begin to do more for themselves. Then, we expect them to do most things without much help. But what about the tasks that are too big for them to take on alone? Children must learn that sometimes individual effort is part of a larger accomplishment by a group. They need to work with others and enjoy the satisfaction of a job well done. Cooperation is important to understand as a Core Value because it confirms our individual worth while emphasizing working toward a shared purpose. Describing real-world examples helps us paint a picture of cooperation that even the youngest child can understand.

THE ORCHESTRA STAGE
One by one the musicians file in to find their appointed chair. They carry music which has only the notes they need to play. A discordant flurry of notes begins as each player prepares his instrument. Each string, key, and reed is finely tuned. There's a hush as the conductor raises his baton. Then from one section comes a quiet melody. The power of the music grows as more instruments and harmony are added. Many parts fit together to make the familiar chords of a great musical piece. Can one member produce the whole sound of the orchestra? No. Would the audience notice if one member played badly? Sure. What is the shared purpose of the orchestra? To perform beautiful and inspiring music, each member playing just his notes while contributing to the whole sound.

THE OPERATING ROOM
The room is brightly lit and cool. Two nurses are preparing rows of carefully cleaned and arranged instruments. The surgeon scrubs his hands before putting on a sterile gown and gloves. Above the patient's head, the anesthesiologist puts the patient off to sleep, carefully monitoring his vital signs and giving drugs when needed. After the operation is complete, a nurse closely observes as the patient begins his recovery. What is the key ingredient in caring for surgery patients? Cooperation - each professional expertly doing their part for the patient's sake. One person cannot do all the tasks it takes to make surgery successful.

THE BASEBALL DIAMOND
The Braves are ahead by two runs in the top of the ninth, one out, with a runner on first. The Marlins are up to bat. John Smoltz is in ready position. He winds up - a 95 mile per hour ball fires toward home plate. Strike one. Lopez tosses the ball back to Smoltz. The batter swings the bat readying himself for the next pitch. In the infield, the first baseman comes into position. The outfielders are watching the batter, ready to react when he makes contact. Smoltz throws, Conine hits a hard line drive to right field. As he heads for first, Tucker scoops up the ball, fires it to Lockhart on second, who tags and then throws to first. A perfect double play! Did Smoltz win the game by himself? No way! Teamwork is cooperation at its finest.

The Value this month is Cooperation - *working together to accomplish more than you could do alone.* Parents can help children recognize and enjoy the chance to cooperate. The objective is for kids to develop an awareness of the way some tasks depend on working together to succeed.

VANDERLYN ELEMENTARY
1877 VANDERLYN DRIVE • DUNWOODY, GEORGIA 30338

TEAM SPORTS

*T*eam sports offer opportunities to learn cooperation and good sportsmanship. Key to the lasting lessons that will be learned are the program and the coach. Make sure that the coach's philosophy is one which supports primarily instruction versus competition for younger children. The coach should emphasize mastery of the sport over winning and encourage the children to reach his or her potential in terms of skill development.

Other things to consider:
- Do all team members get equal playtime?
- What are the time demands (e.g. How many practices per week, length of practice, where are the games held?)
- Does the coach use mistakes as opportunities to gently instruct and are the children praised for their effort?
- Is good sportsmanship emphasized?
- Are safety rules adhered to during games and practices?
- What are the expenses involved?

Not only do team sports teach the valuable lesson of cooperation, they also give your child a great opportunity to build leadership skills, boost self-confidence and help him or her deal with both success and failure.

Culturally WISE

DECEMBER 1620
It was a cold and rainy December morning in 1620 when the Pilgrims landed at Plymouth. They settled in a deserted village of the Pawtuxet Indian tribe. They had heard fantastic stories of Indian tribes and their savagery. Over the harsh winter, many settlers died from diseases and starvation. At last, winter ended and the Pilgrims who remained began their new life as they watched the Mayflower sail out of Plymouth harbor.

The Pilgrims did not wander far from their settlement. They lived isolated from, and in fear of the Indians. One spring day, a so-called "savage" walked into Plymouth. "Welcome Englishmen," he said. The settlers were shocked that he spoke English and seemed so friendly and dignified. How could they have so misjudged their neighbors? A week later, this Native American, Samoset, returned with Chief Massasoit and Squanto, a Pawtuxet Indian who had been kidnapped then returned by the English.

Squanto taught the Pilgrims to plant corn, squash, beans and pumpkins. He also taught them how to fish for native herring. The new crops thrived and the harvest of 1621 was abundant. For three days the Pilgrims and Indians feasted on roasted turkeys, fresh baked breads and the fresh vegetables from their gardens.

Massasoit needed the Pilgrims as much as they needed him. Over half of his tribe had died and he lived in fear of other Indian tribes. By realizing that they were more alike than they were different, two races discovered the benefits of cooperation.

Core Value

COOPERATION

WORKING TOGETHER TO DO MORE

THAN YOU CAN DO ALONE

Stories to Share:

THE FIRST THANKSGIVING
BY JEAN CRAIGHEAD GEORGE

KEEP THE LIGHTS BURNING, ABBIE
BY PETER AND CONNIE ROOP

AND STILL THE TURTLE WATCHED
BY SHEILA MACGILL-CALLAHAN

A CHAIR FOR MY MOTHER
BY VERA B. WILLIAMS

SWISS FAMILY ROBINSON
BY ROBERT LOUIS STEVENSON

Think About It

**HOW WE COOPERATE
TO PROTECT OUR WORLD.**

The **National Wildlife Federation** is our nation's largest, member supported conservation group. Members cooperate to protect nature, wildlife, and the world we share. The NWF suggests several ways that we can create areas which support and protect wildlife. There are four basic elements of a wildlife habitat that we can help protect:

FOOD - Plant trees and shrubs that provide fruits and berries for wildlife. Also, supplement with feeders that provide nectar for hummingbirds in the summer months and provide a variety of seeds for other birds throughout the year.

WATER - A bird bath provides water for drinking and bathing.

COVER - Rock, log, and mulch piles over effective cover. Small mammals, reptiles, amphibians, and a great variety of insects and other small animals find homes here.

PLACES TO RAISE YOUNG - Bird boxes or houses provide protected nest sites for bluebirds, chickadees, wrens and purple martins.

You may choose one of these ideas as a family project.

Mealtime Notes

WEEK 1- DEFINE

Read the Definition
As often as you can at mealtime, have someone read the definition for cooperation.

Define the Value.
During a mealtime this week, attempt to answer the question, "What is cooperation?" Allow family members to put the meaning in their own words. Talk about how we need other people with whom to cooperate to accomplish a task.

Use a Personal Story.
Try to remember an illustration or example of how you cooperated to do more than you could alone. Recall incidents from your childhood, your family, or your work which required cooperation. You might choose to describe a lesson you learned when you chose to cooperate rather than trying alone.

WEEK 2 - EVALUATE

Read the Definition
As often as you can at mealtime, have someone read the definition for cooperation.

Examine the Value.
Go around the table and have everyone answer the question, "Why is it important to cooperate?" Also, "What are some tasks that require cooperation to accomplish?" "What would happen if one person tried to do everything?"

Use a Book, Movie, or Media Source.
Think of something you have learned from a book or story that illustrates cooperation. From the recent movie Apollo 13, talk about the cooperation required to bring the astronauts home. What might have happened if the team on Earth had not cooperated to solve the space capsule's big problems.

WEEK 3 - ENCOURAGE

Read the Definition.
As often as you can at mealtime, have someone read the definition for cooperation.

FAMILY TIME

Spend at least one meal time each week talking about values.

Encourage the Value.
Answer the question, "How have members of our family used cooperation to complete tasks?" Talk about the necessity of cooperation to keep the family going. Have your kids been "caught" cooperating? What tasks are there at home that would allow them to cooperate?

Use an Example from Everyday Situations.
Describe some situations at home, school, or work which require cooperation. Consider such things in your discussion as class plays, school festivals, sports teams, and projects. Also, ask your child how the name of our country describes the cooperation needed to keep the nation running.

WEEK 4 - DECIDE

Read the Definition.
As often as you can at mealtime, have someone read the definition for discipline.

Decide about the Value.
Make some decisions about cooperation in your family. Talk about the cooperation required to accomplish the weekly routine in your home. Discuss how working with others in your family makes big chores seem smaller. Identify some old tasks that cooperation would put new energy into.

Remember a Historical Example.
Choose a historical example of cooperation. You might discuss the Pilgrims and ways they demonstrated cooperation in their lifestyle. Describe the pioneer custom of a "barn raising" to help new settlers.

Nature's Way

ANTS
It doesn't take very long for a group of ants to find your picnic lunch. News travels fast in an ant colony. This is one reason scientists call ants one of the most cooperative species of all animals. People talk by saying words, but ants talk by smelling. When an ant finds something good to eat, it hurries back to the colony leaving behind a special trail. Soon hundreds of ants find their way back to the food by following the trail.

Ants can lift 50 times their own weight. That is like a person lifting two small cars at the same time. The ant lives an average of eight years. That is longer than any other insect known.

Ants live in colonies which are made up of thousands of ants that live and work together. They are called social insects because different ants in the colony do different things to help in the work of the colony. In every ant colony there is usually one queen, a few males and thousands of workers.

Current News

THE MIR SPACE STATION
For the last forty years, the US and Soviet Union have been sending rockets and men into space. What began as a race has become a cooperative alliance of nations united in a common goal. At first, the race was to control space and prevent the use of nuclear weapons. Now we are working together to find solutions to mankind's common problems and sharing knowledge as we pursue this "last frontier."

The year 1975 marked the first cooperative effort of the United States and Russia. The Russian Soyuz and American Apollo 18 docked (connected) in space. Since that time, we have seen the collapse of the Soviet Union and the dawning of full cooperation in space. We began routine launches of the Shuttle in 1981 and the Russians launched the Mir Space Station in 1986. A US astronaut spent four months on Mir in 1995 and we have since shared in many cooperative missions aboard the station. Even though we recognize the risks involved, we continue to share common goals of space research and exploration with Russia.

The US completed the most recent hook-up of a shuttle with the Mir Space Station in September. One of our astronauts, Dr. David Wolf, will spend several months on Mir. He plans to work on three dozen science experiments particularly focusing on the growth of human cancer tissue. Dr. Wolf will also cooperate with his Russian crew-mates to repair and maintain their habitat in space using a new main computer provided by the US.

S	M	T	W	T	F	S

NOVEMBER

| | | | | | | 1 |

Cooperation
WORKING TOGETHER TO DO MORE THAN YOU CAN DO ALONE

| 2 | 3 | 4 | 5 | 6 | 7 | 8 |

Week 1

DEFINE: WHAT IS <u>COOPERATION</u>?
STORY TIME: EXAMPLES FROM FAMILY OR PERSONAL BACKGROUND

| 9 | 10 | 11 | 12 | 13 | 14 | 15 |

Week 2

EXAMINE: WHY IS IT IMPORTANT TO <u>COOPERATE</u>?
STORY TIME: EXAMPLES FROM MOVIES, BOOKS, OR CURRENT EVENTS

| 16 | 17 | 18 | 19 | 20 | 21 | 22 |

Week 3

ENCOURAGE: HOW CAN WE HELP EACH OTHER BE <u>COOPERATIVE</u>?
STORY TIME: EXAMPLES FROM NATURE OR SCIENCE

| 23 | 24 | 25 | 26 | 27 | 28 | 29 |
| 30 | *Week 4* | | | | | |

DECIDE: WHAT HAVE WE DECIDED ABOUT <u>COOPERATION</u>?
STORY TIME: EXAMPLES FROM HISTORY OR EVERYDAY SITUATIONS

EXAMPLES

ORGANIZATIONS THAT SHOW COOPERATION

The **National PTA** is the oldest and largest volunteer association in the United States working exclusively on the behalf of children and youth. The PTA has promoted many projects which coordinate children's key environments - home, school and the community. In 1912, PTA sponsored a hot lunch project in many schools. One of the PTA's most successful volunteer efforts directly effected public health. Many of us remember standing in line for a sugar cube protecting us against polio. The PTA was recognized in 1957 for achieving record acceptance of the Salk vaccine. Throughout its existence, the PTA has forged a vital link between school and home by providing parents and teachers with easy access to one another. Today, the partnership of PTA still provides a mechanism for teachers and parents to agree and act on important issues that effect our children.

To the Rescue - On an average day the **Coast Guard** ... Saves 32 lives ... Assists 308 people ... Saves $8 million in property value ... Conducts 142 Search and Rescue missions ... Seizes 148 pounds of illegal drugs. The Coast Guard is the primary federal agency with maritime authority for the United States. Its four main missions are: Law Enforcement, Maritime Safety, Marine Environ-mental Protection, and National Security. These men and women serve our country by coordinating many activities that respond to public needs.

Millard Fuller gave up a lifestyle of riches and wealth to help other people in need. Under his leadership, a worldwide network has coordinated efforts to provide affordable housing. Volunteers have cooperated with some 60,000 families in need to build homes in more than 1,300 US cities and 50 other countries. This organization ranks in the top 20 builders in the US and is the largest among non-profit builders. More than 300,000 people now have safe, serviceable, and affordable shelter due to their cooperation with **Habitat for Humanity.**

In the summer of 1859, Swiss businessman Jean Henri Dunant visited the northern Italian town of Solferino. He found nearly 40,000 dead and wounded soldiers receiving little or no care, following a massive battle that day between the French and Austrian armies. For the next three days, Dunant did everything he could to help the men who lay dying. He returned to Geneva and put his feelings into words by writing A Memory of Solferino, which would later inspire Clara Barton to found the **American Red Cross.** Today, millions of volunteers participate in the threefold mission of the Red Cross - to improve the quality of human life; to enhance self reliance and concern for others; and to help people avoid, prepare for, and cope with emergencies.

(Discuss how these groups depend on a lot of people.)

Appendix F

Word-of-the-Week Sheets

GENTLE
WORD OF THE WEEK
Using a soft and sweet touch and voice and being kind
when a person or animal might be more upset if you don't.

PUNCTUAL
WORD OF THE WEEK
Getting places and doing things on time.

LOVING
WORD OF THE WEEK
Feeling and showing love, warmth, and caring in a special
way toward a person or animal who is special to you.

COMFORTING
WORD OF THE WEEK
Making someone's sadness, pain, or problem seem
easier by being interested, concerned, and nice.

Appendix G

Religious Expression in the Public Schools

RELIGIOUS EXPRESSION IN THE PUBLIC SCHOOLS

A press release from Education Secretary Richard Riley to all school
superintendents across the country dated July 1995

Student prayer and religious discussion: The Establishment Clause of the First
Amendment does not prohibit purely private religious speech by students.   Students
therefore have the same right to engage in individual or group prayer and religious
discussion during the school day as they do to engage in other comparable activity. For
example, students may read their Bibles or other scriptures, Say grace before meals, and pray
before tests to the same extent they may engage in comparable non-disruptive activities.
Local school authorities possess substantial discretion to impose rules of order and other
pedagogical restrictions on student activities, but they may not structure or administer such
rules to discriminate against religious activity or speech.

Generally, students may pray in a non-disruptive manner when not engaged in school
activities or instruction, and subject to the rules that normally pertain in the applicable
setting. Specifically, students in informal settings, such as cafeterias and hallways, may pray
and discuss their religious views with each other, subject to the same rules of order as apply
to other student activities and speech. Students may not speak to, and attempt to persuade,
their peers about religious topics just as they do with regard to political topics. School
officials, however, should intercede to stop student speech that constitutes harassment aimed
at a student or a group of students.

Students may also participate in before or after school events with religious content, such
as "see you at the flag pole" gatherings, on the same terms as they may participate in other
non-curricular activities on school premises. School officials may neither discourage nor
encourage participation in such an event.

The right to engage in voluntary prayer or religious discussion free from discrimination
does not include the right to have a captive audience listen, or to compel other students to
participate. Teachers and school administrators should ensure that no student is in any way
coerced to participate in religious activity.

Graduation prayer and baccalaureates: Under current Supreme Court decisions, school
officials may not mandate or organize prayer at graduation, nor organize religious
baccalaureate ceremonies. If a school generally opens its facilities to private groups, it must
make its facilities available on the same terms to organizers of privately sponsored religious
baccalaureate services. A school may not extend preferential treatment to baccalaureate
ceremonies and may in some instances be obliged to disclaim official endorsement of such
ceremonies.

Official neutrality regarding religious activity: Teachers and school administrators, when
acting in those capacities, are representatives of the state and are prohibited by the
Establishment Clause from soliciting or encouraging religious activity, and from
participating in such activity with students. Teachers and administrators are also prohibited
from discouraging activity because of its religious content, and from soliciting or
encouraging anti-religious activity.

Teaching about religion: Public schools may not provide religious instruction, but they
may teach <u>about</u> religion, including the Bible or other scripture: the history of religion,

comparative religion, the Bible (or other scripture)-as-literature, and the role of religion in the history of the United States and other countries all are permissible public school subjects. Similarly, it is permissible to consider religious influences on art, music, literature, and social studies. Although public schools may teach about religious holidays, including their religious aspects, and may celebrate the secular aspects of holidays, schools may not observe holidays as religious events or promote such observance by students.

Student assignments: Students may express their beliefs about religion in the form of homework, artwork, and other written and oral assignments free of discrimination based on the religious content of their submissions. Such home and classroom work should be judged by ordinary academic standards of substance and relevance, and against other legitimate pedagogical concerns identified by the school.

Religious literature: Students have a right to distribute religious literature to their schoolmates on the same terms as they are permitted to distribute other literature that is unrelated to school curriculum or activities. Schools may impose the same reasonable time, place, and manner or other constitutional restrictions on distribution of religious literature as they do on non-school literature generally, but they may not single out religious literature for special regulation.

Religious excusals: Subject to applicable State laws, schools enjoy substantial discretion to excuse individual students from lessons that are objectionable to the student or the student's parents on religious or other conscientious grounds. School officials may neither encourage nor discourage students from availing themselves of an excusal option. Under the Religious Freedom Restoration Act, if it is proved that particular lessons substantially burden a student's free exercise of religion and if the school cannot prove a compelling interest in requiring attendance, the school would be legally required to excuse the student.

Release time: Subject to applicable State laws, schools have the discretion to dismiss students to off-premises religious instruction, provided that schools do not encourage or discourage participation or penalize those who do not attend. Schools may not allow religious instruction by outsiders on school premises during the school day.

Teaching values: Though schools must be neutral with respect to religion, they may play an active role with respect to teaching civic values and virtue, and the moral code that holds us together as a community. The fact that some of these values are held also by religions does not make it unlawful to teach them in school.

Student garb: Students may display religious messages on items of clothing to the same extent that they are permitted to display other comparable messages. Religious messages may not be singled out for suppression, but rather are subject to the same rules as generally apply to comparable messages. When wearing particular attire, such as yarmulkes and head scarves, during the school day is part of students' religious practice, under the Religious Freedom Restoration Act schools generally may not prohibit the wearing of such items.

Appendix H

Classroom Observation Form

VESSELS' CLASSROOM OBSERVATION FORM .
OBSERVER INSTRUCTIONS

The VCOF is a three-part, pre-coded observation instrument designed for use in elementary school classrooms. It can be used in middle-school and high-school classrooms as well, but it was not field tested at these levels. The VCOF will work best if used during academic segments in the morning since many activities in the afternoons involve so many interactions that many cannot be recorded. The observation periods will be a minimum of forty-five minutes since there are nine five-minute time intervals in Part One. If time is taken between these time intervals to make recordings, the approximate total time for each observation period will be one hour. It is important for the observer/recorder to be as unobtrusive as possible, and care must be taken to do follow-up observations in each classroom at the exact time of day as the previous observation.

The VCOF can be used as a pre-post or repeated measures instrument; it can also be used to compare teachers and classrooms. In order to make valid within-classroom or repeated measure comparisons and valid between-classroom comparisons, observations and recordings should be made by one person only, and this person needs to have conducted enough practice observations to be familiar with the codes. The use of a single observer is critical when the objective is to draw conclusions about change within a classroom and when the objective is to compare teachers and classrooms. The more observations conducted within each classroom, the more reliable the results will be. If only within-classroom or repeated-measures comparisons are to be made, and the objective is to determine how much the school as a whole is improving classroom by classroom, then using more than one observer may be justifiable provided the observer/recorders are able to demonstrate similar recordings during practice sessions in the same classrooms.

The VCOF has three basic Parts, and there is a legend at the bottom that identifies or defines each available code. The single-letter codes are used only for Part One which is titled "Instruction." These single-letter codes are used for lines four through eight. Part One is structured so that recordings are made for each of nine five-minute intervals. The recorder should use a watch or stopwatch and make recordings at or near the end of each interval. Accuracy with respect to what is recorded is more important than exactness with respect to the five-minute segments.

For lines one through three in Part One, clock minutes are recorded, and the choices are one, two, three, four, and five minutes—no decimals or fractions. For line one, you simply record the number of minutes the teacher was actively teaching. Active Teaching includes moving from group to group to give assistance, giving individual help, and interactive instruction; sitting at a desk while students work quietly and handling a discipline problem without using it as a teaching opportunity are not active teaching. For line two Nonteaching Discipline is defined as time spent on a discipline problem without using this as an opportunity to teach values, rules, or social skills, that is, time spent getting control so that instruction can resume. Teacher Inactivity on line three includes desk time during which help is not being given to students, talking to other teachers, and time spent out of the room.

The codes for Type of Student Activity on line four are T,I,P, and N. Cooperative learning, inter-group competitions, cross-grade inter-class buddy activities, class meetings, group discussions, discovery learning outside the room and building, and special hands-on projects are scored as T, which represents active student participation—when children are asked to go to the board one at a time or to read one at a time, this should be recorded T/P. P is recorded if the group is passively listening to the teacher, to one student, or to a visitor. The I code is defined as interactive teaching, and this is when students are answering teacher questions and asking questions—lecturing that does not include this interchange should not be recorded I and should be recorded P for passive listening. Watching videos and movies and listening to audio tapes should also be recorded P. Observer/recorders should feel free to use any pair of one-letter codes with a slash for any five-minute time interval if two codes reflect what was happening, but no more than two codes for one interval.

The single-letter code options for Student Relations on line six are C (cooperative), X (competitive), L (independent), N (none), or a combination of any two. Cooperation means no competition. When children are competing to be called on by the teacher or they are being asked to read or work a math problem one at a time, this should be coded X. L is recorded when students are working separately and not being compared, and when they are sharing during class meetings. If it is likely that their independent work will be compared in competitive fashion at some later point, you should score L. N is scored when no learning or teaching is taking place—this includes restroom breaks. It does not include average-length transitions from activity to activity. Score these as L unless students have been instructed to work together and are doing so. Once again, pairs of letter codes for each five minute interval are sometimes appropriate.

Instructional Content on line seven is scored A (academic), V (values, character, social skills, rules, virtues), N (none), or a combination of any two. If values or character-related instructional infusion lasts for most of the five-minute segment, score V. Cooperative learning activities should be coded as A/V unless the teacher is taking advantage of opportunities to encourage or teach social skills and virtues. Score V if the topic of the cooperative activity is character-related. Also score V if the class is having a class meeting even if the focus is academic. To make sure that every effort to infuse values/character instruction is recorded irrespective of how much time is spent, the observer/recorder should enter code Y on the final line of this section if any amount of infusion occurs or N if none occurs.

VCOF OBSERVER INSTRUCTIONS (Page 2)

Part Two of the VCOF deals with Interpersonal Interactions and uses the two-letter codes listed in the legend at the bottom of the VCOF. You should place a tally mark in the appropriate box for each interaction you observe. If you cannot decide which of two categories is appropriate for an observed interaction, place a tally mark in both categories. Some of the two-letter codes appear under more than one subheading in Part Two. The student-to-student interaction codes are separated into negative and positive categories with eight codes for each. The descriptions of these codes in the legend are self-explanatory, but a few are similar enough to need clarification. Hostile verbal interactions are divided into those that are angry or extreme (HV) and those that are mild but intentionally provocative (VP). Physical provocation (PP) would involve making faces, grabbing something away from someone, and hand gestures. This is distinguished from PA, which represents minor physical aggression such as pushing. Off-task talk is recorded as either disruptive (OD) or nondisruptive (ON). Nonverbal disruption such as noise making and physical movement is coded ND.

Learning-related student-to-student interactions are recorded as disruptive (LD) or nondisruptive (LN) unless characterized by significant cooperation lasting less than five minutes (BC) or significant teamwork lasting five minutes or more (ET). One tally mark is entered under the ET code for each five-minute period during which students work cooperatively together and interact. Team Building/Leadership (TB) is recorded when one student encourages another to follow the rules, when one student makes a suggestion to the whole group, when a child voluntarily assumes a positive leadership role, and when one student mediates a conflict or tries to calm someone who is upset . FR represents friendly talk and is recorded when at least one person involved in an interaction is smiling, when the nonverbal behavior of at least one student suggests that the interpersonal relationship is valued, and when one student is polite or courteous to another. Helpfulness is separated into solicited (SH) where one student seeks help and receives it, and unsolicited (VH) where one student voluntarily helps another.

The teacher-to-student interactions are recorded on the bottom left side under Interpersonal Interactions, and this section includes both positive and negative interactions—the negative comes first. When a teacher hugs a child or says something affectionate, such as calling a child "sweetie," record a tally mark under KA for kindness/affection. When he or she engages a child in friendly, casual talk that elicits a smile, mark under FR for friendly. PE for praise/ encouragement includes any complimentary positive feedback that is learning related. RR for respectful reprimand/ redirection should be scored any time a teacher gives negative feedback without being demeaning or using a hostile tone. HC is for hostile or unnecessarily harsh criticism. Most interactions will be recorded in the PE and RR categories. Polite or courteous comments such as "thank you," "please," and "excuse me" are scored CO; however, many times teachers will use these terms to either redirect or praise. If this occurs just once or twice during an observation period, both CO and either RR or PE can be scored; if this occurs more than once or twice, the observer/recorder should use either the RR or PE category and not the CO category, and should select either RR or PE based on the apparent intent of the communication.

Student-to-teacher interactions are coded in the bottom right section under Interpersonal Interactions. AH is scored any time a child talks to the teacher in an angry tone and any time a child mumbles angrily in protest. DP is scored when a child is disrespectful of the teacher or tries to provoke by making fun, mocking, and so forth. Learning-related interactions with the teacher that are initiated by the student and thus not in response to a teacher's question are recorded, once again, as either LD or LN. LD represents disruptive communications that are learning-related or on-task; LN represents nondisruptive communications that are learning-related or on-task. When students cause the teacher to stop instruction, choose LD. The off-task OD and ON codes are used the same in the student-to-student and student-to-teacher sections. This is true for the voluntary helpfulness (VH) code as well. The CO, FR, and KA codes are used the same in the teacher-to-student and student-to-teacher sections and represent courteousness, friendliness, and kindness or affection.

Part Three of the VCOF (Quality Ratings) is completed after the hour-long observation period is complete. You will rate the students and teacher by placing checks in the boxes. Preventive-moral discipline refers to management systems that help maintain order, the effective use of teachable moments, taking the time to explain why actions are right or wrong, involving students in conflict resolution, and whether the teacher is being positive and noticing rule violations in the room. The teacher need not be doing didactic character education to receive a high rating for Caring Community/ Character Education if she or he is very positive and is clearly trying to create and maintain a caring community atmosphere.

VESSELS' CLASSROOM OBSERVATION FORM

Teacher: _____ Date: _____ Time: _____ Grade: ____ School: _____

Subject(s): _____

INSTRUCTION	FIVE-MINUTE TIME INTERVALS								
	1	2	3	4	5	6	7	8	9
Minutes of Active Teaching									
Minutes of Nonteaching Discipline									
Minutes of Teacher Inactivity									
Percent of Students on Task									
Student Activity (T,I,P,N)									
Student Relations (C,X,L,N)									
Primary Content (A,V,N)									
Any Amount of Virtue Infusion (Y,N)									

INTERPERSONAL INTERACTIONS

Student-to-Student(s) Negative			Student-to-Student(s) Positive				
FF	PA	HV	LD	LN	BC	ET	TB
VP	PP	ND	OD	ON	FR	SH	VH

Teacher-to-Student(s) Pos. & Neg.			Student-to-Teacher Positive & Negative				
HC	RR	PE	AH	DP	VH	LD	LN
CO	KA	FR	KA	CO	FR	OD	ON

QUALITY RATINGS	Poor - Good							
Teacher Kind & Respectful								
Students Kind & Respectful								
Teacher Motivated & Responsible								
Students Motivated & Responsible								
Preventive/Moral Discipline								
Caring Community/Character Education								

Legend for Instructional and Interactive Codes

Y	=	Yes	PA	=	Physical Aggression (one- or minor two-way)	TB	=	Team Building; Leadership; Conflict Mediation
N	=	No or None	HV	=	Hostile Verbal (extreme one- or two-way)	FR	=	Friendly Talk That Carries or Elicits a Smile
A	=	Academic	LD	=	Learning-Related and Disruptive	SH	=	Solicited Help (one student asks; one gives)
C	=	Cooperative (no individual competition)	LN	=	Learning-Related and Not Disruptive	VH	=	Voluntary Helpfulness
I	=	Interactive Teaching with Students Answering	VP	=	Verbal Provocation	HC	=	Hostile; Harshly Critical; Demeaning
L	=	Independent	PP	=	Physical Provocation	RR	=	Respectful Reprimand or Redirection
P	=	Passive Listening or Quiet Seat Work	ND	=	Nonverbal Disruption (noises and movement)	PE	=	Praise or Encouragement
T	=	Active Student Participation	OD	=	Off-Task Talk That Disrupts the Class	CO	=	Courteousness (please, thanks, excuse me)
V	=	Values; Character; Social Skills; Rules; Virtues	ON	=	Off-Task Talk That Does Not Disrupt the Class	KA	=	Kindness or Affection (touch and talk)
X	=	Competitive (individually)	BC	=	Brief Cooperation (less than five minutes)	AH	=	Angry or Hostile Toward Teacher
FF	=	Fight with More Than One Student Aggressing	ET	=	Extended Teamwork (1 tally for each 5 minutes)	DP	=	Disrespectful or Provocative Toward Teacher

Appendix I

School Climate Survey

VESSELS' SCHOOL CLIMATE SURVEY

GUIDELINES FOR ADMINISTRATION, SCORING, AND INTERPRETATION

Prospective Respondents: The VSCS can be completed by high school students, parents, and any adult working in the school. Within Atlanta, south Georgia, and Louisville where the instrument was field tested, only teachers and paraprofessionals were asked to complete it. Eventually, separate norms or comparison means and standard deviations will need to be obtained for parents, students, teachers, and others in various types of schools and communities. It may be possible for middle-school students to complete the VSCS, but the items were not written with early adolescents in mind.

Operational Definition and Intended Use: The VSCS is designed to assess the climate of elementary, middle, and high schools. School climate is defined as the combination of internal characteristics that give an organization its unique and readily perceptible personality. As reflected by the subscales of the VSCS, it is believed that the principal's community, various types of relationships (student-to-student, student-to-teacher, and teacher-to-teacher), the school-community that is defined in part by connections with the outside community, student discipline and self-discipline, and specific activities related to character building are the key elements of school climate.

Administration Procedures: Since many of the VSCS items concern the school principal, she or he must not be involved in any way in distributing and collecting the surveys and must never be permitted to see them. If respondents who are displeased with or critical of the principal believe there is any chance whatsoever that their honest responses will be revealed to the principal or staff members who strongly support the principal, they may not complete the survey or may choose to protect themselves by not telling the full truth as they see it. An attempt was made in the field testing to use numbers instead of names as a way of protecting the identity of respondents, but many forgot their self-selected number between the pretesting in September and follow-up post-testing in June, and as a result, many of their surveys could not be matched. This approach to protecting the identity of respondents is not recommended. Your only option, therefore, is to find someone to distribute and collect the surveys who will be trusted by all respondents, preferably a researcher who is not involved in any other way with the respondents and the school. Respondents should be assured that the surveys will be quickly removed from the school upon collection and that only total scores for the school as a whole will be shared with the principal, that is, no scores for individual respondents. It is assumed that prospective respondents who are satisfied with the principal and other aspects of the school climate and possibly those who are extremely displeased will be the most likely to turn them in voluntarily. Therefore, it is recommended that all prospective teachers, parapros, and other school staff members be similarly required to complete them. Obviously students and parents cannot be similarly required to complete the survey.

Scoring and Interpretation: An attempt was made to make scoring as easy as possible in case this needs to be done. Where data will be analyzed by computer, numbers need only appear in column A or on a substitute computer scan form. For hand scoring, the numbers placed in column A (1 for strongly disagree, 2 for disagree, 3 for agree, 4 for strongly agree) need to be copied into the boxes that appear under the small letters "a" through "I" on the right-hand side of each page. This should be done row by row with as many numbers entered as there are empty boxes for each in that row. Next, add each of the nine subscale columns (a–i) and the total-score column (A) and transfer these subtotals to page four where the totals for each will be entered. The subtotals are named on page four where instructions for handscoring and computing T scores are provided. For program evaluation purposes, the most useful statistic will be a paired-samples t-test using pretest and post-test scores. The Evaluation section of *Character and Community Development* provides means and standard deviations for various populations including an urban midwest elementary school after several years of a progressive program (mean = 349 and SD of 29), a small-town south Georgia elementary school after a few years of a traditional program (mean = 363; SD = 33), and five Atlanta elementary schools before (combined mean = 290; SD = 39) and after (combined mean = 292; SD = 48) the first year of their programs.

Statistical Properties: Field testing of the VSCS in Atlanta, south Georgia, and Louisville produced encouraging results with respect to reliability and validity. The alpha or internal consistency coefficient was .98 with subscale alphas ranging from .86 for the four-item Physical Environment subscale to .98 for the Quality of Relations subscale. All subscales of the survey. The test-retest stability coefficient was .66 over a nine-month period. With respect to validity, the factor analysis supported the original subscales of the survey. The pre-post paired-samples t-test results revealed that the two schools with the best program implementation showed a significant mean-score increase and that two of the three schools with less impressive implementation did not. The southwest Georgia school with an established program outscored all of the Atlanta schools using their pretest and post-test means; the urban midwest school scored significantly higher than the Atlanta schools using the pretest means, but it did not score significantly higher than two of five using post-test means.

Vessels' School Climate Survey

Name: _____

School: _____

Date: _____   ID #: _____   Position: _____

Instructions: please enter your answer in the column of blocks labeled A. You will have four response choices: **strongly disagree (1), disagree (2), agree (3), strongly agree (4)**.

	A	a	b	c	d	e	f	g	h	i
1 The principal's balance of high expectations and friendliness motivates others.										
2 Rules and consequences for breaking rules are made with student input and are viewed as fair.										
3 Teachers help students work out their conflicts peacefully and use conflicts as teachable moments.										
4 Active student participation is strongly encouraged and is viewed as a necessity for character-building.										
5 Everyone in our school community seems to be pulling together.										
6 Teachers from different backgrounds and age groups work well together.										
7 Students are quick to comfort and console one another.										
8 Our school has an atmosphere of constant change and improvement.										
9 Special recognition for good citizenship and good character is commonplace.										
10 Very few students break rules intentionally to provoke their teachers.										
11 Our school program is adapted to student needs and neighborhood characteristics.										
12 Most students are kind to one another and show concern for one another.										
13 The principal works as hard or harder than anyone else in the school.										
14 Students respect and admire their teachers and want to be like them.										
15 Teachers encourage student autonomy and independent decision making.										
16 A cross-grade, class-to-class buddy system is in place in our school as a community-building strategy.										
17 Teachers in this school reach out rather than staying to themselves.										
18 Students respectfully listen to one another during class meetings and class discussion.										
19 The principal knows about students with special needs and tries to help them.										
20 Most teachers reprimand students privately rather than in front of their peers.										
21 School service and other service learning projects are numerous and expected.										
22 Teachers are ready to help out whenever they are needed.										
23 Students reach out to help new students by being friendly and teaching them routines.										
24 At staff meetings, the principal enthusiastically acknowledges the accomplishments of teachers.										
25 It is common to see students praising students and teachers praising teachers.										
26 Teachers encourage students to be kind to one another and to display good character.										
27 The school grounds are attractive thanks to school service projects.										
28 Our school culture is so strong that it draws in and changes the surrounding community.										
Subtotals (carry over to page 4)										

Vessels' School Climate Survey page 2

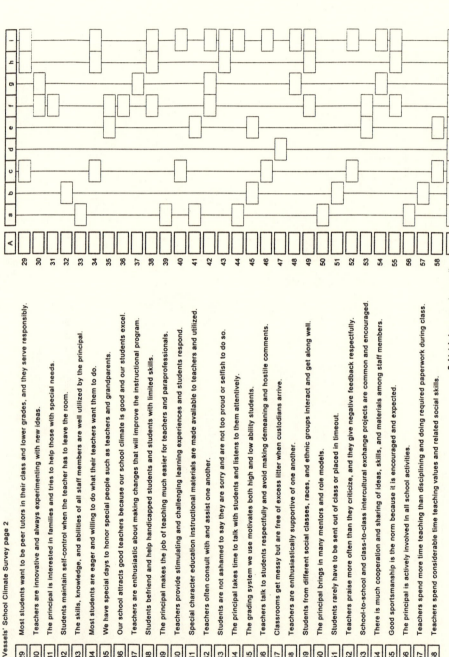

A	a	b	c	d	e	f	g	h	i

29. Most students want to be peer tutors in their class and lower grades, and they serve responsibly.
30. Teachers are innovative and always experimenting with new ideas.
31. The principal is interested in families and tries to help those with special needs.
32. Students maintain self-control when the teacher has to leave the room.
33. The skills, knowledge, and abilities of all staff members are well utilized by the principal.
34. Most students are eager and willing to do what their teachers want them to do.
35. We have special days to honor special people such as teachers and grandparents.
36. Our school attracts good teachers because our school climate is good and our students excel.
37. Teachers are enthusiastic about making changes that will improve the instructional program.
38. Students befriend and help handicapped students and students with limited skills.
39. The principal makes the job of teaching much easier for teachers and paraprofessionals.
40. Teachers provide stimulating and challenging learning experiences and students respond.
41. Special character education instructional materials are made available to teachers and utilized.
42. Teachers often consult with and assist one another.
43. Students are not ashamed to say they are sorry and are not too proud or selfish to do so.
44. The principal takes time to talk with students and listens to them attentively.
45. The grading system we use motivates both high and low ability students.
46. Teachers talk to students respectfully and avoid making demeaning and hostile comments.
47. Classrooms get messy but are free of excess litter when custodians arrive.
48. Teachers are enthusiastically supportive of one another.
49. Students from different social classes, races, and ethnic groups interact and get along well.
50. The principal brings in many mentors and role models.
51. Students rarely have to be sent out of class or placed in timeout.
52. Teachers praise more often than they criticize, and they give negative feedback respectfully.
53. School-to-school and class-to-class intercultural exchange projects are common and encouraged.
54. There is much cooperation and sharing of ideas, skills, and materials among staff members.
55. Good sportsmanship is the norm because it is encouraged and expected.
56. The principal is actively involved in all school activities.
57. Teachers spend more time teaching than disciplining and doing required paperwork during class.
58. Teachers spend considerable time teaching values and related social skills.

Subtotals (carry over to page 4)

234

Vessels' School Climate Survey page 3

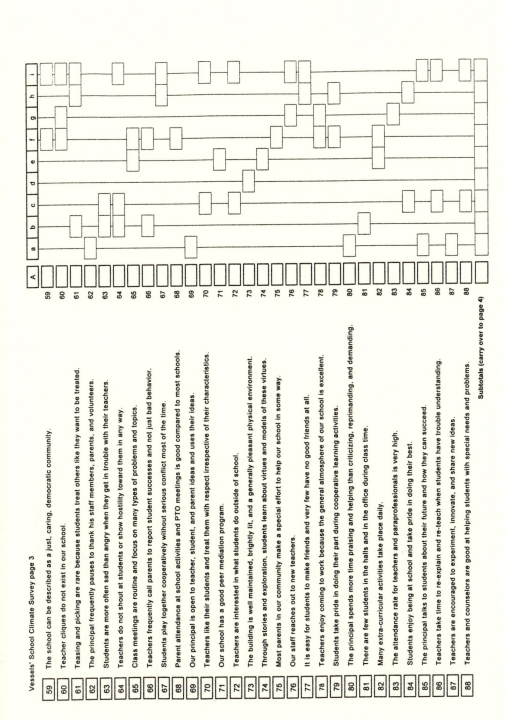

	A	a	b	c	d	e	f	g	h	i
59										
60										
61										
62										
63										
64										
65										
66										
67										
68										
69										
70										
71										
72										
73										
74										
75										
76										
77										
78										
79										
80										
81										
82										
83										
84										
85										
86										
87										
88										

Subtotals (carry over to page 4)

59 The school can be described as a just, caring, democratic community.
60 Teacher cliques do not exist in our school.
61 Teasing and picking are rare because students treat others like they want to be treated.
62 The principal frequently pauses to thank his staff members, parents, and volunteers.
63 Students are more often sad than angry when they get in trouble with their teachers.
64 Teachers do not shout at students or show hostility toward them in any way.
65 Class meetings are routine and focus on many types of problems and topics.
66 Teachers frequently call parents to report student successes and not just bad behavior.
67 Students play together cooperatively without serious conflict most of the time.
68 Parent attendance at school activities and PTO meetings is good compared to most schools.
69 Our principal is open to teacher, student, and parent ideas and uses their ideas.
70 Teachers like their students and treat them with respect irrespective of their characteristics.
71 Our school has a good peer mediation program.
72 Teachers are interested in what students do outside of school.
73 The building is well maintained, brightly lit, and a generally pleasant physical environment.
74 Through stories and exploration, students learn about virtues and models of these virtues.
75 Most parents in our community make a special effort to help our school in some way.
76 Our staff reaches out to new teachers.
77 It is easy for students to make friends and very few have no good friends at all.
78 Teachers enjoy coming to work because the general atmosphere of our school is excellent.
79 Students take pride in doing their part during cooperative learning activities.
80 The principal spends more time praising and helping than criticizing, reprimanding, and demanding.
81 There are few students in the halls and in the office during class time.
82 Many extra-curricular activities take place daily.
83 The attendance rate for teachers and paraprofessionals is very high.
84 Students enjoy being at school and take pride in doing their best.
85 The principal talks to students about their future and how they can succeed.
86 Teachers take time to re-explain and re-teach when students have trouble understanding.
87 Teachers are encouraged to experiment, innovate, and share new ideas.
88 Teachers and counselors are good at helping students with special needs and problems.

235

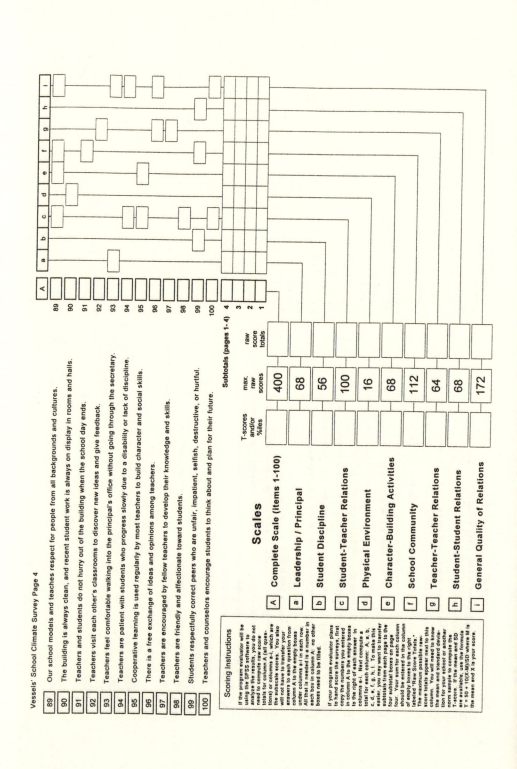

89	Our school models and teaches respect for people from all backgrounds and cultures.
90	The building is always clean, and recent student work is always on display in rooms and halls.
91	Teachers and students do not hurry out of the building when the school day ends.
92	Teachers visit each other's classrooms to discover new ideas and give feedback.
93	Teachers feel comfortable walking into the principal's office without going through the secretary.
94	Teachers are patient with students who progress slowly due to a disability or lack of discipline.
95	Cooperative learning is used regularly by most teachers to build character and social skills.
96	There is a free exchange of ideas and opinions among teachers.
97	Teachers are encouraged by fellow teachers to develop their knowledge and skills.
98	Teachers are friendly and affectionate toward students.
99	Students respectfully correct peers who are unfair, impatient, selfish, destructive, or hurtful.
100	Teachers and counselors encourage students to think about and plan for their future.

Subtotals (pages 1- 4)

Scales		max. raw scores	raw score totals	T-scores and/or %iles
A	Complete Scale (items 1-100)	400		
a	Leadership / Principal	68		
b	Student Discipline	56		
c	Student-Teacher Relations	100		
d	Physical Environment	16		
e	Character-Building Activities	68		
f	School Community	112		
g	Teacher-Teacher Relations	64		
h	Student-Student Relations	68		
i	General Quality of Relations	172		

Scoring Instructions

If the program evaluator will be using the SPSS software to analyze the results, you do not need to compute raw score totals for column A (all questions) or columns a-i, which are the subscale scores. You also will not have to transfer your answers to each question from column A to the many boxes under columns a-i in column A: no other boxes need to be filled.

If your program evaluator plans to hand score the surveys, first copy the numbers you entered in column A to the empty boxes to the right of each answer in columns a-i. Next compute a total for each column: A, a, b, c, d, e, f, g, h, i. To make this easier, you may want to transfer subtotals from each page to the four subtotal boxes on page four. Your sum for each column should be entered in the column of empty boxes to the right labeled "Raw Score Totals." The maximum possible raw-score totals appear next to this column. You will need to know the mean and standard deviation for your school or another norm sample to compute the T-score. If the mean and SD are available, use the formula $T = 50 + 10(X-M)/SD$ where M is the mean and X is your score.

Appendix J

Classroom Climate Surveys

VESSELS' CLASSROOM CLIMATE SURVEY – EARLY AND LATE ELEMENTARY

ADMINISTRATION, SCORING, AND INTERPRETATION GUIDELINES

Target Subjects: The VCCS-EE is designed for use with children in grades one and two. First grade students have diffculty staying focused and on the right question at the beginning of the year, and kindergarten students simply do not have the skills needed to make the results reliable and valid. The VCCS-EE is not recommended for use with kindergarten students. The VCCS-LE is designed for use with children in grades three through five. You can also use it with academically advanced and/or highly socialized second grade students, but many normal second grade students will have difficulty with the questions. The VCCS-LE was not field tested on sixth and seventh grade students, but you may feel the content is appropriate for your students.

Parental Consent: Since the VCCS-EE and VCCS-LE questions are not personal and concern conditions within the classroom, there is no need to obtain parental consent. Nevertheless, you should keep parents informed.

Authorized Use: Until more is learned about the VCCS-EE and VCCS-LE through controled research, they should be used only as research tools and program evaluation tools and not to evaluate individual teachers or schools. Like the student character questions, the validity of the results depends on how honest students respond and whether they will be as truthful the second or third time they answer the questions as they were the first. The questions are straight forward, so it is unlikely that students will be unable to recognize and assess the various aspects of the classroom that the questions address. It is assumed that over-reporting and under-reporting will be the same from administration to administration, with the possible exception of teachers who are very nurturing or hostile toward children during the year.

Statistical Properties: Like the Vessels' Student Character Questionnaires, the VCCS-EE and VCCS-LE were field tested in five Atlanta schools, one southwest Georgia school, and one urban midwest school. The VCCS-EE data yielded an alpha (internal consistency) coefficient of .73 for the post-test and .65 for the pretest—the pre-post difference was greater for first graders than second. The Atlanta means were at or near 11.5 with standard deviations of about 2.5; the means for the comparison schools were 11.9 and 13.1 with similar standard deviations. The VCCS-LE data yielded an alpha of .82 for the pretest and .85 for the post-test plus a test-retest correlation of .52 over nine months. The Atlanta means were 20.4 and 19.0 with a standard deviation of about 5.8; the comparison-school means were 24.6 and 28.9 with a standrad deviation of 5.7 for the former and 3.4 for the latter. The means for the comparison schools were significantly higher, and the Atlanta school with the best implementation scored significantly higher than several other Atlanta schools on the post-test only. Scores in the Atlanta schools (beginning character programs) were lower from grade to grade, while those for the comparison schools (established character programs) were about the same.

Administration Procedures: The VCCS-EE should be administered to groups of about ten students by an adult other than the teacher or principal, and with enough test proctors to maintain a one-to-five ratio. The VCCS-LE can be administered to whole classes with enough proctors to maintain a ten-to-one ratio. It is better to have students sitting at separate desks rather than tables. The reader and proctors have distinctly separate responsibilities. Proctors should not restate questions for individual students, and readers should not look for students who might be on the wrong question or who may have skipped one by accident. It is critical that the reader encourage students to be honest before the reading begins, and it is important for the reader to occasionally ask students to "Please tell the truth." It is also very important for the reader to assure students that their answers will never be known to their teachers or parents and to impress upon them that no laughing in response to questions, and no oral answering or vocalizations of any kind will be tolerated. For the VCCS-EE, the reader should begin by explaining that students should place their left finger on the picture as it is named and then circle the "yes" to the left of the picture or the "no" to the right after the question is read in full. The reader should take plenty of time to illustrate the procedure on the board and should use the first couple of items as guided practice. The reader should ask students if they are ready prior to each item and then say, "Put your finger on the ___." For the VCCS-LE, the reader should instruct students to enter an X or check under the T column for true or the F column for false. Proctors should focus on keeping students on the right question, making sure all items are answered, dealing with inappropriate behavior through nonverbal feedback to the extent possible, giving the reader cues about student readiness for the next item, and removing disrupters. They should also enter identifying information at the top of each questionnaire for first grade students since it will take students fifteen to twenty minutes to do this themselves.

Scoring and Interpretation: The VCCS-EE and VCCS-LE are designed so the total score and subscale scores can be computed by hand fairly easily. For the VCCS-EE, enter a numeric 1 in the empty boxes on the right side of the form for each item where the "yes" is circled and the empty box does not have a small R in the corner; for the empty boxes that have a small R, enter a numeric 1 if the "no" is circled. For the VCCS-LE, the same instructions apply for entering 1s, but adding the scores involves two subscale scores as well as a total-scale score. The empty boxes to the right with a small 1 in the corner comprise the Teacher Support subscale; the empty boxes with a small 2 in the corner comprise the Caring Community subscale. You have been provided comparison group means and standard deviations, but your primary statistic for program evaluation purposes should be a paired-sample t-test. This will tell you if obtained differences between pretest means and post-test means are statistically significant, that is, a fairly certain indicator of real change. If you intend to have the data analyzed by computer using the SPSS program, you do not need to enter 1s in the boxes.

VESSELS' CLASSROOM CLIMATE SURVEY – LATE ELEMENTARY

Name: _____ Teacher: _____ Date: _____

School: _____ Grade: _____

Check T for True or F for False

		T	F	Official Scoring
1	The students in my class help each other without being asked by our teacher.	1		2 T
2	When two kids argue in my room, the teacher listens to both and tries to help them work it out.	2		1 T
3	The kids in my class make fun of me when I make a mistake.	3		2 F
4	Many of the students in my class are selfish and don't seem to care about others.	4		2 F
5	I always get help from the teacher when I need it in my classroom.	5		1 T
6	There are a lot of mean kids in my class.	6		2 F
7	When I do well in class, my classmates are happy for me.	7		2 T
8	Early in the year, we went over and over class rules and routines until everyone knew them.	8		1 T
9	I sometimes get to help the teacher or get to help other students with their work.	9		2 T
10	Students say "excuse me," "I'm sorry," "thank you," and "please" all the time in my room.	10		2 T
11	Our class is such a fun place to be that students sometimes stay after school on their own.	11		1 T
12	The kids in my room care about each other and like to be together just like family members.	12		2 T
13	My teacher talks so mean sometimes that it scares all of us.	13		1 F
14	I know my teacher really cares what I think and how I feel about things because she asks.	14		1 T
15	Students in my class call each other names and try to make each other mad.	15		2 F
16	My teacher hugs me a lot and talks nice to me and to all the kids in my room.	16		1 T
17	I feel important in my room because I sometimes get to choose what to do.	17		2 T
18	Our teacher wants us to work cooperatively in small groups and often lets us work in groups.	18		1 T
19	We have worked together in my class to help others who really need help like the homeless.	19		2 T
20	Our teacher is always joking with us and having fun with us.	20		1 T
21	I can talk to my classmates and teacher about my family and my feelings.	21		2 T
22	It is easy to make friends in my classroom, and everyone seems to have friends.	22		2 T
23	It is easy to stay out of trouble in my classroom.	23		2 T
24	Our teacher sometimes gets very loud when students break the rules or don't do as she asks.	24		1 F
25	When someone in my class makes fun of someone else, others join in.	25		2 F
26	When I do something wrong, my teacher talks to me privately so my classmates can't hear us.	26		1 T
27	We sometimes sit in a circle in my room and talk about real important things.	27		2 T
28	Our classroom is clean and colorful and always has lots of student work on the walls.	28		1 T
29	In my room, students share and take turns.	29		2 T
30	The students in my class remind each other to follow the rules and to be nice to each other.	30		2 T
31	Older students and adults come to our class to work with us sometimes.	31		2 T
32	When someone says or does something dumb or silly in my room, everybody laughs.	32		2 F
33	My teacher would like it if parents visited the classroom every day.	33		1 T
34	The teacher always decides what we will do and never asks us what we would like to do.	34		1 F

Teacher-Support Total (1s) [ ]   Caring-Community Total (2s) [ ]   Scale Total [ ]

ID # : _____   **All About My Classroom**   Vessels' Classroom
Climate Questionnaire –
Early Elementary

Name: _____   Teacher: _____

School: _____   Grade: _____   Date: _____

yes		no	The kids in my class help each other.	1
yes		no	My teacher listens to me.	2
yes		no	Kids in my class laugh when I mess up.	3 R
yes		no	There are mean kids in my class.	4 R
yes		no	Kids say "thank you" in my room.	5
yes		no	My class is a really fun place to be.	6
yes		no	My teacher cares how I feel.	7
yes		no	My teacher hugs me and other kids.	8
yes		no	My teacher laughs and has fun with us.	9
yes		no	The kids in my class fight.	10 R
yes		no	It is easy to make friends in my class.	11
yes		no	Learning in my class is really fun.	12
yes		no	I can stay out of trouble in my room.	13
yes		no	Kids in my class share and take turns.	14
yes		no	The kids in my class follow the rules.	15

Total

Appendix K

Student Character Questionnaire – Early Elementary

VESSELS' STUDENT CHARACTER QUESTIONNAIRE – EARLY ELEMENTARY

ADMINISTRATION, SCORING, AND INTERPRETATION GUIDELINES

Target Subjects: The VSCQ-EE is designed for use with children in grades one and two. First grade students have difficulty staying focused and on the right question at the beginning of the year, and kindergarten students simply do not have the skills needed to make the results reliable and valid. The VSCQ-EE is not recommended for use with kindergarten students.

Parental Consent: Since the VSCQ-EE questions are personal and deal with issues of right and wrong, it is important to obtain parental consent. If you plan to administered the questionnaire to all students, a passive consent letter should be sufficient. Such a letter asks parents to return the bottom portion if they do not want their child questioned. It is best to administer the questionnaire to all students whose parents consent. The number of parents who refuse will be small if the letter is factual, and the questionnaire is made available in the office for parents to review.

Restricted Use: The VSCQ-EE should be used as a program evaluation tool only and should not be used to draw conclusions about the morality of an individual child. Even if future research shows that it can be used for this purpose, it would have to be administered by a person trained in one-on-one assessment, such as a school or clinical psychologist, and it would need to be used with other instruments. Even as a program evaluation tool, it should be one of several measures or change indicators included in your evaluation plan (see Evaluation chapter of *Character and Community Development*). Users should bear in mind that much more data needs to be gathered and many more studies need to be done before we will know with certainty if this instrument measures "character" or "morality" (including the inner workings such as conscience, empathy, and ethical reflection), and whether it is sensitive to the subtle changes in character that might occur as a result of character education programs. One important question is whether enough students will answer honestly to make the results meaningful and valid. Most first and second grade students will not lie intentionally if asked to tell the truth, but they tend to exaggerate their positive qualities and minimize their negative. It is possible that students begin to acknowledge and clarify their values as a first step toward improved character and/or actually improve in character (including honesty) as a result of a character education program. Either of these possibilities could cause scores as a whole to drop or remain the same initially, and this drop or lack of change could be misleading and easily misinterpreted. Researchers are asked to treat these possibilities as hypotheses, and program evaluators are asked to bear them in mind and not rely on the VSCQ-EE too heavily until more is known. The picture with respect to reliability, face validity, and construct validity is more clear as reflected by a total-scale alpha of .69 (internal consistency), a stability coefficient of .38 over nine months, some factorial support for the subscales, and good inter-subscale and subscale-to-total correlations.

Administration Procedures: The VSCQ-EE should be administered to groups of about ten students by an adult other than the teacher or principal, and with enough test proctors to maintain a one-to-five ratio. It is better to have students sitting at separate desks than tables. The reader and proctors have distinctly separate responsibilities. Proctors should not restate questions for individual students, and readers should not look for students who might be on the wrong question or who may have skipped one by accident. It is critical that the reader encourage students to be honest before the reading begins, and it is important for the reader to occasionally ask students to "Please tell the truth." It is also very important for the reader to assure students that their answers will never be known to their teachers or parents and to impress upon them that no laughing in response to questions, and no oral answering or vocalizations of any kind will be tolerated. The reader should begin by explaining that students should place their left finger on the picture as it is named and then circle the letter to the left or right of the picture after the question is read in full. The reader should take plenty of time to illustrate the procedure on the board and should use the first couple of items as guided practice. The reader should ask students if they are ready prior to each item and then say, "Put your finger on the ___." When all have done so, the item should be read followed by a restatement of which answer choice goes with which letter. The two answer options should be read with equal emphasis, and items should be re-read as needed taking care not to allow the administration time to be lengthened too much. Proctors should focus on keeping students on the right question, making sure all items are answered, dealing with inappropriate behavior through nonverbal feedback to the extent possible, giving the reader cues about student readiness for the next item, and removing disrupters. They should also enter identifying information at the top of each questionnaire for first grade students since it will take students fifteen to twenty minutes to do this themselves.

Scoring and Interpretation: The VSCQ-EE is designed so the total score and subscale scores can be computed by hand. In the boxes to the right of each picture and capital-letter pair, enter a numeric one in every empty box if the circled letter is to the left of the picture. Then total the 1s in each column (F,T,S, B, E,C,1,2,3) and add the page subtotals to obtain scale totals on page three. *Character and Community Development* includes a few means and standard deviations you may want to use to make between-subject or inter-school comparisons, but your primary statistic for program evaluation purposes should be a paired-sample t-test. This will tell you if obtained differences between your pretest means and your posttest means are statistically significant, that is, a fairly certain indicator of real change. The empty columns to the right of columns "a" and "b" can be left empty if your data is to be analyzed by computer. For the latter, each answer from each questionnaire will have to be entered into a database and then read by a statistics program.

ID # : _____

All About You. Please Circle What Is True.

Vessels' Student Character
Questionnaire – Early Elementary

Name: _____

School: _____   Grade: _____   Teacher: _____   Date: _____

Circle only one letter for each picture.

A	B	Circle A if it makes you sad to see other kids cry. Circle B if you like to see other kids cry.
C	D	Circle C if you do what you are told right away. Circle D if you try to play for awhile and then do it.
E	F	Circle E if you can listen close when others talk. Circle F if you begin to think about other things.
G	H	Circle G if you help boys or girls who get hurt playing. Circle H if you wait for someone else to help them.
I	J	Circle I if you always do what you should do. Circle J if you only do things you like to do.
K	L	Circle K if you are good because it is fun when kids are good. Circle L if you are good to stay out of trouble.
M	N	Circle M if you are good at helping other kids. Circle N if they sometimes tell you to go away.

Subtotals (carry over to page 3)

Keep your left finger on the picture until you draw a circle.

This part is not for children. Do not write here.

F	T	S	B	E	C	1	2	3

This part is not for children. Do not write here.

F T S B E C 1 2 3

All About You. Please Circle What Is True.

(page 2 of 3)

Circle only one letter for each picture.

O	P	Circle O if you keep working when your teacher helps others. Circle P if she tells you to get back to work.
Q	R	Circle Q if you feel sad when you hear about children who are sad. Circle R if you do not feel sad.
S	T	Circle S if you would choose to work with other kids. Circle T if you would choose to work all by yourself.
U	V	Circle U if you can tell kids how you feel when you are mad and not hit them. Circle V if you hit sometimes.
W	X	Circle W if you say thank you when your teacher helps you. Circle X if you forget most of the time.
Y	Z	Circle Y if you might give one of your holiday presents to a homeless child. Circle Z if you would keep them.
A	B	Circle A if you would go talk to a new boy or girl in your class. Circle B if you let them pick their own friends.
C	D	Circle C if you are good at making friends. Circle D if most children are better at this than you.
E	F	Circle E if you would tell the teacher or try not to fight if a child hit you. Circle F if you would hit them back.
G	H	Circle G if you would help a friend who is being picked on by a big kid. Circle H if you would be too scared.

Keep your left finger on the picture until you draw a circle.

Subtotals (carry over to page 3)

244

F	T	S	B	E	C	1	2	3

All About You. Please Circle What Is True.

(page 3 of 3)

Circle only one letter for each picture.

I	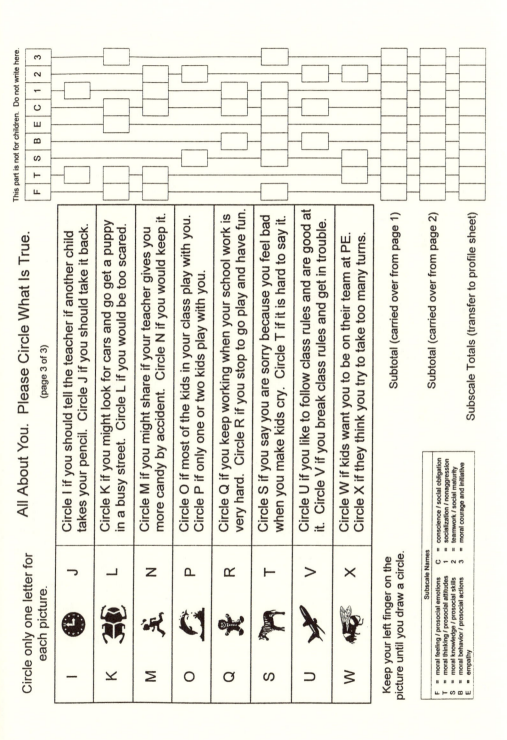 J	Circle I if you should tell the teacher if another child takes your pencil. Circle J if you should take it back.
K	L	Circle K if you might look for cars and go get a puppy in a busy street. Circle L if you would be too scared.
M	N	Circle M if you might share if your teacher gives you more candy by accident. Circle N if you would keep it.
O	P	Circle O if most of the kids in your class play with you. Circle P if only one or two kids play with you.
Q	R	Circle Q if you keep working when your school work is very hard. Circle R if you stop to go play and have fun.
S	T	Circle S if you say you are sorry because you feel bad when you make kids cry. Circle T if it is hard to say it.
U	V	Circle U if you like to follow class rules and are good at it. Circle V if you break class rules and get in trouble.
W	X	Circle W if kids want you to be on their team at PE. Circle X if they think you try to take too many turns.

Keep your left finger on the picture until you draw a circle.

Subtotal (carried over from page 1)

Subtotal (carried over from page 2)

Subscale Totals (transfer to profile sheet)

Subscale Names

F = moral feeling / prosocial emotions
T = moral thinking / prosocial attitudes
S = moral knowledge / prosocial skills
B = moral behavior / prosocial actions
E = empathy

C = conscience / social obligation
1 = socialization / nonaggression
2 = teamwork / social maturity
3 = moral courage and initiative

245

VESSELS' STUDENT CHARACTER QUESTIONNAIRE – EARLY ELEMENTARY
SUMMARY PROFILE SHEET

Scale / Subscales		Pretest Raw	T Score	%ile Score	Post-test Raw	T Score	%ile Score
TS	Student Character Total Score						
F	Moral Feelings / Prosocial Affect						
T	Moral Thinking / Prosocial Attitudes						
S	Prosocial Skills						
B	Moral Behavior / Self-Discipline						
E	Empathy / Caring						
C	Conscience / Obligation						
1	Socialization / Nonaggression						
2	Teamwork / Social Maturity						
3	Moral Initiative / Moral Courage						

T Scores	Student Character	Moral Feelings	Moral Thinking	Prosocial Skills	Moral Behavior	Empathy Caring	Conscience / Moral Obligation	Socialization / Non-Aggression	Teamwork/ Social Maturity	Moral Initiative / Courage	%ile Scores
— 90											
— 80											>99 —
— 70											98 —
— 60											84 —
— 50											50 —
— 40											16 —
— 30											2 —
— 20											<1 —
— 10											

Appendix L

Student Character Questionnaire – Late Elementary

VESSELS' STUDENT CHARACTER QUESTIONNAIRE – LATE ELEMENTARY

ADMINISTRATION, SCORING, AND INTERPRETATION GUIDELINES

Target Subjects: The VSCQ-LE is designed for use with children in grades three through five. You can also use it with academically advanced and/or highly socialized second grade students, but many normal second grade students will have difficulty with the questions. The VSCQ-LE was not field tested on sixth and seventh grade students, but you may feel that the content is more appropriate for them than the VSCQ-MH content.

Parental Consent: Since the VSCQ-LE questions are personal and deal with issues of right and wrong, it is important to obtain parental consent. If your plan is to administer the questionnaire to all students, a passive consent letter should be sufficient. Such a letter asks parents to return the bottom portion if they do not want their child to be questioned. It is best to administer the questionnaire to all students whose parents give consent. The number of parents who refuse will be small if the letter is factual, if parents know about the program, and if the questionnaire is made available in the office for parents to review.

Restricted Use: The VSCQ-LE should be used as a program evaluation tool only and should not be used to draw conclusions about the morality of an individual child. Even if future research shows that it can be used for this purpose, it would have to be administered by a person trained in one-on-one assessment, such as a school or clinical psychologist, and it would need to be used with other instruments. Even as a program evaluation tool, it should be one of several measures or prospective change indicators included in your evaluation plan (see Evaluation chapter of *Character and Community Development*). Users should bear in mind that much more data needs to be gathered and many more studies need to be done before we will know with certainty if this instrument measures "character" or "morality" (including the inner workings such as conscience, empathy, and ethical reflection), and whether it is sensitive to the subtle changes in character that might occur as a result of character education programs. One important question is whether enough students will answer honestly to make the results meaningful and valid. Another is whether honest answering will increase from one administration to the next. It is possible that students will grow more comfortable with the questions, begin to acknowledge and clarify their values as a first step toward improved character, actually improve in character (including honesty) as a result of a character education program, or some combination of the three. Any of these possibilities could cause scores to drop or remain the same, and this drop or lack of change could be misleading and easily misinterpreted. Researchers are asked to treat these possibilities as hypotheses, and program evaluators are asked to bear them in mind and not to rely on the VSCQ-LE too heavily until more is known. The picture with respect to reliability, face validity, and construct or factorial validity is more clear and encouraging as reflected by a total scale alpha of .85 (internal consistency), a stability coefficient of .49 over nine months, good factorial support for the subscales, and good inter-subscale and subscale-to-total correlations (see reference cited above for more detail).

Administration Procedures: The VSCQ-LE should be administered to groups of about twenty students by an adult other than the teacher or principal and with enough test proctors to maintain a one-to-fifteen ratio Students should be sitting at separate desks rather than tables. The reader and proctors have distinctly separate responsibilities. Proctors should not restate questions for individual students, and readers should not look for students who might be on the wrong question. It is critical that the reader encourage students to be honest before the reading begins, and it is important for the reader to give students reminders and encouragement approximately six times during the administration. It is also very important for the reader to assure students that their answers will never be known to their teachers or parents and to impress upon them that no laughing in response to questions, and no oral answering or vocalizations of any kind will be tolerated. Double offenders should be removed from the room as quietly as possible. The reader should begin by explaining that students should place an X or check in the box under "a" or "b" for each item and to put no other marks there. They may want to illustrate this on the chalk board. The reader should then state that students will be asked questions about how they feel, think, and act in various situations and that these questions are sometimes difficult to answer honestly. The reader should then proceed to encourage students to be honest and give assurances of no negative consequences. The two answer options (a and b) should be read with equal emphasis, and items should be re-read as needed taking care not to allow the administration time to be lengthened too much. Proctors should focus on keeping students on the right question, making sure all items are answered, making sure they have entered their name and other required information at the top, dealing with inappropriate behavior through nonverbal feedback to the extent possible, giving the reader cues about student readiness for the next item, and removing disrupters.

Scoring and Interpretation: The VSCQ-LE is designed so the total score and subscale scores can be computed by hand fairly easily. In the boxes to the right of the "a" and "b" columns, enter a numeric 1 in every empty box in a given row if the check or X in that row is in the "a" column. Then total the 1s in each column (F,T,S, B, E,C,1,2,3) and add the subtotals to obtain totals on page three. *Character and Community Development* includes a few means and standard deviations you may want to use to make school-to-school comparisons, but your primary statistic for program-evaluation purposes should be a paired-sample t-test. This will tell you if obtained differences between your pretest means and post-test means are statistically significant. If you plan to analyze your data by computer using SPSS, and you do not use a computer scan form, you will need to enter your data one questionnaire and one item at a time into a database, which will be read by SPSS. If this is the plan, answers need not be moved into the empty boxes.

VESSELS' STUDENT CHARACTER QUESTIONNAIRE – LATE ELEMENTARY

Date: _____ ID #: _____

Name: _____ Grade: _____ School: _____ Teacher: _____

Instructions: You will find the [a] and [b] answer choices in the questions below. For each question, choose the one that is the most true, and mark your answer by placing an X in the empty boxes to the right of each question.

	F	T	S	B	E	C	1	2	3	a	b

1. Do you feel better [a] when you do your best on school work that is very hard or [b] when you do better than others on school work that is easy?

2. When you are told to do to do chores, do you [a] always do them right away or [b] wait awhile before starting them?

3. Are you [a] good at going up to talk to someone for the first time or [b] is this hard for you to do?

4. When your school work is very hard, do you [a] keep trying or [b] stop and do something more fun?

5. [a] Does it make you sad when you see other children cry, or [b] do you like to see them cry?

6. [a] Do you get things done quickly, or [b] does your mother say you are too slow?

7. Can you [a] always listen carefully to others, or [b] do you sometimes start to think about other things?

8. If your friends leave their toys at your house, do you [a] take them back or [b] wait until they ask for them or come to get them?

9. When you hurt someone's feelings, do you [a] feel ashamed or [b] not feel ashamed because you didn't mean to do it?

10. Do you obey your parents [a] because they love you and take care of you or [b] because you don't want to be bad and get in trouble?

11. Are you [a] pretty good at helping other students or [b] do they sometimes tell you to go away?

12. When one of your classmates gets hurt on the playground, do you [a] hate to hear them cry and rush to help them or [b] let someone else help them?

13. When you do something bad and the teacher asks you about it, do you [a] say you did it because you feel bad when you lie or [b] tell a small lie to stay out of trouble?

14. [a] Do you usually play with kids who ask even if they don't know the game rules, or [b] do you only like to play with kids who know the game rules well?

Subtotals (carry over to page 3)

	F	T	S	B	E	C	1	2	3		a	b

15 When someone makes you mad, [a] can you tell them how you feel without getting into a fight or [b] do you talk loud and sometimes get into a fight?

16 At school do you [a] keep working when your teacher is helping others or [b] must she sometimes remind you to get back to work?

17 Do you [a] not feel like laughing when others make mistakes or [b] is it hard to keep from laughing?

18 When you act good in class, is it [a] because it is more fun when everyone behaves as they should or [b] because you might get in trouble if you're bad?

19 [a] Do you know how to ask other children if you can play with them or [b] do you usually wait until they ask you to play?

20 [a] Do you say thank you when your teacher finishes helping you or [b] do you sometimes forget?

21 Do you [a] do things you feel you should do even though you don't want to, or [b] only things you like to do?

22 Would you rather [a] work with a group of children your own age or [b] work all by yourself?

23 Are you [a] pretty good at telling people how you feel or [b] do you usually stay quiet when something is bothering you?

24 When someone tries to fight with you, do you [a] tell the teacher and try not to fight, or [b] hit them back if they hit you?

25 When you hear about someone who is very sad, do you [a] feel sad too or [b] not feel sad?

26 Do you do your school work and homework [a] the best that you can or [b] just good enough that the teacher will take it?

27 Are you [a] usually polite when asking the teacher for help or [b] does she sometimes have to tell you not to interrupt while she is helping someone else?

28 If your teacher passes out holiday stockings and you accidentally get more candy than your classmates, would you [a] tell the teacher and share or [b] not say anything.

29 If your mother asks you if you would like to give one of your holiday season gifts to a child who isn't going to get any, would you [a] agree or [b] keep your presents?

30 If you are in a store and you see a ten dollar bill on the floor, should you [a] take it to the cashier or [b] keep it since anyone might claim it?

Subtotals (carry over to page 3)

250

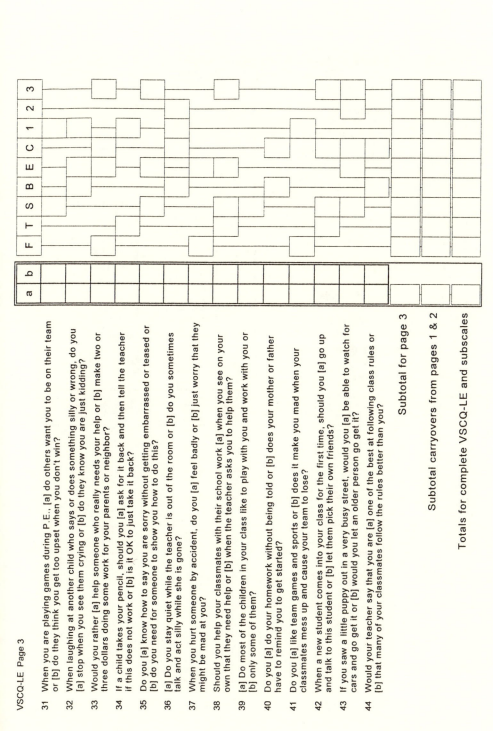

31 When you are playing games during P.E., [a] do others want you to be on their team or [b] do they think you get too upset when you don't win?

32 When laughing at another child who says or does something silly or wrong, do you [a] stop when you see them crying or [b] do they know you are just kidding?

33 Would you rather [a] help someone who really needs your help or [b] make two or three dollars doing some work for your parents or neighbor?

34 If a child takes your pencil, should you [a] ask for it back and then tell the teacher if this does not work or [b] is it OK to just take it back?

35 Do you [a] know how to say you are sorry without getting embarrassed or teased or [b] do you need for someone to show you how to do this?

36 [a] Do you stay quiet while the teacher is out of the room or [b] do you sometimes talk and act silly while she is gone?

37 When you hurt someone by accident, do you [a] feel badly or [b] just worry that they might be mad at you?

38 Should you help your classmates with their school work [a] when you see on your own that they need help or [b] when the teacher asks you to help them?

39 [a] Do most of the children in your class like to play with you and work with you or [b] only some of them?

40 Do you [a] do your homework without being told or [b] does your mother or father have to remind you to get started?

41 Do you [a] like team games and sports or [b] does it make you mad when your classmates mess up and cause your team to lose?

42 When a new student comes into your class for the first time, should you [a] go up and talk to this student or [b] let them pick their own friends?

43 If you saw a little puppy out in a very busy street, would you [a] be able to watch for cars and go get it or [b] would you let an older person go get it?

44 Would your teacher say that you are [a] one of the best at following class rules or [b] that many of your classmates follow the rules better than you?

Subtotal for page 3

Subtotal carryovers from pages 1 & 2

Totals for complete VSCQ-LE and subscales

251

VESSELS' STUDENT CHARACTER QUESTIONNAIRE – LATE ELEMENTARY
SUMMARY PROFILE SHEET

Scale / Subscales		Pretest Raw	T Score	%ile Score	Post-test Raw	T Score	%ile Score
a	Student Character Total Score						
F	Moral Feelings / Moral Maturity						
T	Moral Thinking / Prosocial Attitudes						
S	Prosocial Skills						
B	Moral Behavior / Self-Discipline						
E	Empathy / Caring						
C	Conscience / Moral Obligation						
1	Socialization / Self-Control						
2	Honesty / Exaggerated Responses						
3	Moral Initiative / Moral Courage						

T Scores	Student Character	Moral Feelings	Moral Thinking	Prosocial Skills	Moral Behavior	Empathy Caring	Conscience / Moral Obligation	Socialization / Self-Control	Honesty / Exaggerated Responses	Moral Courage	%ile Scores
90											
80											>99
70											98
60											84
50											50
40											16
30											2
20											<1
10											

Appendix M

Student Character Questionnaire – Middle-High

VESSELS' STUDENT CHARACTER QUESTIONNAIRE – MIDDLE/HIGH SCHOOL

ADMINISTRATION, SCORING, AND INTERPRETATION GUIDELINES

Target Subjects: The VSCQ-HS is designed for use with high school students but can be used with middle school students who are on grade level and have the knowledge to answer questions about the government, the UN, and AIDS. Most eighth graders should have this knowledge. The LE version of the VSCQ may be more appropriate for sixth grade.

Parental Consent: Since the VSCQ-HS questions are personal and deal with issues of right and wrong, it is important to obtain parental consent. If you plan to administer the questionnaire to all students, a passive consent letter is sufficient. Such a letter asks parents to return the bottom portion if they do not want their son or daughter questioned. It is best to administer the questionnaire to all students whose parents consent. The number of parents who decline will be small if the letter is factual, if parents know about the program, and if the questionnaire is made available in the office for parents to review.

Restricted Use: The VSCQ-HS should only be used as a program evaluation tool and should not be used to draw conclusions about the morality of an individual student. Even if future research shows that it can be used for this purpose, it would have to be administered by a person trained in one-on-one assessment, such as a school or clinical psychologist, and it would need to be used with other instruments. Even as a program evaluation tool, it should be one of several measures or change indicators included in your evaluation plan (see Evaluation chapter of *Character and Community Development*). Users should bear in mind that much more data needs to be gathered and many more studies need to be done before we will know with certainty if this instrument measures "character" or "morality" (including the inner workings such as conscience, empathy, and ethical reflection), and whether it is sensitive to the subtle changes in character that might occur as a result of character education programs. One important question is whether enough students will answer honestly to make the results meaningful and valid. Another is whether students will answer more honestly with each administration. It is possible that students will grow more comfortable with the questions, begin to acknowledge and clarify their values as a first step toward improved character, actually improve in character (including honesty) as a result of a character education program, or some combination of the three. Any of these possibilities could cause scores to drop or remain the same, and this drop or lack of change could be misleading and easily misinterpreted. Researchers are asked to treat these possibilities as hypotheses, and program evaluators are asked to bear them in mind and not to rely on the VSCQ-HS too heavily until more is known. Since the piloting of the VSCQ-HS involved only 155 seventeen- and eighteen-year-old students who completed it only once, and since the item analysis and factor analysis resulted in the re-wording of many moral thinking items, relatively little is known about the statistical properties. It is reasonable to expect that internal consistency coefficients will remain at or near .86 and that the subscale alphas, excluding Moral Thinking, will remain in the .62 to .85 range. It is anticipated that the Moral Thinking alpha will rise from .46. Inter-subscale and subscale-to-total correlations are also expected to stay in the .79 to .88 range, excluding Moral Thinking, which will probably remain in the .30 to .60 range. A larger N should add clarity to the factor analysis results. Thus far, these results support the original four components and justify the inclusion of three new factor-based subscales.

Administration Procedures: The VSCQ-HS can be administered to any size group at the high school level; middle school groups should probably be kept to class size since students may need to have terms defined. Students are to read and answer the questions on their own in a silent atmosphere. Students must sit at separate desks and not tables. Proctors should not be needed since there is no advantage to copying off others. It is critical that the test administrator encourage students to be honest and to assure students that their answers will never be known to their teachers or parents. It is important to maintain silence since the questions tend to elicit comments and other reactions such as laughing that could affect how others answer. Double offenders should be removed from the room as quietly as possible. The test administrator should explain the four answer choices (Strongly Disagree, Disagree, Agree, Strongly Agree) and instruct students to place a check or an X in one of the four corresponding boxes just to the right of each question. They should explain that all of the remaining boxes on the right-hand side of the form are for official scoring. Students who are reluctant to enter their name should be reassured of confidentiality and encouraged to enter their name since efforts to match code numbers in pre-post assessment have proven difficult.

Scoring and Interpretation: The VSCQ-HS is designed so the total score and subscale scores can be computed by hand fairly easily. In the boxes to the right of the SD, D, A, SA boxes, you will find the RS column, which is the reverse-score-conversion column. If the RS box does not have a small R in the corner, enter the number corresponding to the student's response. If it does have an R, convert the SA choice that has a value of 4 to a value of 1. Convert the SD choice that has a value of 1 to a value of 4. The A choice with a value of 3 should be converted to a 2; the D choice with a value of 2 should be converted to a 3. Once this RS column is filled, each number should be copied into all empty boxes in the same row. Then add the numbers in each column (F,T,S, B, E,C,1,2,3) and add the page subtotals to obtain totals on page three. If you have means from different schools, you can compare them, but your primary statistic for program-evaluation purposes should be a paired-sample t-test that will tell you if obtained differences between your pretest means and your post-test means are statistically significant. For computer scoring, you should complete the RS column and then procede to enter these numbers one at a time from each questionnaire into a database that will be read by the SPSS program. The only way to avoid this is to develop a computer scan form.

Date: _____

VESSELS' STUDENT CHARACTER QUESTIONNAIRE – MIDDLE/HIGH SCHOOL   ID No. _____

Name: _____   Grade: _____   School: _____   Teacher: _____

Instructions: For each of the following statements, you have four answer choices: (1) **Strongly Disagree**
(2) **Disagree** (3) **Agree** (4) **Strongly Agree.** These choices are shown in the first four columns to the right labeled SD-1, D-2, A-3, SA-4. Place a check or X in the empty box to the right of each statement. Please be honest.

	Place check or X below				For use by official scorer only unless entries are requested									
	SD 1	D 2	A 3	SA 4	RS	F	T	S	B	E	C	M	R	I

1. Learning about people who have shown unusual kindness and compassion has given me a desire to be like them.

2. I don't think it is possible for me to ever be down and out like homeless people because I am different.

3. If two people cannot trust one another and share their most personal feelings, they are not true friends.

4. When I am with one of my friends who talks badly about another one of my friends, I usually don't say anything.

5. It upsets me to see or hear about young children who were left alone by an alcoholic or drug addicted mother.

6. I look up to and want to be like people who are rich, famous, and popular, like professional athletes and rock stars.

7. The best type of hero is a person who takes personal risks and makes personal sacrifices to make the world better.

8. In cooperative learning and committee work, I tend to dominate others and annoy them by coming on too strong.

9. I could easily risk my life to help or save someone I really care about.

10. Disabled people and poor people depend too much on others and the government and need to do more for themselves.

11. My ability to help my peers solve their conflicts without violence is pretty good because I have had some training.

12. During my community service work, I got to know the people I helped and now understand them better.

13. When I get in an argument with someone, I don't worry about upsetting anyone. I just think about winning.

14. I can't understand why people who make good money have to pay more taxes than people who make less.

15. I would describe as weak my ability to keep myself organized in my work, personal life, and planning for the future.

16. I must admit that I usually give in when my friends pressure me to do things I should not do.

17. After my team wins a hard fought game or contest, I think about how the losing team members must feel.

18. I can't see how getting volunteers from the community is better than paying people to do what needs to be done.

19. I believe others would describe me as a responsible and productive team member.

20. My community service experiences through school inspired me to help others on my own.

Subtotals (carry over to page 3)

VSCQ-MH Page 2   (1) Strongly Disagree (2) Disagree (3) Agree (4) Strongly Agree

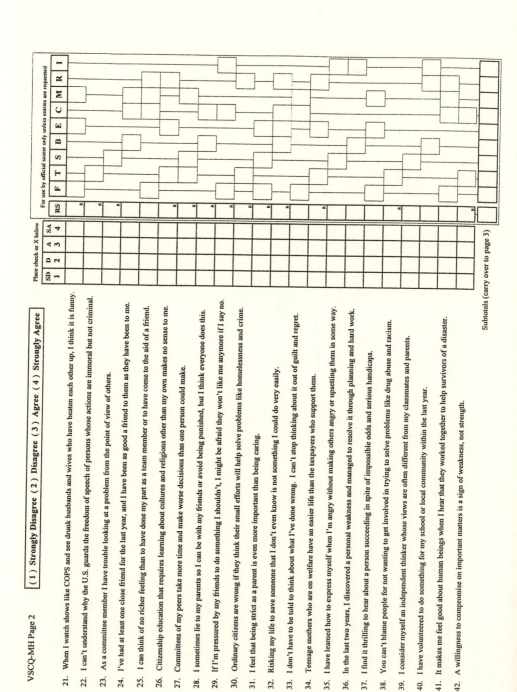

For use by official scorer only unless entries are requested

Place check or X below

	SD 1	D 2	A 3	SA 4

21. When I watch shows like COPS and see drunk husbands and wives who have beaten each other up, I think it is funny.

22. I can't understand why the U.S. guards the freedom of speech of persons whose actions are immoral but not criminal.

23. As a committee member I have trouble looking at a problem from the point of view of others.

24. I've had at least one close friend for the last year, and I have been as good a friend to them as they have been to me.

25. I can think of no richer feeling than to have done my part as a team member or to have come to the aid of a friend.

26. Citizenship education that requires learning about cultures and religions other than my own makes no sense to me.

27. Committees of my peers take more time and make worse decisions than one person could make.

28. I sometimes lie to my parents so I can be with my friends or avoid being punished, but I think everyone does this.

29. If I'm pressured by my friends to do something I shouldn't, I might be afraid they won't like me anymore if I say no.

30. Ordinary citizens are wrong if they think their small efforts will help solve problems like homelessness and crime.

31. I feel that being strict as a parent is even more important than being caring.

32. Risking my life to save someone that I don't even know is not something I could do very easily.

33. I don't have to be told to think about what I've done wrong. I can't stop thinking about it out of guilt and regret.

34. Teenage mothers who are on welfare have an easier life than the taxpayers who support them.

35. I have learned how to express myself when I'm angry without making others angry or upsetting them in some way.

36. In the last two years, I discovered a personal weakness and managed to resolve it through planning and hard work.

37. I find it thrilling to hear about a person succeeding in spite of impossible odds and serious handicaps.

38. You can't blame people for not wanting to get involved in trying to solve problems like drug abuse and racism.

39. I consider myself an independent thinker whose views are often different from my classmates and parents.

40. I have volunteered to do something for my school or local community within the last year.

41. It makes me feel good about human beings when I hear that they worked together to help survivors of a disaster.

42. A willingness to compromise on important matters is a sign of weakness, not strength.

Subtotals (carry over to page 3)

256

VSCQ-MH page 3

(1) Strongly Disagree (2) Disagree (3) Agree (4) Strongly Agree

Place check or X below

For use by official scorer only unless entries are requested

| | SD 1 | D 2 | A 3 | SA 4 | | RS | F | T | S | B | E | C | M | R | I |

43. I am able to express myself in a group without becoming uneasy and without finding it hard to say what I think.

44. I can recall a time when I stood up for someone whose rights were being violated or whose feelings were being hurt.

45. Giving up makes me more miserable than hanging in there and not quitting when the going gets tough.

46. Cheating a little on tests is not that big of a deal if the person is willing to pay the price if caught.

47. Little kids and old people like to be around me because I listen closely and try to understand their situation.

48. Self-control and moderation are not in my vocabulary. I overdo things and sometimes run over others in the process.

49. If my friend or someone in my school had AIDS, I would worry more about getting infected than anything else.

50. It would be excusable if a doctor chose his father for an organ transplant rather than an unrelated young mother.

51. Others who have worked with me in a group would say that I change my position if others have made a strong case.

52. I haven't made any specific plans for my future after high school and haven't really thought about it very much.

53. Sharing inner feelings and talking openly about personal weaknesses is for whimps and not for me.

54. Sending UN forces to keep peace around the world makes no sense to me regardless of the circumstances.

55. Students from other races and social classes would describe me as a person who always treats them with respect.

56. I think my teachers would describe me as selfish rather than quick to notice and help others in need.

57. I have enough problems of my own without having to worry about the problems of the world and other people.

58. If a woman finds out that her husband murdered someone in his past, she should turn him in to the police.

59. When I have hurt someone's feelings, I always apologize because it bothers me until I do.

60. If people do not want to look after their own health, they should be left alone since they are only hurting themselves.

61. My parents and friends would describe me as a responsible and competent family member and community member.

62. World and social problems like war, hunger, racism, crime, and environmental destruction should concern everyone.

Subtotal for page 3

Subtotal carryover from pages 1 & 2

Complete Scale & Subscale Totals

Scoring Instruction: For "reverse score" questions (identified in column RS with small Rs in the lower right hand corner of otherwise empty boxes), the number corresponding to the student's check or X must be changed in the following manner: 1a become 4s, 4s become 1s, 2s become 3s, 3s become 2s. The new score corresponding to all other questions should also be transferred to the RS column using the boxes that do not have a small R in the lower right-hand corner. For the VSCQ-MH total, simply add the numbers in column RS on each page and then add these subtotals on page three. For subscales F,T,S,B,E,C,M,R, and I, copy the number score from column RS for each question to the empty boxes to the right of column RS in each row, add the numbers in each column on each page, and then sum these subtotals on page three. Transfer these number totals for the complete scale and subscales to the summary profile sheet, which defines the subscales.

VESSELS' STUDENT CHARACTER QUESTIONNAIRE – MIDDLE/HIGH SCHOOL
SUMMARY PROFILE SHEET

Scale / Subscales		Pretest Raw	T Score	%ile Score	Post-test Raw	T Score	%ile Score
TS	Student Character Total Score						
F	Moral Feelings / Moral Maturity						
T	Moral Thinking / Prosocial Attitudes						
S	Prosocial Skills						
B	Moral Behavior / Self-Discipline						
E	Empathy / Caring						
C	Conscience / Moral Obligation						
1	Moral Maturity						
2	Social Consciousness / Responsibility						
3	Moral Initiative / Moral Courage						

T Scores	Student Character	Moral Feelings	Moral Thinking	Prosocial Skills	Moral Behavior	Empathy Caring	Conscience / Moral Obligation	Moral Maturity	Social Responsi-bility	Moral Courage	%ile Scores
90											
80											>99
70											98
60											84
50											50
40											16
30											2
20											<1
10											

Index

About the Author

GORDON G. VESSELS is a school psychologist who recently directed a character education grant project in the Atlanta Public Schools, funded by the Georgia Humanities Council. Currently he is working on related research articles and consulting with schools and school systems that are interested in initiating or improving character education programs. Dr. Vessels is a former teacher and social worker with leadership certification and 25 years of experience as an educator.